T0339888

When Slavery and Rebellion Are Destroyed

New Perspectives on the Civil War Era

SERIES EDITORS
Judkin Browning, Appalachian State University
Susanna Lee, North Carolina State University

SERIES ADVISORY BOARD
Stephen Berry, University of Georgia
Jane Turner Censer, George Mason University
Paul Escott, Wake Forest University
Lorien Foote, Texas A&M University
Anne Marshall, Mississippi State University
Barton Myers, Washington & Lee University
Michael Thomas Smith, McNeese State University
Susannah Ural, University of Southern Mississippi
Heather Andrea Williams, University of Pennsylvania
Kidada Williams, Wayne State University

When Slavery and Rebellion Are Destroyed

A Michigan Woman's Civil War Journal

Edited by Jack Dempsey

The University of Georgia Press
ATHENS

Library of Congress Cataloging-in-Publication Data

Names: Woodworth, Ellen Preston, 1833–1914. | Dempsey, Jack, 1952– editor.
Title: When slavery and rebellion are destroyed : a Michigan
woman's Civil War journal / edited by Jack Dempsey.
Description: Athens : The University of Georgia Press,
[2023] | Series: New perspectives on the Civil War era |
Includes bibliographical references and index.
Identifiers: LCCN 2023019306 | ISBN 9780820365619
(hardback) | ISBN 9780820365602 (paperback) | ISBN
9780820365626 (epub) | ISBN 9780820365633 (pdf)
Subjects: LCSH: Woodworth, Ellen Preston, 1833–1914—Correspondence.
| Woodworth, Samuel, 1832–1899—Correspondence. | Michigan—
History—Civil War, 1861–1865—Personal narratives. | Michigan—
History—Civil War, 1861–1865—Social conditions. | Women—Michigan—
Isabella County—Biography. | United States. Army. Michigan
Engineers and Mechanics Regiment, 1st (1861–1865). Company M. |
Woodworth family. | United States—History—Civil War, 1861–1865—
Personal narratives. | Isabella County (Mich.)—Biography
Classification: LCC F572.17 W66 2023 | DDC 977.4/03092—dc23/eng/20230502
LC record available at https://lccn.loc.gov/2023019306

To the loyal women of the Union
for their devotion
on behalf of
one free American nation

Contents

When Slavery and Rebellion Are Destroyed

Introduction

The old letters were fraying, and their wartime words were fading. An irreplaceable record of family conversations might become lost to posterity; Ellen Preston Woodworth could not countenance such an outcome. Twenty years had elapsed since her veteran husband had risked his life for the Union during the Southern Rebellion. Ellen's part of the story during his twenty months of absence was equally compelling. So she opened a bound volume of blank pages and began painstakingly copying each word of the more than one hundred letters they had exchanged during the Civil War. Once completed, this irreplaceable journal would await the attention of a historiography that would not be limited to battles, strategy, guns, and men.[1]

The journal that Ellen compiled out of that carefully preserved correspondence provides a window into the rural life of a young wife and mother during the gravest crisis to befall the United States, a civil war that took the lives of over three quarters of a million soldiers. Though Ellen and her children were far from the front lines, that war's traumatic effects become powerfully felt through Ellen's faithful witnessing by ink on paper. The journal is an intimate record, revealing Ellen's thoughts, emotions, and convictions as she lived in a sparsely populated midwestern locale, enabling readers to grasp the grassroots reality and stresses of a military family during wartime thanks to a voice rarely saved for publication.

In 1992, Pulitzer Prize–winning historian James McPherson introduced *Divided Houses*, "the first book" (according to the back cover) to thoroughly examine wartime gender issues by affirming that "the Civil War affected the female half of the population as profoundly as the

---

1. The original correspondence has vanished, but the manuscript journal and typescript are preserved in the Clarke Historical Library in Isabella County, Michigan, where the Woodworths lived during the war. The journal was donated in 1966.

male half."[2] The volume's coeditors, Catherine Clinton and Nina Silber, sought "to weave gender into the tapestry of the war" and demonstrate its "centrality."[3] In 1998, McPherson and William Cooper surveyed the writing of Civil War history and maintained that "a great deal remains to be done" to paint a comprehensive picture of those times, including "the role of religion" and the "impact on families, children, and marriage patterns."[4] Especially in the new millennium, scholarship has brought to the forefront a recognition that "women are not just witnesses to history but actors and makers of it."[5] Primary source collections and focused studies on women's experiences have expanded and enriched the narrative of this pivotal era.

The rapid growth in literature on women during the Civil War has roots in the mid-twentieth century. Contrary to popular histories that had "overwhelmingly focused on armies and generals," two epic studies of the everyday Union and Confederate soldier became classics for concentrating on the words and actions of men in the ranks.[6] The motivations of individual soldiers as revealed in diaries and correspondence informed works that garnered critical praise.[7] Historians began to "probe connections between the men on the battlefield and the civilians at home."[8] A new body of scholarship sought to address how women shaped events, sustained the soldiers, supplied the war machine, and participated, through a multiplicity of roles, in remaking America. This "explosion" of scholarship helped increase the understanding of women and gender in the Civil War but also began

---

2. McPherson, "Foreword," xv. That assertion may have exaggerated. Some early chroniclers saluted the "nobleness and self-sacrificing spirit" of women who were "patriot workers in quiet country homes." Brockett and Vaughan, *Woman's Work in the Civil War*, 591–592. Other historians acknowledged that "families waited wearily at home," their male members gone, with "women taking their places." Hubbart, *Older Middle West*, 237. In 1991, a monograph sought to remedy how historians "gloss over the experiences of women." Culpepper, *Trials and Triumphs*, 1; a review termed it a "major comprehensive survey of women in the Civil War." Caffrey, *Register of the Kentucky Historical Society*, 100.

3. Clinton and Silber, *Divided Houses*, 335.

4. McPherson and Cooper, "Introduction" in *Writing the Civil War*, 6.

5. McCurry, *Women's War*, 3.

6. Gallagher, *Union War*, 121; Jordan, Robertson, and Segards, *The Bell Irvin Wiley Reader*, 14–15. The two books were *The Life of Johnny Reb* (Indianapolis: Bobbs-Merrill Co., 1943) and *The Life of Billy Yank* (Indianapolis: Bobbs-Merrill Co., 1952).

7. Linderman, *Embattled Courage*; Reid Mitchell, *Vacant Chair*; McPherson, *What They Fought For*; Noe, *Reluctant Rebels*; Carmichael, *War for the Common Soldier*.

8. McPherson and Cooper, "Introduction," 3.

to demonstrate its complicated and diverse nature.[9] This current work opens the door into a woman's rarely examined life through an extraordinarily revealing correspondence.

The broad development of studies on female participation has come accompanied by inquiry into the experiences of Union women differentiated by factors such as race and region.[10] In "the Heart of the Union"—the Midwest—agriculture "most profoundly shaped" identity, more so than for the rest of the North.[11] When the Civil War came, and midwestern males flocked to defend the U.S. flag, the region became "a place of struggle and hardship for the largely agrarian women and families" who coped with their absence. The experience of midwestern women who "negotiated" a "rapidly destabilizing" world has been "overshadowed"—yet deserves telling.[12] In some rural areas, a particular factor came into play: the presence of Native Americans.

The 1860 population of Wisconsin and Michigan each amounted to approximately 750,000 to 775,000 persons, with Minnesota's around 175,000. Ohio (2.3 million), Illinois (1.7), and Indiana (1.35) were far more populous.[13] Settlement in the Upper Midwest had accelerated during the previous decade, encroaching on traditional homelands of Native Americans and replicating the clash of cultures that had transpired in the lower three states. One midwestern wife wrote her deployed husband that "many persons here are afraid that the Indians in Mich[igan] will make trouble" during the soldiers' absence.[14] Events such as the so-called Sioux War in Minnesota during 1862–1863 could stoke such fear.[15] But how might someone in Ellen Woodworth's straits process that Native men from nearby would volunteer, like her husband, and be accounted as "gallant" and "brave" though suffering "dreadfully, but never faltered nor moved" in battle?[16]

An impediment to such inquiry has been the comparatively few documents remaining from women that reveal their contributions. Collec-

9. Faust, "'Ours as Well as that of the Men,'" 228, 239–240; Giesberg, "Future of Civil War Era Studies."

10. On race, see, e.g., Glymph, *Women's Fight*.

11. Aley and Anderson, *Union Heartland*, 3.

12. Ibid., 6; Aley, "Inescapable Realities," 126–129.

13. Kennedy, *Population of the United States*, iv.

14. Quist, *Michigan's War*, 106.

15. Connolly, *Thrilling Narrative*.

16. Lanman, *Red Book of Michigan*, 307.

tions of everyday letters and diaries originating from the southern home front are numerous and occupy much of Civil War scholarship and publication inventories.[17] Initially, as Elizabeth Leonard argued, one of the "few aspects of Northern women's Civil War experience that has received focused scholarly attention" has been of ladies' soldiers' aid societies.[18] These organizations were more typical in cities and towns. Correspondence between eastern men and women is also more extant.[19]

The expanding literature on Civil War women since the 1990s has helped correct a skewed record, but rural midwestern women's voices remain largely silent compared to those of southern white women or middle-class eastern women. The experience of Union farm women is lesser known, allegedly because they "were strikingly silent and unseen" and since "scant literature documented their trials and travails."[20] In addition to the scarcity, scholars judged writing by such "common folk" as "excessively routine, poorly expressed, and irregularly kept."[21] A century after the war, a study of its effects on a Union state's agriculture made no mention of the role of women.[22] The participation in the war by women of the rural Midwest where Indigenous people still lived remains obscure.

Ellen Woodworth's Civil War journal helps fill such gaps. Her letters originated from a farm homestead in a small community in central lower Michigan. Farming alone would not sustain the family while the husband and father went off to war, prompting Ellen into a different resourcefulness. Her point of view serves to reveal a predominant understanding of the population, since nearly nine out of ten Michiganders could call themselves "rural."[23] After twelve years of marriage, Samuel Woodworth's enlistment left the thirty-year-old mother to raise their two young children and manage family affairs during a crisis

---

17. See generally Glymph, *Women's Fight*; McCurry, *Women's War*; Monson, *Women of the Blue & Gray*; Berry and Elder, *Practical Strangers*; Marshall, "'Sisters' War'" 481; Chestnut, *Mary Chestnut's Diary*.

18. Leonard, *Yankee Women*, 163.

19. See, e.g., Keating, *Greatest Trials I Ever Had*.

20. Weiner, "Rural Women," 150; Silber, *Gender and the Sectional Conflict*, 83, 94.

21. Mohr, *Cormany Diaries*, x–xi.

22. Marks, *Effects of the Civil War*, 22 [bibliography]. This Commission did publish a farm wife's diary, but it only covered a three-month period. McCune, *Mary Austin Wallace*. It was incorporated into another slim monograph embracing a fuller survey. *Michigan Women in the Civil War*.

23. *Historical Statistics*, 29.

that, in historian Nina Silber's words, "severely tested the marital stability of many Northern couples."[24] As George Rable has argued, this "trauma of separation" might be eased through regular and mutual correspondence, which itself "became a test of love and devotion." By contrast, "irregular mail threatened relationships."[25] Ellen would fulfill her promise to be a regular correspondent; after the war, she would ensure her letters, and her soldier husband's, would not be lost.[26]

Ellen L. Preston was born on July 7, 1833, in Strafford, Vermont, to William (1803–1881) and Mary Fisk Preston (1806–1888), members of "a sterling old Eastern family."[27] Samuel Woodworth was born September 20, 1832, in New York State to Charles (1804–1861) and Nancy Whitney Woodworth (1806–1878). They were married on April 13, 1851. Their first child, Vesper Lagrande Woodworth, was born on November 9, 1854, in Java Center, Wyoming County, New York. Dallas Charles Woodworth, their second child, was born on December 26, 1859, in the same western New York community. On the eve of the Civil War, the couple decided to relocate westward and came to Isabella County, Michigan. They followed in the footsteps of other easterners seeking "a better country, where land was cheap" and "wild grapes and other wild fruit grew in abundance" in rich soil.[28] They were among the first white inhabitants in a region long inhabited by the Ojibwe people (usually called "Chippewa" by non-Natives); Isabella County was home to the second-largest Native American population in Michigan.[29] Due to federal policy that opened Indigenous lands to non-Native settlement, the Woodworths were able to stake a claim, despite having few financial assets, on 160 acres of land "in the southeast quarter of section eleven in what is today Lincoln Township." An 1838 U.S. survey described the property "as second rate and rolling."[30]

---

24. Silber, *Daughters of the Union*, 111. Approximately one-third of Union enlistees were married, but many had not started families. Gallman, *Defining Duty*, 8.

25. Rable, "Hearth, Home and Family," 88–89.

26. A 1989 local history relied on the journal for a chapter titled "The First Schoolteacher." Cumming, *This Place Mount Pleasant*, 24–26.

27. Fancher, *Past and Present*, 466.

28. Nowlin, *Bark Covered House*, 18.

29. Dunbar, *Michigan*, 351. The county name came at the suggestion of Henry R. Schoolcraft (1793–1864; U.S. government agent who married a Native American) "for Queen Isabella, of Spain, patron of Columbus." Romig, *Michigan Place Names*, 288.

30. *Portrait and Biographical Album*, 556; Fancher, *Past and Present*, 325; Miles, *School ma'm*, 17.

The couple would own their farm outright once they secured a patent under the Homestead Act. That statute, signed by President Abraham Lincoln on May 20, 1862, encouraged migration by enabling settlers to make a claim on surveyed public land in exchange for constructing a dwelling, living in it, and farming it for five continuous years.[31] The program was justified as an incentive for the spread of free labor.[32]

The Woodworths' opportunity at land ownership in newly named Lincoln Township was made possible by a series of treaties with the resident Indigenous people.[33] The first, in 1819, ceded Ojibwe land in the east-central portion of the Lower Peninsula.[34] The second, in 1836, involved even larger cessions in the northwestern Lower Peninsula and eastern Upper Peninsula.[35] As to the latter, Odawa councilor Mack-e-te-be-nessy (Andrew J. Blackbird) wrote of "watching our people as they were about going off in a long bark canoe . . . to Washington to see the Great Father, the President of the United States, to tell him to have mercy on the Ottawa and Chippewa Indians in Michigan, not to take all the land away from them." The disappointing result, he recounted, was a treaty "signed at Washington, not with the free will of the Indians, but by compulsion."[36] Blackbird participated in negotiations over a treaty in 1855, which from the Native perspective sought to forestall forced emigration from their remaining Michigan homes.[37] As

---

31. Alternatively, a homesteader could purchase land from the U.S. Government for $1.25 per acre, an option the Woodworths did not pursue. Hyman, *American Singularity*, 35. "Singular" means "unusual" or "exceptional," here reflecting that "a nation caught up in such a trauma as our Civil War" nonetheless legislated "on the greater access of its citizens" to land. Ibid.

32. Foner, *Free Soil*, 28; *United States Statutes at Large*, Vol. XII, 392 ff. The program could benefit African Americans: a nearby official State marker recounts that "In the 1860s Negroes from southern Michigan, Ohio and southwest Ontario settled in this region as farmers and woodsmen." Michigan Historic Register Site L81, Nine Mile Road at Ninetieth Avenue, Morton Township, Mecosta County, http://www.michmarkers.com [Negro Settlers]. See Hyman, *American Singularity*, 38, 40, 45–46, 48.

33. The township name was adopted October 16, 1863. *Isabella County, Michigan*, 19. This adoption shows a greater level of support for the war than apparent from the 1860 presidential election returns. Isabella County cast 123 votes for Lincoln (48.5%), 131 for his chief opponent, Stephen A. Douglas (51.5%). Dubin, *United States Presidential Elections, 1788–1860*, 171.

34. Peters, *Public Statutes*, Vol. VII, 203.

35. Kappler, *Indian Affairs*, 461.

36. Blackbird, *History of the Ottawa and Chippewa*, 51.

37. Michigan Historical Marker, State Historic Register No. 352, 368 East Main Street, Harbor Springs, http://www.michmarkers.com [Andrew J. Blackbird House].

for the Ojibwe, the treaty withdrew from alienation to settlers all un-sold land in six Isabella County townships "to be selected by said Indi-ans" for their own eighty-acre homesteads, a step to resolve "legal and equitable claims" they had against the United States.[38] The territory en-compassed nearly one hundred thousand acres—much less than they once enjoyed but a successful outcome given the context.[39]

Once settled into their "woodland home," the Woodworths' situa-tion brought major differences from life back East. The 1860 Census recorded an exiguous county population of approximately 1,500 (of whom 848 were recorded as "Indian," likely Ojibwe).[40] The county seat, initially placed at its geographic center, was not divided into sell-able lots and lacked access to water transportation.[41] Roads were few and rail transportation distant.[42] Women often braided their hats out of straw.[43] Since non-Native homes were scattered, fashionable enter-tainment meant hitching a "team of oxen, [and] go[ing] to a neighbor's to spend the entire day and eat dinner with them." The fare at these gatherings further emphasized the area's remoteness. Coffee and tea were scarce, requiring the use of substitutes including pine bark, dried strawberry leaves, scorched peas, beans, barley, and corn. As with the Native peoples, maple sugar became the staple sweetener.[44]

The Civil War, which began in April 1861, only indirectly affected the Woodworth family until President Lincoln signed a compulsory mil-itary service system into law on March 3, 1863. Males between twenty and forty-five years of age were subjected to enrollment and poten-tial conscription into the Union army.[45] Each congressional district re-

---

38. Minot and Sanger, *Statutes at Large* , 633.

39. The Michigan Ojibwe story is part of "a more complex and less linear narrative" than typically told. White, *Middle Ground*, ix; McDonnell, *Masters of Empire*, 327; Dan-ziger, *Great Lakes Indian Accommodation*. The Museum of Ojibwa Culture is located in St. Ignace, Michigan.

40. United States Census Bureau, "Population of the United States in 1860: Michigan," accessed January 30, 2023, https://www2.census.gov/library/publications/decennial /1860/population/1860a-20.pdf This summary document listed no "Colored," an inaccu-racy. For example, Joseph Lett enlisted in the First Michigan Colored Infantry on January 11, 1864, for 3 years, age 17, and served until September 1865. *Record of Service*, vol. 46, 61. He resided northwest of Mount Pleasant. *Isabella County, Michigan*, 18.

41. Fancher, *Past and Present*, 86, 88.

42. The closest depots were in Owosso and Ionia, at least sixty miles away.

43. *Portrait and Biographical Album*, 540, 563.

44. Id., 563.

45. *United States Statutes at Large*, XII, 731–737.

ceived a quota, which, if unmet by enough volunteers, would require a draft. The law could have the effect of spurring communities "to more aggressive recruiting."[46] Six months after passage of the law, a recruiting officer came to Isabella County seeking volunteers to enlist in advance of the draft taking place.[47]

Samuel Woodworth—five foot seven, with light hair, a light complexion, and blue eyes—had suffered from a respiratory condition, potentially enabling a physician to find him unfit for duty if conscripted.[48] Generally, no married man could be drafted until all eligible unmarried men had been taken. Despite such factors, on September 22, 1863, without his wife's full assent,[49] Samuel, a carpenter by trade, voluntarily enlisted for a three-year tour of duty in Company M of the 1st Michigan Engineers & Mechanics Volunteer Regiment. The enlisting officer was "Sergt Nelson."[50] Samuel was "paid 25 Dollars Bounty and four Dollars prem[ium]."[51]

The contributions of this unit "were specially valuable to the government" and earned for it "a national as well as State reputation."[52] Its members were trained for warfare but devoted to construction projects and logistical support through road and rail building, bridge and tunnel maintenance, and military operations. Like many of his comrades who were experienced in clearing forests and using the lumber produced,[53] Samuel's experience in clearing his homestead land helped qualify him for duty. He also brought an enthusiasm for service—measured by how he escorted the recruiting officer through the settlements. He sought to foster enlistment by his neighbors by taking part in "war meetings" where "old patriotic songs were sung, speeches made and papers read," exhorting volunteerism.[54]

---

46. Gallman, *Defining Duty*, 252.

47. *Portrait and Biographical Album*, 312-313.

48. Draftees "had numerous options for avoiding service." One could become exempt from serving through medical disability, pay a commutation fee, or supply a substitute. A draftee might also fail to report. Gallman, *North Fights the Civil War*, 68–70. See Murdock, *Patriotism Limited*.

49. Letter of Ellen to Samuel, October 12, 1863.

50. *Descriptive Roll of Company M*, 170. His enlistment papers list "Sargt D[?] Nelson" as Recruiting Officer. Service Record, National Archives. Nelson resurfaces later in the correspondence.

51. Service Record.

52. Robertson, *Michigan in the War*, 507.

53. Hoffman, *Among the Enemy*, 1; Hoffman, *My Brave Mechanics*, 4–6, 17.

54. Fancher, *Past and Present*, 312–313.

Ironically, another of the State's specialized regiments—the 1st Michigan Sharpshooters—was bolstered during 1863 by the formation of a unit composed of marksman from several tribes.[55] The Isabella reservation furnished several.[56] Some sixty-seven Indigenous males enlisted, primarily for service in that regiment.[57] Company K was composed almost entirely of members of three major tribes in Michigan: Ojibwe, Odawa, and Potawatomi. They did not hold U.S. citizenship, though the 1850 Michigan Constitution afforded voting rights to "every civilized male inhabitant of Indian descent, a native of the United States and not a member of any tribe."[58] The unit "was the largest all-Native company" east of the Mississippi.[59] They participated in some of the bloodiest and most consequential battles late in the war, and their heroism proved second to none.[60]

Samuel's enlistment came at a challenging juncture. Two July victories, at Gettysburg and Vicksburg, had boosted Union morale, countered by Confederate victory at the Battle of Chickamauga in north Georgia on September 19–20. The formidable Confederate Army of Northern Virginia continued to stalemate the war in the East. Samuel was mustered in on October 7 in Detroit as "artificer," a craftsman or carpenter.[61] He reached his first duty station at Louisville, Kentucky, later that month, then joined the regiment at Elk River near the Alabama/Tennessee border. Deep in the South, it was the site of the unit's largest construction project, a bridge more than five hundred feet long. If the Union army was to prevail, the rail supply line to Chattanooga, and beyond, would have to be maintained through such efforts. As Earl Hess has noted, the interior of the Deep South was "a kind of citadel of resistance" for the Rebels, requiring "an almost superhuman effort" of perseverance by Union soldiers to keep the supply artery open.[62]

The responsibility of the Engineers & Mechanics for constructing and protecting Union military communications coincidentally enabled

55. See generally Hauptman, *Between Two Fires*; Sutton and Latschar, *American Indians and the Civil War*; Herek, *These Men Have Seen*; Czopek, *Who Was Who*; Walker, *Deadly Aim*.

56. Herek, *These Men Have Seen*, 35.

57. Fancher, *Past and Present*, 310.

58. Art. VII, sec. 1, *Revised Constitution*, 18. The name of the state had derived from a Native term. Romig, *Michigan Place Names*, 366.

59. Hemenway, "Foreword," viii.

60. Walker, *Deadly Aim*, 243.

61. *Record of Service*, vol. 43, 229.

62. Hess, *Civil War Supply and Strategy*, 6–7, 10, 139.

the Woodworths to correspond regularly, though several interruptions brought anxiety for each of them. Ellen wanted "all the particulars" attending her husband's situation: "if its only where you sleep—who with, who you eat with, talk with—what you talk about—think about— what you do evenings, where you sit, what you sit on, how you look, how you feel—& how you are treated; any thing concerning you is of great interest to me. Tell me about every thing."[63] When trips to the rural post office found no letter waiting, Ellen's heart sank.

With Samuel's enlistment, Ellen had to assume nearly total responsibility for the family's well-being for the first time. Doing so brought her into a similar sphere with many other women in the North and poor white women of the South who "sent their sons to war, sewed for the soldiers, sacrificed, and suffered for the war effort."[64] Her letters about the home situation demonstrate management of financial, social, educational, and other necessary aspects of family welfare. She coped with the harsh conditions of a midwestern winter. She encountered the inflationary effects of the war on food prices, necessitating substitutes for staples, especially difficult in such a remote locale. Without consistent income from farming or in pay envelopes from Samuel, she looked for opportunities to improve the family's financial resources.[65]

In January 1864, the new community seat of Mount (or "Mt.") Pleasant held a meeting to discuss constructing a schoolhouse and hiring a teacher. Ellen applied for the position, after spending Christmas there and having written Samuel that "I almost wish I had a house up there, to live in, & rent our place here, while you are away."[66] On May 1, she was hired for that summer's session. The income was significant: "there was paid to the teacher, Mrs. Woodworth, during 1864 at one time thirty-six dollars and fifty cents, and at another time thirty-four dollars and twenty-five cents."[67] Her resourcefulness did not end there. With-

63. Letter of Ellen to Samuel, September 26, 1864.

64. Glymph, *Women's Fight*, 59.

65. For Civil War era economic matters, see: Unger, *Greenback Era*; Lowenstein, *Ways and Means*. Unlike Northern farmers and growers who harvested their crops and produce for sale in a bountiful market, Hurt, *Food and Agriculture*, 78, Ellen grew for subsistence and had to be a net purchaser rather than producer.

66. Letter of Ellen to Samuel, November 30, 1863.

67. Fancher, *Past and Present*, 145–146. The 1850 Michigan Constitution provided for a system of public instruction for children under which a school must be kept without tuition, at least three months in each year, in every school district in the State. *Revised Constitution*, 23.

out her husband's foreknowledge, she determined on, bargained for, and acquired a house near the school. It would be a good investment, she wrote him. Samuel expressed surprise "at your buying so expensive a place at present."[68] She insisted her plans were well considered: "I thought it better to be earning something & not be wholly dependent on you."[69] He relented: "I will do all I can to help you pay for it."[70]

Supplemental aid came from local government. In February 1864, Isabella County acted to provide a bounty of two hundred dollars to families whose breadwinners had gone off to war. Half would be paid one year from enlistment and the rest at the two-year mark. When it arrived that fall, the bonus payment aided Ellen's efforts at balancing their books. Still, she expressed concern about accepting aid and becoming known as a "war-widow."[71] That label came home when she supported widows at their husbands' funerals.

The dangers inherent in service at a post deep in enemy territory informed the couple's writings. Maintaining the supply lifeline subjected Samuel's company to organized raids by Confederate cavalry and to ambushes from guerilla forces.[72] The dangers from "bushwhackers" were so pronounced that Samuel frequently slept with his weapon nearby. A number of his comrades were killed, and his frankness about the wounds incurred in hostilities—witnessing Union soldiers being transported to hospital from the front, "cut to pieces in all shapes"[73]—made vivid the combat he could face at a moment's notice. Still, illness took most lives in uniform during the war.[74] Samuel was not immune. He wrote Ellen after only a few months in uniform about suffering from "a regular Camp sickness, attended with fever & dysentery."[75] "O, Samuel, are you seriously ill?" she replied.[76] When he wrote a month later about having "a hard week of it,"[77] the implications underscored that his return home had no guarantee.

Unable to help nurse her husband, Ellen freely confessed to the

---

68. Letter of Samuel to Ellen, October 9, 1864.
69. Letter of Ellen to Samuel, April 18, 1864.
70. Letter of Samuel to Ellen, October 9, 1864.
71. Letter of Ellen to Samuel, February 14, 1864.
72. Dyer, *Compendium*, 162; Robertson, *Michigan in the War*, 498–499.
73. Letter of Samuel to Ellen, June 3, 1864.
74. "There were just so many bodies to count." Faust, *This Republic of Suffering*, 260.
75. Letter of Samuel to Ellen, January 3, 1864.
76. Letter of Ellen to Samuel, January 11, 1864.
77. Letter of Samuel to Ellen, February 7, 1864.

"weight of anxiety" that her "nervous system" constantly experienced.[78] Her fortitude was bolstered by the couple's two young boys—"all I have left to comfort me, now that you are gone."[79] Their illnesses and injuries were yet another problem to bear, and Ellen sought to involve Samuel by inviting him to write fatherly counsel to "Veppy & Dallie." The older, in turn, penned a note to "My Dear Papa." The letters from home sought to keep Samuel apprised of the boys' behavior, including the mischievous. Her vivid writing of how "the children now both stand beside me—Vesper with his slate & pencil—and Dallie with a book,"[80] re-created homelife for the absent father. The war came home to the family: Ellen wrote of how one child "has got his Geography out, to find where the last battles are being fought" while the other "has got some large illustrations of battle scenes spread out on the floor, & trying to find his papa among the Soldiers."[81] Samuel's descriptions of military events helped inspire such interest.

The proximity of friends and family also served to help ease Ellen's loneliness. She attended "Singing School at the Court House," went to meetings and on visits to other homes, came home in a neighbor's "horses, & sleigh." When a sister and her friends paid a call, Ellen "warmed a mince pie . . . served some refreshments & then had some music from an Accordeon."[82] Advance notice of "a Surprise Party" by a visit of fifteen late one evening tested her hospitality, but she wrote about rising to the occasion. Still, she wrote Samuel, "if *you* had been present I should have enjoyed it much better than I did."[83]

Her husband wrote about the novelty of meeting southerners and "Negroes," and Ellen reveled in sharing and reacting to his experiences. "[W]hen I get home I will tell you some of their sad history," he promised.[84] She replied: "I am also glad to see that your views on the question of Slavery, and the justness of the course pursued by our leaders in this war, is changing—from what your belief was formerly."[85] When

78. Letter of Ellen to Samuel, December 4, 1864.

79. Letter of Ellen to Samuel, January 11, 1864. For studies on children and the Civil War, see Marten, *Civil War America*, and *The Children's Civil War*.

80. Letter of Ellen to Samuel, November 29, 1864.

81. Letter of Ellen to Samuel, September 3, 1864.

82. Letter of Ellen to Samuel, February 2, 1864.

83. Letter of Ellen to Samuel, February 9, 1864.

84. Letter of Samuel to Ellen, October 15, 1864.

85. Letter of Ellen to Samuel, November 21, 1864.

he revealed danger from Confederate raiders, the news prompted far different feelings. Her emotional stress was heightened when Samuel's letters told of becoming seriously ill. Recuperation, albeit a slow one, became a theme in the rather brief letters next received at home. Ellen's lengthier reports sought to reassure her husband of how the family longed for his health and his eventual return and to encourage upholding moral strictures. Eventually, Samuel would reveal the full circumstances of his afflictions: vermin infestation, boils, hair and weight loss. He also told the family of his messmates' surprise at the invalid's recovery.

Religious beliefs helped foster endurance, especially for Ellen. Membership in the Methodist church placed her in the religious mainstream since it was among "the more populist denominations."[86] Its network of itinerant ministers who preached the faith in rural places produced, as David Reynolds states, "almost as many Methodist churches in the United States as there were post offices."[87] Ellen's views on key issues—rebellion, slavery, and postwar welfare of the newly freed—placed her squarely within the moral framework of her denomination, which held that "the destruction of slavery was the chief object of the war," unequivocally defended the Union, and urged support of Freedmen's aid societies to ease the transition from bondage to freedom.[88] Religious grounding, however, did not eliminate her anxiety, as shown by a lament: "Why am I so apprehensive?"[89]

Ellen consistently invoked biblical injunctions and urged her husband to become a better moral agent than he had been before enlistment.[90] She was far from unique: both sides relied on Bible texts for endurance and justification. Leaders including Frederick Douglass and Abraham Lincoln invoked scripture, the latter most iconically in his Second Inaugural speech.[91] Military service in the Deep South afforded Samuel the opportunity to reconsider his spiritual framework in light

---

86. Reynolds, *America, Empire of Liberty*, 104.

87. Id., 104.

88. Macmillan, *Methodist Episcopal Church*, 59.

89. Letter of Ellen to Samuel, December 20, 1864.

90. For studies on how the war intersected expectations on morality and social conventions, see Stout, *Upon the Altar* and Foote, *Gentleman and the Roughs*.

91. See, e.g., Byrd, *Holy Baptism*; Woodworth, *While God Is Marching On*. Many battlefields are known by their religious landmarks or connotations: the Dunker church at Antietam; Shiloh; New Hope Church; New Bethel; the Wilderness (to name a few).

of Ellen's continuing encouragement. Samuel had his first encounter with African Americans in a church setting by attending "Negro meetings" of the formerly enslaved. He concluded "there are some very inteligent [sic] Negroes."[92] His letters revealed that while he had held no abolitionist sentiment at enlistment, his outlook changed: "I have come to the conclusion that it is a just war—I have had an opportunity to learn something of the horrid institution of Slavery. O how wicked; how cruel! I have conversed with a great many, from all parts of the south that have come into our lines for protection—& it has drawn tears from my eyes to listen to their sad story."[93]

Samuel's approach to spiritual matters underwent something of a transformation. He was not much of a believer or of any particular faith at enlistment, a significant difference from his wife's fervor evidenced from her first epistle. Ellen's letters recounted how he had engaged in pursuits, such as card playing, that she thought less than virtuous. Military service caused him to rethink his behavior and beliefs. Receiving "a Testament & hymn book" not long after enlisting, his mention of the gift evoked this response from Ellen: "I hope you will *read* your books that you spoke of, that had been given you; for your sake, & mine."[94] She longed that he "might become a christian."[95] His letters do show change, exemplified by news that "I sent Vesper a soldiers hymn book this week."[96] Eventually, he would write home: "It is pretty hard to be a christian, among what we have to contend with."[97]

Ellen wrote of gratification that his politics had come into alignment with hers. "You will now call me an abolishionist," he confessed.[98] She affirmed his change of heart: "if any one will listen to reason and look for the right, they will not be governed by party spirit, when truth, & *Justice* tells them they are in error."[99] Her defense of the Union and opposition to slavery remained constant. Not until 1881 did Michigan

---

92. Letter of Samuel to Ellen, October 15, 1864. He did not employ terminology in his letters disrespectful by contemporary standards.

93. Letter of Samuel to Ellen, October 15, 1864.

94. Letter of Ellen to Samuel, November 10, 1863.

95. Letter of Ellen to Samuel, April 12, 1864.

96. Letter of Samuel to Ellen, March 18, 1864.

97. Letter of Samuel to Ellen, April 30, 1864.

98. Letter of Samuel to Ellen, October 15, 1864.

99. Letter of Ellen to Samuel, November 21, 1864.

women gain a limited right to vote, a precursor to broader achievements in 1918–1920.[100] Without the right to vote, Ellen Woodworth's
letter writing gave her an avenue to express political views and influence her husband in a new, meaningful way.

Though neighbors were few and far between in Lincoln Township,
Ellen's letters speak of visits among neighbors and social interactions
that proved critical to a sense of community. Her move to Mount Pleasant began to widen her circle of contacts, though the town featured
only nine structures.[101] She was called on to take in and nurse an injured lumberman; she took in a boarder, a new arrival who launched
a town newspaper. Her repeated mentions of a brother-in-law who
was becoming a leading citizen, other community leaders, and their
spouses demonstrated the interconnectedness of the rural inhabitants.

As in her husband's, Ellen's letters spoke of novel cultural experiences. Like his, they first occurred in a religious context. Unlike his,
her reactions were mixed. On the one hand, she could speak of Native
congregants as her "brothers, & sisters."[102] On the other hand, employing a descriptive term of them as "dusky" revealed something less than
full acceptance as fellow children of God. When visiting Native children at the Mission School, she regarded "some of them quite intelligent looking." But calling them "filthy and disobedient," and express-
ing a preference for teaching "white children, at less remuneration,"
revealed an attitude that bore markings of prejudice.[103] There was not
much Christian compassion in her complaining about higher prices for
fruit because "the Squaws" had more enterprise in picking it first.[104]
Still, she did not refer to Native people as a "menace" as did persons
of prominence, raised in a "pioneer" environment, such as suffragette

---

100. The 1881 change permitted "[e]very person" (with some additional requirements)
in "any school district" and who held property "liable to assessment for school taxes," or
who was a parent of a child, to vote at "any school meeting." Act No. 164, effective May
21, 1881, *Public Acts*, 163, 168; voter approval of HJR 14 on November 5, 1918, extended the
franchise to women; Nineteenth Amendment to the U.S. Constitution, effective August
1920.

101. Cumming, *This Place Mount Pleasant*, 29. See Ellen's sketch later in this volume. For
a period map of Lincoln Township, see Hayes, *Atlas of Isabella County, Michigan*, 19.

102. Letter of Ellen to Samuel, June 14, 1864.

103. Letter of Ellen to Samuel, June 28, 1864.

104. Letter of Ellen to Samuel, August 9, 1864.

Anna Howard Shaw.[105] Nor did she express fear about their proximity as did other midwestern women.[106]

Missing from her written observations is awareness of the varied and parallel lives of Native families in the county. As documented in the 1860 Census, male heads of Native families principally maintained two occupations, "Farmer" and "Hunter." They shared such "jobs" with Euro-Americans. Three males were recorded in religious roles, as Methodist preachers. Several told the enumerator that their occupation was "Conncilor"—a tribal leadership designation—or "Ex Chief," and one woman described herself as "Chiefs' widow." Names were listed in Native as well as European forms. Family units ranged in size from that of the Woodworths to larger numbers.[107] Native women and children had to cope with their family members' absence in blue uniform just as much—including their deaths.[108]

After the initial twelve months apart, Ellen could express pride in her contribution to the Union war effort. The challenges of separation were felt daily, sharpened by a visit to their farmstead when she "could not stay there long" because of reminders of Samuel in his "work on every hand."[109] Yet, such hardships could be endured on account of the cause:

> When I think of the lonely hours I have passed since you went away, and still must pass—I feel that I too am doing something for our Coun-

---

105. Shaw, *Story of a Pioneer*, 34.

106. Works that examine prevalent views of nineteenth-century white individuals toward Native Americans, and help explain Ellen's, include Drinnon, *Facing West*; and Berkhofer, *White Man's Indian*. Even for abolitionists—those seeking the eradication of human slavery—the issue of extending rights to others (including women voting) took later priority.

107. See schedules for Isabella Township, Isabella County, Michigan, in the *Eighth United States Decennial Census*. Other lines of work included "Boatman," "Com[mon] Laborer," "Ind[ian] Trader," "Sawier" (Sawyer), and "Interpreter."

108. One poignant example is the "Maishcaw" or "Mash-kaw" family of Elbridge Township, Oceana County, almost due west. James (Kahkuhgewa/Kaw-gaw-ge-way) enlisted on July 4, 1863, in Company K, 1st Michigan Sharpshooters, age thirty-one. Younger brother John, age twenty-two, did the same. Both volunteered for three years; both were killed in action on the same day, May 12, 1864, at Spotsylvania Court House. *Record of Service*, vol. 44, 61; Herek, *These Men Have Seen*, 148, 343. Both are interred in the Fredericksburg National Cemetery, according to one database. They left behind bereaved parents and James's widow. Herek, *These Men Have Seen*, 346; "Mash-kaw Brothers," *Company K 1st Michigan Sharpshooters* blog, November 16, 2018, https://nativesharpshooters. blogspot.com/2018/11/mash-kaw-brothers.html (a roster of death on this website indicates they died "while charging the enemies works").

109. Letter of Ellen to Samuel, May 30, 1864.

try. I have given all I had to give, for the cause of Liberty & freedom; and should the happy hour come when we can welcome our brave Soldiers home, we can truly unite in the glad anthem of gratitude & praise that will burst from the national heart, & feel that we have *helped* hasten the happy era, & borne a share in this great & fearful struggle. God bless you, my dear Husband.[110]

Ellen's views on contemporary politics found expression in anticipating the day when "a prosperous & *purified Nation*" would emerge.[111] She looked to "restoration of our noble Union"[112] and denigrated those of the "Copperhead" party,[113] counting them as southern sympathizers arrayed against her husband. She opined on the 1864 presidential election, clearly favoring Lincoln's reelection over his opponent, Union general George B. McClellan, who ran on a platform without emancipation. Samuel lagged behind; he did not vote and initially suggested that "Uncle Abraham is losing friends among the Soldiers—he may be all right but he will lose votes by the course he is taking."[114] When the canvass concluded, Samuel observed: "Abraham has a firm hold of me, so I shall have to stay; yet he clothes me well, & feeds us—such as it is."[115]

Despite a fairly dependable delivery system, the vagaries of the mail compounded the difficulty of separation.[116] As Ellen waited "two long weeks in suspense" for a letter, the dearth of news from her distant spouse caused her to confess that it "makes me nearly sick."[117] At the lowest emotional point early in the winter of 1864–1865, she did ask him to "come home on furlough," a need so powerfully felt that "it has seemed the past few days as though you were coming—so much so that I sat up Saturday night till past 12 o clock watching for you."[118] Her candor revealed a state almost of desperation: "Three weeks of sus-

---

110. Letter of Ellen to Samuel, July 12, 1864.

111. Letter of Ellen to Samuel, June 14, 1864.

112. Letter of Ellen to Samuel, July 12, 1864.

113. Letter of Ellen to Samuel, November 21, 1864. Copperheads were an element of the Democratic Party who opposed war and sought a settlement without emancipation. Weber, *Copperheads*, 1.

114. Letter of Samuel to Ellen, September 4, 1864.

115. Letter of Samuel to Ellen, November 16, 1864.

116. For information on the U.S. mail system during the Civil War, see Hager, *I Remain Yours*; Woods, "Neither Snow Nor Rain"; John, *Spreading the News*.

117. Letter of Ellen to Samuel, July 19, 1864.

118. Letter of Ellen to Samuel, December 20, 1864.

pense—what can be the reason—Are you sick, or a prisoner—or—O what! Not dead!"[119]

Samuel complained of not receiving correspondence from home, but he expressed willingness to sacrifice, temporarily, if the lack of letters was due to military necessity, such as trains being occupied with carrying munitions. When an envelope did arrive, his well-being was buttressed: "the letter I received to day pays me for waiting—so full of hope and good news it cheers me on."[120] Can you "ever realize," he replied, "how much good they do me"?[121] Ellen's constancy in corresponding inspired Samuel to remain in uniform until war's end. He received his discharge on May 17, 1865.[122] A week later, his regiment paraded through the streets of Washington, D.C., in a victory celebration tempered by Lincoln's assassination. Samuel's recuperation from lingering illness prevented his participation but brought him home quicker.

In addition to teaching for an income, Ellen's other pursuits were representative of women "[a]cross the Old Northwest" who "increasingly moved from their traditional domestic roles" into formerly exclusive male domains because they and their families and the Union required it: "necessity knew no law." Like Ellen, there were those who received advice from absent soldiers but "acted independently from necessity."[123] Such forbearance against obstacles entitled them, in the words of the sixteenth president, to be counted as among "the best women" in America.[124]

After his discharge, Samuel Woodworth became a veterinarian in Mount Pleasant and, like many veterans, joined the local post of the Grand Army of the Republic.[125] He and Ellen had a third son, Raymond Preston, who was born on July 20, 1871. In 1888, since two sons had homesteads nearby, the couple relocated to Emmet County, Mich-

---

119. Letter of Ellen to Samuel, December 27, 1864.

120. Letter of Samuel to Ellen, October 5, 1864.

121. Letter of Samuel to Ellen, January 1, 1865.

122. *Record of Service*, vol. 43, 229 (at Nashville).

123. Hurt, *Food and Agriculture*, 51–52, 86.

124. Basler, *Collected Works of Abraham Lincoln*, vol. 5, 326–327.

125. *Portrait and Biographical Album*, 497. For postwar experiences of Union soldiers like Samuel, see Jordan, *Marching Home*; McConnell, *Glorious Contentment*; *Michigan in the American Civil War*.

igan, and lived in the Village of Petoskey.[126] Samuel died there in 1899; Ellen was still living and working in Petoskey the next year, teaching German.[127] She moved back to Mount Pleasant during the next decade.[128] Ellen received a veteran widow's pension until she died in 1914 at her son Dallas's home in Illinois.[129] The couple's graves are found together in section 3 of Riverside Cemetery in Mount Pleasant.

Vesper Lagrande Woodworth, born on November 9, 1854, in Java Center, Wyoming County, New York, died on December 1, 1950, in Ashland County, Ohio, at the age of ninety-six. He was buried in Brookside Cemetery in Charlevoix, Michigan. He had been a farmer and a United States Post Office mail carrier.[130]

Dallas Charles Woodworth, born in Java Center on December 26, 1859, died July 17, 1916, at Rock Island, Illinois, at the age of fifty-six. He had worked as a tailor and as a motion picture operator and inventor.[131] He coauthored a dramatic production titled *The Pioneer: A Game of Hearts*.[132] He was buried in Chippiannock Cemetery, Rock Island, Illinois.

Raymond Preston Woodworth died September 30, 1948, in Ashland County, Ohio, at the age of seventy-seven. In 1900, he was employed as a "musician (show)" and was living in Birmingham, Alabama.[133] A decade later, that was still his occupation, but he had moved to Ann Arbor, Michigan.[134]

---

126. *Census of the State of Michigan 1894*, 86.

127. Miles, *School ma'm*, 40; Twelfth United States Decennial Census; Place: Petoskey, Emmet County, Michigan; p. 4; Enumeration District 89.

128. Thirteenth United States Decennial Census; Place: Mt. Pleasant, Isabella County, Michigan; p. 2; Enumeration District 96.

129. *United States General Index to Pension Files*, 1861–1934, https://www.familysearch.org/search/collection/

130. *Twelfth United States Decennial Census*—Place: Springvale, Emmet County, Michigan, p. 15, Enumeration District 0091; *Official Register, 1909*, vol. II, 696.

131. *Twelfth United States Decennial Census*—Place: Petoskey, Emmet County, Michigan, p. 29, Enumeration District 90; *Thirteenth United States Decennial Census*—Place: Chicago Ward 21, Cook County, Illinois, p. 9B, Enumeration District 0921; Fraprie, *American Photography*, vol. III, 436, 497.

132. *Dramatic Compositions*, 1825.

133. *Twelfth United States Decennial Census*—Place: Birmingham Ward 8, Jefferson County, Ala., 2, Enumeration District 0153.

134. *Thirteenth United States Decennial Census*—Place: Ann Arbor Ward 1, Washtenaw County, Michigan, Roll: T624_677, p. 7A, Enumeration District 0111.

The field of academic study known as "Civil War Memory" has yet to give fully proper attention to the service and sacrifice of the rural women of the Midwest. As Nina Silber notes, southern women have obtained "an exaggerated presence in our memory," leaving their Union counterparts "with barely a memorial or tribute worth noticing." Ostensibly, this uneven reckoning was due to an insufficient record to document (for Union farm women) "their trials and travails."[135] Even if recorded, readability might suffer from insufficient education. Not with the Woodworths as authors. Their writing is descriptive—Ellen, a teacher, penning a letter "to the constant patter of the rain against the window pane"[136]—Samuel, a woodworker, making keen observations about the destitution of the southern society he is helping to reform.

The Woodworths' correspondence may serve as among the "few monuments" of tribute earned by the women of the Union and, especially, those of the rural Midwest. Ellen Woodworth's writings demonstrated her resourcefulness and determination as she engaged in bartering, trading, borrowing, and investing, stood ready to litigate her family's rights, and sought not to be dependent on her deployed husband. She did not submit "to perform as 'women'" were expected.[137]

Samuel Woodworth would confess that, in retrospect, "I did not realize what I was doing when I enlisted."[138] It was an admission applicable to the extensive burden he shifted onto his wife by volunteering. Ellen Preston Woodworth appreciated her husband gaining comprehension of "some thing of the anguish that wrung my soul when you enlisted; but heaven forbid that you should ever feel the intensity of grief that filled my heart at that time."[139] Her anguish "wasn't because I lacked Patriotism; for I felt & knew that your Country needed you, & every other such brave heart as yours; but O, how much we needed you too."[140] Her constancy served to reinforce her husband's endurance, perhaps in no better way than in her envisioning a glorious conclusion to their separation: "Keep a brave heart—my Boy—for the day

---

135. Silber, *Gender and the Sectional Conflict*, 83, 94.
136. Letter of Ellen to Samuel, April 24, 1864.
137. Attie, *Patriotic Toil*, 5.
138. Letter of Samuel to Ellen, September 22, 1864.
139. Letter of Ellen to Samuel, September 3, 1864.
140. Ibid.

will dawn, ere long—when slavery—& rebellion will be wiped out—and the heroes of this war come proudly marching home."[141]

Immediately after organized fighting ceased in 1865, an insightful commenter offered a challenge to those who would chronicle the War of the Rebellion: "The story of the war will never be fully or fairly written if the achievements of women in it are untold."[142] With this volume, an important chapter in that complex story is supplied in aid of comprehending the full historical truth of America's greatest crisis.

---

141. Letter of Ellen to Samuel, October 9, 1864.
142. Moore, *Women of the War*, v.

Editorial Method

The personal letters that fill the next four chapters are essentially unchanged from their appearance in Ellen Woodworth's journal. This approach enables the couple to speak for themselves, and it provides immediacy by approaching each letter as written by the author and received by the addressee.

Ellen's journal notations indicate her letter of March 6, 1865, was not preserved and thus unable to be copied. Several others appear to be missing, including the first one she mailed between his departure and October 12, 1863, and letters from the children.

One consistent revision is use of a full proper name in place of an abbreviation or bracket. Other bracketed names have been taken from either the original or typescript copy.

Other changes include the addition of brackets for clarity, which are noted; the insertion of the day of the week of a letter where none was given; the arrangement of the letters in chronological order of their dating, a slight reordering from the journal. Superscriptions are not repeated.

Spelling and format remain largely unchanged from the original. In most cases, misspelling does not interfere with readability. The term "[sic]" has been used only when essential. A comma used for a decimal point is unchanged. Underlining in the original has been converted to italics.

Footnotes have been added to provide necessary background, context, and clarity.

This volume contains the entirety of the journal. The original of both versions are held by the Clarke Historical Library at Central Michigan University, Mount Pleasant, Michigan. The autograph version is in very clear handwriting and is legible despite the passage of time. The typescript was prepared with care and accuracy; it was proofed for errors, and handwritten proofing notes on the typescript are accurate corrections of the few typos that crept into it. The primary material in this book is accompanied by a digital component, a website that allows students and scholars to interact with the volume's content. Search for this book on www.ugapress.org for links to the bonus material.

CHAPTER 1

September–December 1863

Compiled from correspondence during the war. Principally, through the year 1864.

In our cottage home.

Lincoln, Mich.[1]

Ellen to Samuel[2]

Sept 24th 1863 [Thursday].

My Dear Husband:

You will be far away, perhaps in a strange land, when your eye first rests upon these lines; And I, where shall *I* be. Thinking of you, with an intense yearning to see your dear face, to hear your loving voice & to breathe words of council & admonition into your ear that my heart prompts me to do now, but when I fain would speak, grief chokes my utterance, & the words are smothered in sobs & tears, & remain unspoken.

But if I have no control over my feelings, I can still guide my pen, while it traces, in feeble language, a few, of the many things I *would* say to you if I could. First let me thank you for the sacred promise you made me, last night that you would be *firm* in your principles, and never be led to do aught that would cast a shadow on your good name as a citizen, or Soldier: And above all, would strictly regard the Sabbath as a day of rest, contemplation, & meditation; so far as the for-

---

1. Originally, in the Township of Coe, Isabella County.

2. Ellen prefaced this entry with the following: "First, a letter written to S.—by his wife with the request to not open, until he was on his way to the seat of war."

tunes of war will permit; and never indulge in wicked and idle games, on that sacred day. O, Samuel my heart thanks you for those blessed words; and they will cheer me in many a dark & lonely hour; & cause me to look forward with pride & joy, when I can claim again my noble soldier husband: and I will nightly pray God to watch over you, & shield you from all harm, & teach our little ones to do the same. And O, may you so live, that should it become necessary that your life should be sacrificed for your country, you would be ready to meet the stern summons, & enter into the presence of your Maker: O my Husband, do this & you will soon see many of your Comrades imitating your noble example and then the sweet assurance will be yours that you have done your duty to yourself, your Country & to your God. I will, for your sake, try to be more cheerful in our seperation, & will aim to live for you, & our precious children, & make them as comfortable as possible; Ever praying that kind heaven will guard you from every ill, & bring you safely to the loving embrace of your devoted family.

God bless thee, & with pleasure rife,
Grant thee a long & happy life:
But think of me in joys blest hour
Remember too, if dark clouds lower
That she in days of youth, thy friend
Will be the same till time shall end.
Ellen

Samuel to Ellen

Detroit. Oct. 2nd 1863 [Friday].

Dear Friends & Home,
Here I am in camp,[3] not knowing yet whether I shall be accepted,[4] or not: I have been examined once, but have got to be again to day by two Surgeons: Those that came with me have passed, all but C[aswell].[5]

---

3. At the military installation named Fort Wayne along the Detroit River on the near west side of that city. As evidenced by his next letter, Samuel had his photograph taken here and sent it home.

4. I.e., mustered into service, which did occur on October 7. *Descriptive Roll*, 170.

5. David Caswell, age forty-six, enlisted in the regiment at Adrian, Michigan, on October 3, 1863, for a three-year term, and was mustered in on October 14, evidently finding

I have had a pleasant time, so far—& am feeling well: and hope these few lines will find you the same. I cannot tell you where to direct, as we shall soon leave here. Should not have written to-day—only you would not have got it till next week; will write again soon.

Love to all—Truly Yours
Samuel

Samuel to Ellen

Louisville, Ky.[6] *Oct 9th 1863 [Friday].*

Dear Ellen

As I have a few moments to write I will drop a line to let you know how, & where I am. We left Detroit Wednesday night & arrived here this morning; have had good luck, & no accidents. was kept rather too close to suit me, but feel well. I sent a letter by B[rickley][7] with my likeness, some money, & directions. You may think strange that I did not send more; but I see so many poor fellows that do not get any thing, but bread & meat, to eat—that I do not mean to be without money. I hope to hear from you soon; and to hear that you are well; I cannot write much with 300 men around me; Good bye for this time.

Samuel

Ellen to Samuel

In our little Home—

Oct 12th 1863 [Monday].

My Dear Husband.

It is two weeks to day, since I parted from you, but it seems like two, *long*, month[s]. I have held up bravely so far; hoping that you would

a less strict examiner. He survived the war and mustered out on September 22, 1865. *Record of Service*, vol. 43, 32.

6. A staging location where the Union Army of the Cumberland was posted to organize new recruits for the front. See Daniel, *Days of Glory*. The short time since Samuel's first letter indicates sparse instruction or training in camp.

7. Likely Daniel Brickley, one of the early landowners who served as coroner of Isabella County. *Portrait and Biographical Album*, 542–543.

not go[8]—& I should soon see you again: but to-day that hope is torn
from me, & the bitter hour has come that tells me you are far away—
hundreds of miles from your home—your wife, & little ones. O, My
God, how *can* I have it so? Yet I must bow to the inevitable, for you
have gone, & cannot be recalled—

You will say where is your patriotism? O I fear I have none—we are
left so lonely—so entirely unprotected: I hope you may never know
such loneliness—or weep such bitter tears as now scald my cheeks,
while I gaze upon your picture. And yet you are a noble looking soldier! just such an one, as I am proud to call my husband and when I
know that you are well, & not in danger, I will not murmur—but look
to the bright future, when we shall once more be united in our own little home;

Mr. B[rickley] brought your letter containing the money; I will do
as you direct, with it: I cannot tell when I shall go to New York State[9];
Mr. B[rickley] said he would carry us to Johns,[10] as he was going out
to get some salt—Your Citizens clothes are in Midland;[11] Can we ever
bear to have them come home—just as you wore them away—and shall
we ever see you again? These are questions that are continually in my
mind. Who *can* answer them for me? I wrote you a letter last week &
sent by Mr. C[aswell]. I told you, in it, that Hattie E[stee] was very sick
with Diphtheria.[12] She has since died, & will be buried tomorrow at 10
clock. I am very careful of our children; so you must not worry about
them. Little D[allas] asks for papa, very often & wishes he would come,
sometime. He is well, & so is V[esper]. They are all the comfort I have
left now. May kind Heaven spare them to me, & ever watch over &
care for the absent one, & bring him safely home again, is my constant
prayer. I will now bid you good night & seek my pillow, where my pre-

---

8. Ellen apparently held out hope that Samuel would either not actually take the oath
and thus might return home after declining to be mustered in or not passing the physical.
From the letter of November 15, 1863, it appears he had suffered chronically from a respiratory condition, referring to it as asthma.

9. It appears that Ellen considered moving back East. See her letter of October 20,
1863.

10. St. Johns, Michigan, south in adjacent Clinton County.

11. Located approximately thirty miles to the east.

12. Hattie Estee Dana, born January 26, 1854, died October 12, 1863, age nine. "Hattie
Estee Dana," Find a Grave, https://www.findagrave.com/memorial/171758264/hattie-dana.
Diphtheria is a highly contagious bacterial infection typically accompanied by fever that
affects the ability to breathe.

cious children are sweetly sleeping. What a blessing is sleep, if it had no bitter awakening: I hope I may not always write so sorrowful a letter, but "out of the abundance of the heart the mouth speaketh."[13] Let me once more beg you to take good care of your health, & if any thing befalls you, let me know at once. Write me every week, if possible, & then it seems a long while till mail day—to wait *seven long* days, without hearing from you. Accept my best wishes, & blessing, & believe me, your ever devoted,

Ellen

Samuel to Ellen

Elk-River Tenn.[14] *Oct 19th 1863 [Monday]*.[15]

My Dear E[llen] & Children;

I have not heard one word from you since I left you at the Indian Mills, you were feeling badly, & as our raft floated down the river,[16] and round the bend, out of sight of my little family, standing there upon the bridge, you may be sure I felt the parting—keenly.[17] We had a pleasant voyage & if it were not for being so far away—I should enjoy my-

13. A quote from the Bible, King James Version, Matthew 12:34 (hereafter "KJV" with book, chapter, and verse).

14. Near Estill Springs, Tenn., on the Nashville & Chattanooga Railroad, the key supply line for Union forces operating in southeastern Tennessee and northwestern Georgia. *Atlas to Accompany the Official Records*, plate 34, map 4; *The War of the Rebellion*, Series 1 [hereafter "*OR*"], vol. 30, pt. IV, 399–400 (includes a sketch of Union fortifications); Hoffman, *My Brave Mechanics*, 157.

15. Unbeknown to those of Samuel's rank, on this day Major-General William S. Rosecrans was relieved of duty as commander of the Army of the Cumberland and replaced by Major-General George H. Thomas. The change came by order of Major-General Ulysses S. Grant, who, two days earlier, had traveled to Louisville for a meeting with Secretary of War Edwin V. Stanton, where he was informed of his elevation to command the Military Division of the Mississippi. Rosecrans had allowed his army to be besieged in Chattanooga. See Daniel, *Days of Glory*. Grant's mission was to lift the siege and initiate offensive operations.

16. The "faster-running" Chippewa River carried traffic east to the Tittabawassee and Saginaw Rivers. Lewis, *West to Far Michigan*, 263. Indian Mills was the site of the government-sponsored mill required in the 1855 treaty, and a Council House built in 1857 to transact business; it soon became the platted town of Isabella City with hotel, tavern, store, and post office. A plaque affixed to a boulder at the intersection of Mission Road and Craig Hill Road commemorates the location.

17. See the appendix for more detail on the leave-taking.

self pretty well. And when I hear from you that you are all well, I will be quite contented.

The weather is very pleasant here now; we have a nice camping ground: It is on Elk River, about 85 miles from Nashville.[18] We have good water, enough to eat—& a pretty good place to sleep: There are about 3000 soldiers camped here—one New York regiment, one Wisconsin, & the remainder are Michigan troops.[19] There has been no fighting very near here: Some of the Engineers & Mech[anics] left here thursday to repair the road about 40 miles south of here:[20] They were taken prisoners & the train burned.[21] They were a part of Co. E. I will try & take good care of myself—I have good warm clothes, & you must not worry about me. I must close & go to drill. Take good care of our children & yourself—Good bye

Yours as Ever.

Samuel

1st Mich Eng, & Mech.

Ellen to Samuel

Lincoln, Oct 20th 1863 [Tuesday].

(Cottage Home.)

My Dear Husband,

I wrote you one week ago, but wrote such a gloomy letter, I am going to try & write a more cheerful one; I certainly do not want you to feel badly about us,—now that you are there—by any means—and if I could only know that you were well, & *comfortable* & free from danger, then I would be content. We are all well now, although I have been sick three days with sore-throat,—am about well now. I dont think it was diphthe-

18. This location served as the regiment's headquarters as of October 31. Robertson, *Michigan in the War*, 498; *History of the Michigan Organizations*, 156.

19. Likely the 107th or 150th New York Volunteers and the 3rd Wisconsin Volunteers of the 3rd Brigade of the 1st Division, Brigadier-General Alpheus S. Williams commanding, of the XII Corps of the Army of the Cumberland, Major-General George H. Thomas commanding. *OR*, vol. 31, pt. 1, 801, 805; Quaife, *From the Cannon's Mouth*, 267.

20. The road referenced is the Nashville & Chattanooga Railroad.

21. Stationed on this supply line in the rear, Union troops were subjected to raids by Confederate cavalry units and by guerillas ("bushwhackers"). Working parties were ambushed, track was torn up, and bridges were destroyed. Hoffman, *Among the Enemy*, 48.

ria, although the neighbors think it would have been, if I had not broken it up at the beginning.[22] You may believe I wanted you here to care
for me—but the neighbors were very kind & came in to see me, & did
what they could. Yesterday Mrs McL[ane] & Mrs H[ollan]d, were here;
to day Mrs I[ve]s, Mrs D[unha]m, Mrs H[oa]g & Mrs K[ro]ll[23] have
been here, so you see I have some company yet, as usual.

Our friend[s] from Wisconsin have not arrived yet, but shall expect
them this week: I have sold the cook stove for 16 dollars—cash—& have
it to use while I remain here. This morning I sold the old cow for 23
dollars—have paid some little debts, so that we are square with the
world & have $75.00 to go home with: The children are both well, & are
good boys. Vesper does all he can to help me, & we get along very well:
I shall have some maple sugar to dispose of—also fodder—I think with
a little experience I shall prove quite a succesful manager. If it were not
for the *loneliness*, we should be very comfortable—I hope you wont get
homesick,—for you could not come home, if you did, unless you came
without permission—and that would be a *crime*. I would rather *never*
see you than to have you dessert. Do your duty as a true Soldier in the
sight of man, & the fear of God; and when peace once more smiles
upon us (which I hope may be *soon*) then you will return with bright
honor, to be welcomed to the glad hearts & happy home of your wife
& children who will ever pray God to watch over you & keep you from
every harm, & guard you from temptation, and crown your labors with
success. O my Dear Samuel how happy shall we all be, if a kind Providence bring[s] this war to a speedy close, & each dear Soldier returns
to home & fireside—no more to be disturbed by the fearful cry of *war*.
I am exceedingly anxious to hear that you are landed in safety—and to
know how you like your occupation; also what kind of fare you have in
your new quarters. You know I am very particular so write all the little events of your journey; just how you were treated, & how you bore
it. I received a letter from your brother J[ohn][24] last week:—they were

---

22. Ellen's self-care treatment apparently caused her fever to "break" as her body
fought off the infection and returned to a more normal temperature.

23. Female relatives of enlistees from the community, specifically, Alonzo and Lou Holland, Leonard Ives, Charles Dunham, and James Hoag. Fancher, *Past and Present*, 314.

24. Perhaps John W. Woodworth (1835–1910). Find a Grave, https://www.findagrave
.com/memorial/24313440/john-whitney-woodworth. He appears in the *Eighth United
States Decennial Census* for Java, Wyoming County, N.Y., 855.

all well, & much surprised that you had enlisted. Your Mother wants
you to be a *good boy*, & write to her.[25] Our town has been organized,
& named Lincoln: but my P.O. address will be Wiota[26] until you hear
from me in [New] York State. The children are playing hide-&-seek,
& make so much noise I can hardly write. Remember and write often,
very often, & mention all you think I might wish to hear—I wish I could
send you a nice ball of home made butter, & a mince pie for your dinner. We think of you every time we eat & wonder what papa has to eat,
& where he sleeps.

 Good bye—Affectionately
Ellen & the Children.

Samuel to Ellen

Elk-River Oct 27th 1863 [Tuesday]

My Dear Wife & children; I received yours of the 12th ult, & was very
glad to hear from you, but sorry to have you feel so badly: I wish you
would not worry about me; for I am having an easy time, & feel well.
I stay with the Officers, & get a good many extras that the other boys
dont have. I do not feel in any more danger than I would at home. I
have not seen but 35 armed rebels, & they were running from us. There
were about 100 of us; we were on the cars[27] & had our guns pointing
out of the windows. They came back night before last & tore up the
track; and the cars ran off & Capt. Sly had his legs broken.[28] There was
a negro caught last night tearing up the track about half a mile from
here: he is to be shot tomorrow.[29] One of the boys fell off the bridge

---

25. Samuel's stepmother, Julia M. Woodworth; his biological mother died in 1842.

26. In the northwest corner of Coe Township, the most southeastern portion of Isabella County. Romig, *Michigan Place Names*, 609. It appears Ellen had ideas of relocating
to live with family back in New York during her husband's absence.

27. I.e., aboard railroad cars.

28. James W. Sligh of Grand Rapids, Michigan, native of Scotland, joined Company
F of the regiment at its organization, age thirty-nine, and was commissioned captain on
September 12, 1861. He died at Tallahoma, Tennessee, from injuries he sustained in the
crash. *Record of Service*, vol. 43, 185; Hoffman, *My Brave Mechanics*, 173.

29. The first mention of an African American in the correspondence; all references employed contemporary usage showing respect rather than slurs, in contrast to others in the
regiment. See Hoffman, *Among the Enemy*, 98.

last Friday—fell 60 feet & struck on the stone;[30] I was the first to get to him; I thought he was dead, as he was black in the face & did not revive until we reached the hospital. I wish you could have been here last night & listened to the Band playing: it was grand music, & a splendid evening—

C[aswell] brought me the letter you sent; Try & enjoy self with the children & do not fret about me. Rest assured I shall take as good care of myself as possible; I have no doubt, but that I shall see you all again within one year: I have just heard that Grant has issued orders to burn every house within five miles of the road.[31] The day I left Nashville there was a fellow killed himself—He had been taken for a deserter; he went to the window on the third story & jumped to the pavement; killing himself on the spot.[32] I have a Testament & hymn book that was given me. I have not played a game of any kind; nor shall not.[33] I think I have done well—for me, in writing—this time. I want Vesper to write to papa—& I should like to hear from little master Dallas. Write often & a little more cheerful—I will close & go to drill. Good bye

From your Absent Husband.

Samuel

Vesper to Samuel[34]

Letter from Vesper 9 years old.—to his Papa.

My Dear Papa. I want to see you very much. It seems a long time since you went away—I havn't got my new boots yet, & I dont know whether Mr Bentl[e]y[35] has got them done, yet; but I hope he has.

---

30. Fred Smith, Company B, "while crossing the [rail] bridge missed his footing and fell 53 feet" into the Elk River. Hoffman, *Among the Enemy*, 106.

31. Samuel mistakenly believed Grant issued the order. On October 13, Major-General William T. Sherman issued the order to deal with Confederate raids on the Union rail supply line. He directed the "cavalry to take all horses and mules between the railroad and the Tallahatchie, burn all mills and corn-fields, and let them feel that to attack our road will be surely followed by vengeance." *OR*, vol. 30, pt. 4, 304. See Marszalek, *Sherman*.

32. See generally Lonn, *Desertion during the Civil War*; Fantina, *Desertion and the American Soldier*; Dean, *Shook Over Hell*.

33. Playing cards was held to be sinful by mainline Christian denominations. Woodworth, *While God Is Marching On*, 71–72, 84, 219.

34. Undated.

35. Most likely Langdon Bentley, who "came to the county in 1855" and was elected

Mama & I are very lonesome; we have staid all alone ever since you went away, but 3 or 4 nights, & Mama cries every day. Mama got the money & your likeness—It looks like you, but not as well as you do. Please write to me next time,

So good bye; from Vesper to Papa.

Ellen to Samuel

Lincoln. Oct 27th 1863 [Tuesday].

Dear Samuel I dont know but I write oftener than you will care to hear from me, but it seems that I cannot let more than one week pass without writing; as that is the only means left me now of conversing with you.

I received your letter last week that you sent from Louisville, Ky. I was so glad to hear that you were well: We are all well & not alone now. Our friends from Wis, came last Thursday. Came with their own team around the Lake [Michigan]—visited in Buchanan,[36] & were 17 days on the road. I wrote you last week that I had made arrangements to go to [New] York State & stay this winter; but I got a letter since, that our folks have sold there & are coming here in Feb. & brother W[allace][37] is on the way now—A[lbert][38] started for St Johns[39] yesterday morning to bring him & his goods, & I expect them next Saturday. He & wife[40] will stay with me this winter, so I shall not go East.

---

county supervisor in 1861 and county treasurer in 1864. He was also "a good shoemaker." Fancher, *Past and Present*, 323, 328–329; *Portrait and Biographical Album*, 551.

36. A town in southwest lower Michigan.

37. Wallace Worth Preston, Ellen's younger brother, born October 9, 1837. He married Samuel Woodworth's younger sister Arsenath. Died September 8, 1916. Gravestone, Riverside Cemetery, Mt. Pleasant. He served as county clerk, register of deeds, and treasurer, as well as treasurer and supervisor of Union Township. *Portrait and Biographical Album*, 228–229.

38. Albert A. Preston, Ellen's older brother, born in 1828 and died July 22, 1885, age fifty-seven. Gravestone, Riverside Cemetery, Mt. Pleasant; Fancher, *Past and Present*, 325. He came to Isabella County in March 1863 and brought his family there in May. Ibid., 467.

39. The town of St. Johns was approximately fifty miles south of Mount Pleasant.

40. Martha A. (Nichols) Preston (1833–1900). They were married in 1851. Fancher, *Past and Present*, 325, 467; *Portrait and Biographical Album*, 497; "Martha A Nichols Preston," Find a Grave, https://www.findagrave.com/memorial/61060919/martha-a-preston.

They all feel disappointed to not have you here. The children are well—I wrote you last week that I had a sore throat, but it is entirely well now. F[ancher][41] has been fixing up the house to day—putting in chinking between the logs & plastering on the out side with clay—as the nights are getting cold—This makes 4 letters that I have written you; I hope you have received them all, or some of them, at least, by this time: It is most ten o clock, & I must close for tonight—All are sleeping quietly, in happy unconciousness—but me. If I could know to night that you were safe & well—I too, would be happy—Tomorrow is mail day—& I shall go to the [Post] Office, & will finish my letter there—Good night, & Heaven protect thee from all harm:—Oct 28th (at the [Post] Office), Wednesday morning. I have walked to the office (two miles)—& am doomed to *disappointment*. "*No letter*," the postman said, in answer to my anxious inquiry. Why did you not write? O I fear you are sick: another whole week of suspense before I can know.

I have not received your clothes yet—expect Mr. B[rickley] will bring them soon.—The draft came off here[42]—last monday—have not learned the result. One thing sure—I have not had to worry about your being drafted. Do write *often*. Tell me how you like soldiering: & take good care of yourself—Yours as Ever—Lovingly

Ellen

Samuel to Ellen

Nov 1st 1863 [Sunday]. Camp—Elk River.

My Dear Wife, & Children.

It is a beautiful day to day, & altho it is the Sabbath—we have had inspection of arms this morning: How I would like to see you all but as I *cannot*, I will devote a part of this lovely day to writing: Do not

---

41. Isaac Alger Fancher, husband of Althea Preston. Born September 30, 1833; died March 19, 1934. https://mdoe.state.mi.us/legislators/Legislator/LegislatorDetail/5121Lawyer; surveyor; postmaster; Isabella County prosecuting attorney; Circuit Court commissioner; member, Michigan House of Representatives, Michigan Senate; aided in founding of Central Michigan University; author. Fancher, *Past and Present*, 528–533; Cumming, *This Place Mount Pleasant*, 21, 28.

42. Ellen refers to the local implementation of conscription under the Enrollment Act, which passed Congress in March 1863.

worry for fear that I shall acquire the bad habits, so common in Camp life. I have sworn off & quit playing Cards entirely—& even checkers. There is so much of it, going on, it sickened me; & I am resolved never to play another game, nor utter an *oath* while I am in the Army:[43] I received your letter of Oct the 21st last Friday night. I was glad to hear that you were doing so well—but surprised that you had not received my letter that I wrote at Nashville. I have written two before this since I came here. Was sorry to hear you had sore-throat—it made me tremble for fear you might have a second attack, or the children would get it. I am well at present, & so are the boys that came with me. There was a boy died this morning; he has been sick ever since he came here; he was a poor little fellow, never made any complaint, & only went to the hospital yesterday.—The fellow that fell through the bridge is getting better—You wanted to know what I have to eat—? We have a plenty, if it was only cooked properly—have biscuit, fried cakes, salt pork—bacon, coffee, sugar, molasses, hardtack & sometimes tea.[44] I sleep in a tent: have a lounge with some straw on it. I have a rubber blanket—one heavy woolen blanket, an over coat, woolen drawers & shirt; We have a fire-place at one end of the tent & can keep warm the coldest nights. Tell Mother that I will be a good boy, & do my duty, if I know it, & will write to her soon.

I hope you will have a good time to go home in; dont travel when you, or the children are tired, or hungry—or when it storms—for the sake of saving a few dollars—but take good care of your selves—I am glad to hear that Vesper & my little Dallas are such good boys to their Mama. Good bye for this time, they are calling me to dinner—

Ever Yours,

Samuel

---

43. Swearing was seen as a practice to be avoided. Woodworth, *While God Is Marching On*, 88.

44. Hardtack is a "plain flour-and-water biscuit." Billings, *Hardtack and Coffee*, 113–118.

Ellen to Samuel

Lincoln, Nov 1st 1863 [Sunday].

Dear Samuel I shall write you this week to let you know that we are well & also of the changes that have taken place, since you went away. I wrote you last week that F[ancher] & family were here, & that W[allace] & wife were coming—well they are here also: got here Friday safe & well. A[lbert] went out to St Johns & brought them in; their goods are not all here yet—Your Sister[45] likes the place well, but makes her homesick to have you gone:

Tuesday evening [Nov. 3]: The clock is just striking 9. & the children are in bed & asleep;—but I must write my letter so as to have it ready to send to the [Post] Office in the morning. I began it Sunday but did not write much—W[allace] has been up to the County Seat to day & is much taken with the place;[46] he thinks he shall buy a couple of lots & put up a grocery store. So, I fear I shall be alone this winter, after all; for he is anxious to be at work for himself, & there is no farm that he can get now, that suits him.

F[ancher']s folks moved up a load of goods this morning & will commence housekeeping to-morrow.

W[allace] & wife will stay with us a few days longer, & will then go up & stay to F[ancher']s while he, W[allace], puts up his house. It makes me feel doubly lonely to see them so happy in each others society, & I alone—& you so far away—But I shall stay here this winter & try & make myself & children as comfortable as possible—but should have made different calculations, had I known sooner how things were shaping—should certainly have kept my stove.—As it is, will have to send out to St Johns, when they go for goods, and buy me a new one. Every thing is dear now. Flour is 18 dollars a barrel—wheat 14 shilling per bushell.[47]

---

45. Arsenath Woodworth Preston, Samuel's younger sister. Born June 21, 1841, Java, Wyoming County, New York. Married Wallace Worth Preston, Ellen's younger brother. Died February 17, 1916. Gravestone, Riverside Cemetery, Mount Pleasant.

46. The site of Mount Pleasant became the county seat in 1860. Fancher, *Past and Present*, 87.

47. Both a barrel and a bushel constituted a measure of weight; one bushel of wheat

I sent up to day & got Vesper[']s boots. They cost 2,50. He feels very proud of them. It is quite comfortable weather here yet—have no snow, but considerable rain. Vesper wants me to remind his papa that next monday will be his 9th birthday. & wishes he was here to have a piece of his birthday cake. Little Dallas grows stout every day—he is a little stave-about. He often asks me if Tennessee is farther away than Chippewa[48]? & wonders *why* Papa dont come home to see him. I hear that you are going into active battle? O I hope not, but tell me the truth about it when you write Wednesday morning; I am at the [Post] Office now—& have the happiness of hearing from you: have got your letter dated Oct 22nd & am glad to hear that you are *well*, but sorry to hear some have been taken prisoners; What should I do, if you had been one of the number? Be vigilant, & keep out of danger if possible. I had a houseful to day—but came & left them all I was so anxious to get your letter—F[ancher] & wife came down this morning—W[allace] & wife are still there, & sister C[elia].[49] She sends her love to you—and is a dear good girl. The Children are well—Be a good boy & write often to

Your ever true & loving

Ellen

Samuel to Ellen

Elk River Nov 7th 1863 [Saturday].

Dear Friends—One, & All. I received your letter of the 28th ult, to day: Am glad to hear that you are well, & that F[ancher] had got there, & C[elia]. Would much like to see *her* & the rest. I feel well & am growing fleshy every day. The troops have been leaving here lately, & we had to do picket duty. I have just come in to Camp; have been out since early yesterday morning; I though [sic] of you, & home as I was

---

equaled thirty-two pounds. Traditionally, a "shilling" equaled twelve pennies. On November 16, Ellen wrote that a bushel of wheat cost two dollars. Hale, *Good Housekeeper*, viii, 13.

48. Likely a community and post office within Lincoln Township, also known as Crawford P.O. The township bearing that name was off the customary traveling routes. Romig, *Michigan Place Names*, 138.

49. Celia E. Preston, born June 26, 1846, was Ellen's younger sister. She married Emory Bradley (1843–1901), "the minister's son, in October, 1864, which was the first wedding in the village" of Mount Pleasant. *Portrait and Biographical Album*, 568. She died March 25, 1867, age twenty. Gravestone, Riverside Cemetery, Mount Pleasant.

pacing backwards & forward, in the middle of the night; we expect to leave here tomorrow & go about 100 miles north, to work on the north-western road.[50] You will direct your letters, the same that you have. I have written every week, & don't see why you dont get them. I hope W[allace] wont get homesick: Tell them that when I get home we will have good times: I hope your Father will buy a farm near you—wish he would buy the Ives farm—I should like to hear from all of you there—I think I have done well for me, at letter writing—must close as it is get-ting dark & I am some what sleepy—It was most sun down when I got back to Camp—I have written this in a hurry—& will try to write more news next time—Take good care of yourself—& my dear little boys—O you better believe I would like to see you all tonight—Good bye.—Love to all—

Samuel

Ellen to Samuel

Lincoln. Nov 10th 1863 [Tuesday].

My Dear Husband—This evening finds me seated with pen in hand & paper before me—thinking of you far away in the dreadful land of war. How much we would like to see you to night.—We are all well & sincerely hope you are enjoying the same blessing. W[allace] & wife are here with us to night. F[ancher] & family have moved into their new home, & like very well. W[allace] is going up in the morning to stay awhile, working on his—F[ancher']s building (a barn)—but sister C[elia] is with us, so we will not be left alone. W[allace] has bought the Calkins farm—paid $350,00 & has possession in 4 weeks. Levi was drafted, & they sold the farm to pay $300 for a substitute.[51] Among the

50. The Nashville and Northwestern Railroad, a line originally from Nashville to Kingston Springs but completed by the Union army to the Tennessee River. *OR*, series 3, vol. 5, 943–944.

51. Levi Jerome Calkins (1844–1914), son of Elias Burton Calkins (1818–1898) and Lemira Fairchild Calkins (1822–1902), who by 1861 "had settled in the woods five miles south of Mt. Pleasant" with their family. *Isabella County, Michigan*, 97; various entries in the findagrave.com database.

drafted men are Charley Youngs,[52] Mr Kunkler,[53] David Drake[54] & others to the number of 15 in the township of Coe.

The children are both well, & I have made them some warm winter clothes, & Vesper has got a good pair of boots. I have knit him mittens & am knitting them both woolen stockings from yarn that our folks sent me from [New] York State, so we shall all be comfortably clothed. I have got a 12 lighted window put in the west end of the house. We have got all the turnips gathered, & buried. Had 76 bushel.[55]

I am now at the [post] office writing; have just received your letter of Oct 30th. I feel very thankful that you are well, & enjoy yourself so well. I hope you will *read* your books that you spoke of, that had been given you; for your sake, & mine. I feel to trust you that you will strive to ever be morally & religiously strict in keeping an unblemished character; which you will ever maintain if you heed the admonitions of your pure & noble heart. May kind Heaven ever watch over you, & safely keep you from all harm. Vesper will write again next week. He is a good boy & does well. Little Dallas often speaks of papa, & says when you get home he is going to help you work. He grows fast, & is a chubby boy. Vesper was 9 years old last monday. I presume you thought of it: write often—Be a good & true soldier, & when peace is restored, I hope to welcome once more

my brave & noble husband.

Ever Yours,

Ellen

---

52. Charles H. Young, mustered December 31, 1863, age twenty-one. *Record of Service*, vol. 43, 231.

53. Although drafted, this individual appears to have secured a substitute; his name does not appear in any records of Michigan Civil War soldiers; see the letter of November 16.

54. Similar to Kunkler, this individual apparently procured a substitute by payment of money or securing an individual to serve in his place.

55. See the appendix.

Samuel to Ellen

Poplar Springs,[56] *Nov 15th 1863 [Sunday].*

Dear Ones at Home. I thought I would write you this pleasant Sabbath morning, but had hardly made a beginning, when the order came for inspection of arms. I received a letter from you last night, & was glad to hear that you were well.

The past-week has been a busy one with us. We started from Elk River last Sunday morning & went to Nashville, & Tuesday took the cars & came out 40 miles, & went to work getting out railroad ties.[57]— we do not have to work very hard; If you could see the effects of war, as I do—in this place, you would realize what it is to suffer: There is not an able-bodied man to be found here, & their families are fearfully destitute. Last Thursday we heard that a rebel captain had come home to get some negroes; so at night six of us got on to the horses & went about 7 miles through the woods, to his house to capture him: we arrived about 8 o clock, & when near his house, two big ferocious dogs came at us on double quick; but they met a dose of cold lead which soon quieted them: we went into the house, & found five women, & 8 children: & a more scared set of beings I never saw. They were all crying, & thought their last hour had come. One little girl came near having spasms. The women told a pitiful story, said they had not heard from their husbands since last Spring: were destitute of provisions; but were as afraid of us, as you would be of a band of wild Indians: I saw 15 deserters from Braggs Army,[58] & you may believe they were a hard looking set. The talk is here that by the 1st of March we shall be sent home. I hope it may be so; still there are some things that I like in soldiering, & some that I dont. I have not felt the Asthma since coming here. The boys are well & send their best respects to you, & C[elia]. Tell Vesper that his papa thought of him many times [on] his birthday & would have like to been with you all & had a piece of his birthday cake.—You may be sure that I think of home, many times a day: and hope to come back a

---

56. Approximately one mile west of White Bluff, Tennessee.

57. Repairing and replacing wooden rail ties, especially if damaged or burned by the enemy, was key to "the maintenance of a reliable supply line." Also important was "getting out ties and timbers for duplicate bridges." Hoffman, *My Brave Mechanics*, 56, 172, 175.

58. The Confederate Army of Tennessee, commanded by Major-General Braxton Bragg. Hess, *Braxton Bragg*.

wiser & a better man—Keep up good courage, & let me hear often from you—The weather is getting pretty cool to night & I must close,

Good night, & good bye—

To my Wife, & children.

Samuel

Ellen to Samuel

Lincoln—Nov 16th 1863 [Monday].

My Dear Husband,

Another week has nearly passed & I am again indulging in the blessed privilege of writing to you: We are all usually well, & trying to get every thing ready for winter—as you would if you were here—We have got the fall vegetables all secured—have 100 bushel of baga's[59] & turnips—or Michigan apples, as we call them. I have just purchased 200 weight of flour of Charley Y[oung]s had to pay $5,00 per hundred.[60] Provisions are growing dearer:—Wheat is 2,00 per bushel: & other things in proportion. Mr. *Brickley* has just got in to the woods with W[allace']s goods: he brings the Telegraphic news from St Johns that there are two Iron clads (rebel gun-boats) on Lake Erie: Came by the Welland Canal through Canada, & had liberated some 2000 rebel prisoners that were in our possession. I do not credit it myself—but the rumor is circulating through the settlements here, & many believe it.[61] Charley Y[oungs] feels bad about being drafted & will try & hire a substitute & Charley D_____ talks of going for him—Mr. Kunkler has gone out of the woods to get money to pay his[62], & Harvey Wardwell[63] will go in place of his brother Warren,[64] who is drafted—I have just received your clothes—to day—your Coat & pants are all that came: Lit-

---

59. Rutabaga.

60. Since flour sold at eight or nine dollars a barrel in 1863 in upper Michigan, Ellen appears to have purchased one barrel's worth.

61. The report was false.

62. "The woods" referred to the largely forested and uncleared areas of antebellum Michigan. See, e.g., Fancher, *Past and Present*, 43-44.

63. Harvey D. Wardwell was drafted from Caledonia in Shiawasee County, age twenty-four. Mustered October 30, 1863, and assigned to company M, Second [Michigan] Cavalry, he was discharged June 3, 1865. *Record of Service*, vol. 32, 165.

64. Blacksmith Warren Wardwell was born in 1832 in New York and died April 3, 1887,

tle Dallas went through your pockets & found a nut;—said he guessed you sent it to him, so he cracked, & ate it. Your cousin Jack F_____ was here to see us last Friday—from Lansing[65]—came out to sell his oxen: he felt sorry not to see you at home.—His sympathies are *not* with republicans in this war—he sends kindest regards to you;—thought the children looked as you did at their age.—He wishes you to come & see him, when you get home; but I imagine if you ever get *home*, you will be contented to stay here.

When you write again tell me what you have to eat, how much you are allowed to have—what you eat *on*, &c. You say you have given up playing games: I am truly glad to hear it.—I am looking to see you yet aspire to my ideal of morality, & religion. & trust & believe if your life is spared you will not disappoint me—when once more you are permitted to assume the responsibility of guiding the youthful minds of your dear children—& setting those examples which we may all be proud to follow. O my dear Samuel Ever trust & believe in the love & ruling power of an All-wise Creator, & be guided in all things by His will: Be true to Him, to your-self, & your Country; and God will bless you. Good night.

Ever yours, E. L. W.

Samuel to Ellen

Alabama. Nov 28th 1863 [Saturday].

Dear Ellen. I take my pen in hand to let you know how, & *where* I am. I am now at Bridgeport—125 miles south of Nashville; on the Tennessee river; 25 miles from Chatanooga—at work building a large store house.[66] I am well at present; but we left Alonzo [Holland],[67] & Joe A[t-

---

age fifty-four. *Eighth United States Decennial Census*, Homer, Calhoun County, Mich., 29; gravestone, Riverside Cemetery, Mt. Pleasant.

65. The editor has not been able to identify "Jack F." Lansing was the State's capital city some seventy miles south.

66. From Elk River, the Union rail supply line ran through Stevenson, Alabama, to Bridgeport, Alabama, on the Tennessee River. On taking command, Grant put in place new arrangements for supplies to be carried up river from here, restoring full rations and supplies to his troops around Chattanooga. Grant, *Personal Memoirs*, vol. II, 24–38.

67. Alonzo D. Holland enlisted in Company M at Coe, Michigan, on September 22, 1863, for a three-year term, age twenty-one. He survived the war and mustered out as corporal on September 22, 1865. *Record of Service*, vol. 43, 101.

kins]⁶⁸ (also [Joseph] Miser)⁶⁹ at the Hospital at Nashville: they were
not very sick. I was sorry to leave them, & shall expect them here in a
few days. I wrote to you a week ago that we were going to leave, but did
not expect to come here. I like this place, the best, of any I have been
in. The battle has been fought at Chatanooga,[70] & our men whipped
them badly. We took about Ten thousand prisoners.[71] Our loss was
not very heavy. I received a letter from you last Saturday & it done me
much good; for it looked as though you were trying to be more cheerful. It is very hard for me to be so far away from all that I love, but if
we can all be well I can stand it a short time; for this war must come to
a close before long. I hope to hear from you to day, but dont know as I
shall, I have to keep very busy now; If it had not rained this morning, I
could not have written.

I tell you there are a great number of rebs here now, besides all the
prisoners, there are some 2000 deserters, & more negroes than we know
what to do with.[72] The weather is fine just like spring at home. The
news has just reached us, that we have captured 15000 rebels, 60 pieces
of canon, & small arms without number & Hooker[73] is after Bragg yet.
I guess his army is gone to pieces. The sun is shining & they are calling
me to duty. Tell Veppy & Dallie to be good Boys.

Ever yours,

S.

---

68. Joseph Atkins enlisted in Company M at Coe, Michigan, on September 23, 1863,
for a three-year term, age seventeen. He survived the war and mustered out on September
22, 1865. *Record of Service*, vol. 43, 5.

69. Joseph Miser (or Mixer) enlisted in Company M at Union, Michigan, on September 26, 1863, for a three-year term, age thirty-two. He was listed as "absent, sick" on November 22, 1863, with "no further record." Ibid., 141. *Census of the State of Michigan 1894,
Soldiers, Sailors and Marines*, vol. III, 122, shows a Joseph Miser living in Coe Township,
Isabella County, Michigan.

70. On November 25, 1863, Union forces under Grant achieved a major victory over
Bragg's army, driving it from its strong position overlooking Chattanooga into northern
Georgia. See Cozzens, *Shipwreck of Their Hopes*.

71. The Confederate army indeed "had met great disaster," and "some six thousand
troops, mostly prisoners, had been left behind at Chattanooga." Connelly, *Autumn of
Glory*, 276–277.

72. An encampment of "contrabands"—terminology for escapees from slavery—existed
at Bridgeport. Cooper, "Interactive Map of Contraband Camps," History Digital Projects
(2014), 1, http://repository.upenn.edu/hist_digital/1. See also Manning, *Troubled Refuge*;
and Taylor, *Embattled Freedom*.

73. Major-General Joseph Hooker, commanding the Union XI and XII Corps.

Ellen to Samuel

Lincoln. Nov 30th 1863 [Monday].

My Dear Husband. This cold, dreary, wintry day—finds me as usual, thinking of you: so I draw my chair nearer the stove, & with pen & ink try to pass away time as comfortably as possible—by writing to you; as I omitted writing you last week, by Arsenath writing in my stead. We are left alone to day for the first time in several weeks. Wallace has gone to take a load of Hay up to Fancher, & Celia went with him, to stay awhile, & A[rsenath] has gone down to Alberts. Vesper & Dallas sit by the stove with each a book in their hands & it seems quite a relief to be with them alone once more—after having company so long: Only my heart yearns for the presence of one, far-far away. Can you imagine how glad I am to receive a letter every week, telling me you are well & comfortable; & also what is so gratifying to my feelings, to know from your own pen that you have given up entirely the habit of using profane language. Now indeed have I cause for great thankfulness as such a course will ever influence your comrades for good, & your example will do much toward purifying the morals of others. I believe the prayer of my heart is being answered, & if you are spared to return I shall deem myself one of the happiest of women.

We are all usually well. I went up to make my first visit to Fanchers last week; stayed two days & had a good visit. They have got a pleasant little home & I almost wish I had a house up there, to live in, & rent our place here, while you are away; it would be so much better for the children to attend school, & pleasanter for us all. I went to Chippewa & traded five dollars; but it did not buy much. Only a print dress for me— Vesper a cap & comforter, a few groceries—a broom, & some little notions for Christmas.[74] The children are counting every day, & wonder if Papa will get any presents from Santa Claus, this year.

Wallace went to Lansing to deed his land (the Calkins place), took one of Fanchers horses & went horse back: was gone just 4 days. Pa sent him 100,00 Dollars, this week—Albert 50,00, Celia 2,00 & me 1,00 so you see we are all provided for (?). Oscar, Cyrus, & George Nichols[75] came up to work in the lumber woods—got here Friday noon. They

---

74. A "notion" was a small item sold by a shop, sometimes referred to as "sundries."
75. Brothers of Martha Nichols Preston, wife of Ellen's older brother Albert.

have hired out for $26,00 per month apiece, in Arnolds Camp, one mile from the County Seat.

It is very cold to day & snows some; Fancher has not taken the cow away yet; he paid me $85,00 for her & what fodder there was. I will have to buy me another stove when W[allace] & A[rsenath] move away they have been with me five weeks—They like this place very much. How I dread this long cold winter—alone with my little boys—with no one to go ahead & smooth the way for us. Perhaps it will teach me self reliance—though I have never known what it was to battle with a cold unfeeling, world, & bravely meet every contingency—alone. And when the happy day dawns that our little family are reunited in our little home—though ever so humble, will it not be a joyous household. Celia—& all our friends send love, & best wishes. Take good care of your self & when on picket-duty be doubly vigilant.

Write often; & remember kindly, yours ever—

E L. W.

Samuel to Vesper

Bridgeport, Ala. Dec 7th 1863 [Monday].

My Dear Vesper—As I have received your, & your Aunt Arsene's letter I will take this first opportunity to answer it. I am well, & hope this may find you all the same. I rec'd a nice letter from your Mama a week ago yesterday; but I hav'nt time to write much, we are so busy. For nearly four weeks it has been fine weather, except a couple of hours & we have worked all the time, Sunday's & all. To day I am loading timber, & catch a few moments to write while the teams are unloading.[76] I think you would like to be here awhile & see the men & horses. There are some 40 000 Soldiers here, most of them were engaged in the great battle at Chatanooga[77] & are now going down the river to Stevenson, & on out into Georgia. They have whipped the Reb's *hard*, this time. I saw 6000 prisoners that they were taking through this place & talked with some of them: they say they are whipped & don't want to fight any

---

76. Likely, harvesting of felled trees in surrounding woods to be milled into planks for bridge building and other construction projects. Hoffman, *My Brave Mechanics*, 46.

77. See n. 75.

more. There were 165 Officers among them. Breckenridge's son[78] was one of them: he is a nice looking boy, about 18 years of age, I should judge—but I never want you or Dallie to ever be soldiers; Tell Mama to keep up good courage. I shall come home, some time: be a good boy & help her all you can. The team has come & I must close; shall write a long letter soon. We had 50 large Canon brought in to day, that our men captured. Bragg has resigned & left for—no one knows where[79]— write soon & often.

Love to all—from Papa.

Samuel to Ellen

Bridgeport Ala. Dec. 15th 1863 [Tuesday].

Dear Ellen, It seems a long time since I heard from you; have not received a letter from you since two weeks ago last Sunday. I have written every week. Looked for one from you yesterday, but was disappointed. There has much happened that would interest you. This last battle at Chatanooga was a great victory; I saw 6000 Reb's myself as they were marched through this place, including 165 Officers: Some of them came down on boats, other were compelled to march; when they were crossing the river, the pontoon bridge gave way & let several into the water—6 of them & one union soldier were drownded. It looked sad to see the poor fellows struggling for their lives. This is the first day, but what I have been able to work; I had an attack of cholera morbus[80] last night, & to day I feel rather weak, but hope to be all right in the morning: You asked me what we have to eat? I think I have told you, but will tell you again, as you may not have received that letter. We have light bread, biscuit, fried cakes, pork & beans, bacon, hard crackers—rice, fresh beef & sometimes coffee & sugar—have had tea once a week: have

---

78. Confederate major general John C. Breckinridge, former vice president of the United States and unsuccessful candidate of the Democratic Party for the presidency in 1860. His eldest son, Joseph Cabell Breckinridge, born in 1844, held a commission in the Confederate army. James C. Klotter, *Breckinridges of Kentucky*, xvii, 122–123.

79. Bragg resigned from command of the Army of Tennessee on November 29. Woodworth, *Jefferson Davis and His Generals*, 252–253.

80. Cholera morbus is a historical term referring to gastroenteritis, a painful inflammation or irritation of the intestinal tract, and cholera, a bacterial infection. Welsh, *Medical Histories of Union Generals*, 400.

had potatoes & onions once. We have plenty of material but it is not cooked much, as you would cook it; & you may imagine I would give something to be at home to day with my family. But I feel that I shall sometime: I am rather lonesome since the boys left us—They are still in Hospital at Louisville K.Y. Our Captain has not come yet, & we cannot draw pay until he brings our discriptive lists.[81] I have money enough to last me this winter, the way I use it: but many have none. From my rations, I have sold over a dollars worth of sugar, & I bought me a rubber blanket for a dollar, & in ten minutes I was offered 4,00 for it, so I took it. The Sutler gets nearly all of the soldiers money.[82] I will tell you his prices for some things. Butter 75 cts per pound. Cheese 60. Tea $5,00. Maple Sugar one dollar a pound. Dried Apples & peaches 40 cts & upwards, & green apples 10 cts apiece. I bought 6 for 40 cts & sold 3 of them for 30 cts. I have not slept on a bed since the first night that we staid in Detroit, nor sat on a chair. I would enjoy myself in our rocking chair,—to day. You said I did not look well in my likeness I sent from Detroit? I did not feel well. I would liked to have sent you some presents from Detroit but did not receive my pay in time. McLane is well & a good soldier.[83] I dont know how long we shall stay at this place. I think some time yet, as we are building a large ware-house: it is 900 feet long, & is built along the river. There are a great many of the wounded, brought here from Chatanooga: *there*, is where one can see some of the horrors of war. I would rather bury *my* sons, than ever see them in the army. I will send 50 cts for their Christmas presents, as it is close at hand. Give my love to all my friends there, & especially, to my own little family—

Write Often to

Your Absent Husband—

81. Commissioned on October 5, 1863, Edson P. Clifford of Grand Rapids joined Company M in the field in March 1864. Hoffman, *My Brave Mechanics*, 137.

82. A sutler was a civilian merchant who traveled with an army and sold them food, clothing, and other various provisions.

83. Walter McLain enlisted in Company M, Samuel's regiment, on September 25, 1863, for three years, age forty-two. He mustered out on September 22, 1865. *Record of Service*, vol. 43, 132.

Ellen to Samuel

Dec 22ond 1863 [Tuesday] Lincoln, Mich.

My Dear Husband. This evening finds me again writing to you, & it is my greatest pleasure—in your absence. We are all well, except Vesper had a hard cold. You will see that Wallace has moved, & we are at his place now. He is at the County Seat helping Fancher. The children sit by the table looking at a picture book, & keep such a chattering, I hardly know what I am writing.

We have not had much sleighing yet; but it is snowing to night, which may give us a plenty for Christmas. O how I wish you were here to spend the holidays with us. I dreamed of seeing you last night, & you looked well & happy. Where are you to night my dear Samuel? May God watch over you where ever you are, & never permit you to be led astray by evil companions. Be true to the promise you gave me, & He will bless, & reward you; & when this cruel war is over, may we welcome home a noble, & gallant *christian Soldier*. Do not worry about us, & be of good courage. I am going up to Fanchers[84] & will stay until Albert goes to St Johns after the pork that our folks are going to send—& he will get me a stove, so I can go to house keeping again. For it is not pleasant for me, or others, living around with my children: I have made Vesper a black velvet blouse & Dallie a waist, braided with blue—which looks very pretty. I made them from my velvet cape. They feel proud of them & wish *Papa* was here to see them. Wallace has come & brought my shoes from Bentleys. He measured my foot 4 weeks ago & has just finished them. They are not very fine, & cost $2,00. I expect our folks will be here in Feb & move to the County Seat. Write me all the news, & how you fare, in Alabama. Are you in constant danger? I shall send this to Blunt P.O. in the morning by David Caswell. W[allace] & A[rsenath] send love to you. Please write often, & accept the same, from your ever devoted

Ellen

---

84. In Mount Pleasant, the county seat established in 1860 to replace one found too remote. Fancher, *Past and Present*, 87.

Samuel to Ellen

Bridgeport Ala. Dec 23d 1863 [Wednesday].

Dear Wife & Children—I have received two letters from you, & have had all the reading that I needed for a week. You out-done yourself, almost this time, & I will not try to compete with you in writing: The day I wrote you last, I was not feeling well, & have not yet got so that I feel exactly right; but hope to soon.

I should like to be with you Christmas week, & help devour some of the nice things that I am sure you will prepare: but a Soldiers hopes & wishes, for home & loved ones, are in vain; & he only prays more earnestly for victory, to bring this cruel war to a speedy end. But you must excuse a short letter this time; my head feels badly & I cannot write, will do better next time.

God bless you all—
From your Absent Husband,
and Father—S.W.

Samuel to Ellen

Bridgeport, Ala. Dec 28th 1863 [Monday].

Dear Ellen—I take my pen again to inform you of my health, which I am sorry to say is not much improved. I have been quite sick, but expect to be better soon. I worked to hard, & exposed myself which is unavoidable in a soldiers life. For five weeks I worked every day & slept on the ground *every night*. The last day it rained all day, & it was too much for me. I took a severe cold. I dont want you to worry, for it wont do any good; I shall try & not get sick again, if it is possible to keep from it. Keep up a brave heart, & good courage—my time is passing along—slowly, but surely, & by fall I expect we will all be sent home. I fear you will have a hard time this winter; get a good stove, & keep as comfortable as possible. The weather is not cold here, & except for the rain, it is very comfortable. I dont expect to have to fight—or go into great danger, so dont worry. I have received 3 letters from you in the past 2 weeks. Direct as before. Love to your self—& my little boys.

Good bye from
S. to E.

Ellen to Samuel

Mt. Pleasant. Mich. Dec. 30th 1863. [Wednesday]

My Dear Samuel

You will see by the date of this, that we are up to Fanchers. We came up last Friday to spend Christmas with them, & are still here. We are all as well as usual, & I sincerely hope this may find you much better than when you last wrote.

I expect to go home to house keeping, as soon as the sleighing gets a little better, so that Albert can go out to St Johns. He is going out to get him some provisions & me a stove; as I have none yet. O why cannot this dreadful war be ended, & you come home, to go to living with us when we get ready to go back? It is very lonely there without you,— yet if we can all be *well* I will not murmur: so that you may be spared to return, ere long.

The children enjoyed the Christmas Tree wonderfully. Vesper got a nice comforter, an apple, a china toy & candy pitcher filled with candy drops: Dallie got some new calico for a waist,[85] an apple, bunch of raisins, a toy that he calls John Brown,[86] a little pitcher of candies & a nice little hand-sled. The other children had presents accordingly. I had a collar, a lead pencil & case, & a "housewife" (if you know what that is),[87] made of morrocco & silk, for keeping thread & needles. The day passed pleasantly, only for the thoughts of him absent, while all the others were united.

Last night I attended Singing School at the Court House. Mr Fancher is teacher & Althea[88] & I took the children & went over[.] Celia is down at Alberts & Wallaces visiting. They are all well & very much contented. Vesper was pleased to receive the letter you sent him last week. I hope to get one to day. Fancher is going to Chippewa to the [Post] Office & I must hasten so as to send this. The weather is quite

---

85. Calico refers to a cotton fabric, typically inexpensive, from which clothes were sewn. "Waist" likely means "waistcoat," a garment in the shape of a vest or short jacket. Fee, *Cloth That Changed the World.*

86. John Brown's attack on the federal arsenal at Harpers Ferry, Virginia, in October 1859 was one of the critical events leading up to the Civil War. See Oates, *To Purge This Land* and Reynolds, *John Brown, Abolitionist.*

87. A sewing kit. See Billings, *Hardtack and Coffee*, 85-86.

88. Althea M. Preston, younger sister of Ellen Woodworth. Born 1841, died September 30, 1900. Gravestone, Riverside Cemetery, Mt. Pleasant.

cold, but not much snow. I suppose it is warm & pleasant where you are, & when the weather gets warm here, I shall look for you *home*: be careful of your health. I dreamed again last night of seeing you here, but Fancher laughed when I told my dream, & said that was a sure sign that you wouldn't come, & called me an old widow; but I dont care for his teasing. I shall cling to the hope of seeing you soon.

I expect our folks will move here next month; Tell me if you are well clothed, & *where*, & how you sleep. I think of you every time I lay my head on a pillow, thinking that your dear head rests upon the damp-hard ground. Heaven pity the poor Soldier, & guard him while he sleeps. The children send much love to papa, & Fancher & Allie send kindest wishes. Be a good boy, & remember ever with hope, your affectionate

Wife, & Children.

CHAPTER 2

January–April 1864

"MUST YOU STAY THERE & DIE!"

Samuel to Ellen

Bridgeport, Ala. Jan 3d 1864. [Sunday]

Dear Wife, & children.

Once more I take up my pen, to let you know how I am, but cannot say that I feel very *smart* yet. I have been taking medicine nearly three weeks; my head is seemingly on a whirl & though I do not suffer much pain, I can scarcely stand up, some of the time. I have had a poor appetite, some times eating nothing, & of course it leaves me pretty weak. The boys have been good to me, & done every thing they could. I have no cough but a regular Camp sickness, attended with fever & dysentery.[1] I think I feel better this morning, & hope soon to be all right.

We mustered for pay New Years day but shall not get it under two or three weeks: when I get it shall send it to you, as I have no use for it here. I shall try & write once a week, but they may not be very long letters until I get more strength.

I must close for this time
From your Ever true Husband.
Samuel Woodworth

---

1. Use of this term suggests a diagnosis of that disease; Samuel may have intended "diarrhea" since the terms were closely linked, and he mentions that symptom subsequently. McPherson, *Battle Cry of Freedom*, 487–488; Welsh, *Medical Histories of Union Generals*, 401–402.

Ellen to Samuel

Wyota.[2]

Jan 6th 1864 [Wednesday]

My Dear Samuel—Another year has dawned upon us, & as in the past, finds me writing to the absent one, which I have not failed to do each week since you went away. Your last letter contained 50 cts, which I suppose means postage money. We are all well except the humor in Vespers blood has broken out in large sores on his shins & are quite painful.[3] Albert starts for St Johns to morrow & I shall send for a bottle of "Kennedys discovery" for him to take, as Wallace thinks it will cleanse his blood & cure his sores.[4] It will cost 1,00, but I think it better to get it now before he gets worse. We are now at Wallaces. Came down from Fanchers last night; were there two weeks, nearly.—& will stay here until we can get to house keeping again in our own little home. O, what happy anticipation it would give us if you too, were here to go back to our "little cabin home" with us. Why will this thought keep coming, when I *know*, it cannot be? But I can pray, & trust it is not far distant ere the happy day will dawn on many a re-united family. Our folks are expecting to come in a few weeks & then Fathers family will all be together once more.

My fingers are so cold I can scarcely hold my pen to write.—The weather since Christmas has been extremely cold. Wallace has boarded up his fireplace & set his cook stove out in the middle of the room, which makes it very cosy. They have two beds in the room, & while I am writing, Arsene is flying around doing up the work, & singing; The children are playing horse, (Dallie is Vespers horse) & he kicks up occasionally very viciously, which they seem to heartily enjoy: but the noise they make is anything but helpful to my writing. There is a Donation

---

2. In the northwest corner of Coe Township, the most southeastern portion of Isabella County. Romig, *Michigan Place Names*, 609.

3. The idea that four humors (black bile, yellow bile, phlegm, and blood), corresponding to the four elements in nature (earth, air, fire, and water), needed to be kept in balance for good health had been a traditional understanding. See Freemon, *Gangrene and Glory*; Devine, *Learning from the Wounded*.

4. Kennedy's Medical Discovery, ca. 1854 advertisement online at the Library of Congress, https://www.loc.gov/item/rbpe.06104000/.

to Mr Estee's[5] next friday, for "Brother Sias."[6] Wallace & Arsene talk of going for the visit, & contribute their mite towards his support.[7] Cyrus & Oscar[8] will get a team & carry them up if *Celia* will go. Wallace received a good letter this week from Melvin,[9] & he put in a few lines to us. He said "Oh how many hearts are *yearning* for Sams safe return," he tells me to keep up good courage, & I will be paid threefold for all the sacrifices I have been compelled to make; for he has *faith*, that you will return before long. I hope you are well again, I was very sorry to hear of your sickness. be careful what you eat. I wish I could send you some of our butter, & maple sugar. It finds ready market at 25 cts for butter, & one shilling for sugar. The children send much love to you, we are praying for you.

Accept this poor letter from your ever affectionate
Ellen

Samuel to Ellen

Bridgeport, Ala. Jan 10th 1864. [Sunday]

Dear Ones at home. I am getting my health again, though not able to work yet. We have had some very cool weather, & this morning is decidedly cold. I am laying around Camp & get along very easy. The boys bring me every thing they think I would like—I have fresh eggs, apple pie—ginger cakes, crackers, & fresh bread—& coffee. The Dr thinks I will soon be *well*. I would much like to be with my dear family, to day—instead of trying to write, & hope to receive a letter from you. Last Thursday there came into our Camp, 2000 rebels, & gave themselves up to our men:—they were poor looking Soldiers. The opinion here is that fighting is pretty nearly over. I hope it is, I have seen enough

---

5. Perry H. Estee, born in New York, September 9, 1824; died March 31, 1907. Find a Grave, https://www.findagrave.com/memorial/9763407/perry-harley-estee. He came to the County in 1854 and claimed land in section 18 of Coe Township. *Portrait and Biographical Album*, 255.

6. Unknown.

7. A reference to the "widow's mites" found in KJV, Mark 12.

8. Cyrus and Oscar Nichols, previously mentioned.

9. Melvin Woodworth was a resident of Java, Wyoming Township, New York, in the 1860 Census, age thirty-two, married and with two children. *Eighth United States Decennial Census*, Java, Wyoming, N.Y., 855.

wounded, & dead Soldiers to last me, a life time. I expect to get pay up to Jan 1st, this week. It will amount to $44,00 only. Monday morning Jan 11th. It is a cold day, but I have a warm tent & a little stove to sit by, so I do not feel the cold, much. I am gaining strength every day, would like to have been home these last 4 weeks; I get along pretty well, except doing without a pillow. My Knapsack gets pretty hard, & makes my ears sore, lying down so much. There are a good many sick now, in our company. How did Fancher get along about his draft? Is he building—write all the particulars when you write. I hope you have enough means to get along until I can send some—provisions are so high, there. Who cuts your wood, & how do you get along? Tell me all. I have not received any letter since I wrote last, hoping you are not sick, I must close this, & say good bye to you & my dear Boys—

From your Affectionate Husband

S. W.

(Answer to the above missing.)[10]

Ellen to Samuel

Lincoln. Jan 11th 1864. [Monday]

Dear Husband. I received your very brief letter last week, stating, that your "head felt so bad you could not write" and you may be sure it has been an anxious week to me, since. O, Samuel, are you seriously ill? and what is it that ails you. Why did you not tell me what made your head feel so badly? You have been constantly in my thoughts, ever since & if I could only fly to you, & care for you, how gladly would I come; but it is impossible: the privilege of being near you in "sickness & sorrow" is denied me.

I, & the children are now at Alberts. He & Martha are up to Fanchers to day & will stay until tomorrow, so I am here caring for their children. It is now four o'clock, we have just come over from Wallaces. I have done a large washing for Arsene to day, & if my hand does tremble, you must excuse it. She is not feeling very well, & I want to help them what I can. We all went up to Barnharts[11] yesterday to meeting

---

10. Ellen's notation in the journal.

11. Family of Jeremiah Barnhart.

& the walk was to much for her. Elder Sheldon[12] preached, & will, every two weeks. I did not attend the Donation, but Celia went, & Mr. Wilsey[13] sent me an invitation to come & visit them, & stay a week, & he would bring me home. Guess I will go this week & visit around a few days before I settle down to housekeeping. Celia has taken the school again, she taught last summer, & commences to day. Has three dollars a week, & board.

Our folks will start the first of Feb. Fancher has bargained for the "Dr. Burt house"[14] for them to live in when they come. I must leave my writing & get supper. Willie & Vesper are playing puzzle, on the slate, & Allie & our Dallie are having fine times with the puppy. Martha took her Dallie with her. (Evening). I will now try & finish my letter, while the children are playing "ring round a row" but I have a tedious toothache to comfort me: melted snow to wash with & took a little cold: dont suppose you have snow enough there to wash your hands with? How I wish you were here with us to night—wouldn't we be happy to hear your well known footstep, & see your dear face coming in at the door? "O when shall we all meet again."[15] I can hardly wait until another mail-day comes, to hear how you are. Do be exceedingly careful of what you eat & drink, & dont expose yourself to damp night air if you can avoid it. It is beautiful sleighing here: snow about 18 inches deep, & as firm as a pavement. The weather more moderate than it was a week ago.

Albert is hauling logs to Chippewa mill. Lumber is $10,00 per M, Fancher sold his horses to Mr Payne[16] for $190, & bought an Indian Pony for $25.[17] Albert rode it down home last night & the children all took turns riding. Vesper felt quite proud of his horsemanship, but lit-

---

12. "Rev. R. P. Sheldon . . . one of the first ministers who came to Isabella County" and in 1863 "was assigned" by the Methodist church organization to the area. *Portrait and Biographical Album*, 571.

13. James Wilsey (1811–1882), New York born and "a prominent and popular man," public official, and church member. *Portrait and Biographical Album*, 464.

14. "The first dwelling house built in Mt. Pleasant was by Dr. E. Burt, afterward bought by William Preston." Fancher, *Past and Present*, 103.

15. First line from a contemporary hymn. Myers, *Zion Songster*, 32 (hymn 30).

16. Perhaps Norman C. Payne of Chippewa, first supervisor of Chippewa Township and a member of the Board of Supervisors for Isabella County. *Isabella County, Michigan*, 18; *Portrait and Biographical Album*, 537.

17. "Indian Pony" likely refers to a hardy, gentle, small riding horse bred by the Ojibwe people, and also known as the Ojibwe pony.

tle Dallie reigned him into deep snow & didn't succeed as well. He is a splendid boy & you would feel proud of him. Precious child: he came near being seriously hurt this forenoon,[18] he was up stairs with me, at Wallaces & a board tipped & let him down through to the foot of the stairs: he was very much frightened, as well as myself—but it only made his nose bleed & bruised his lip slightly; to night he has forgotten all about it, and is singing as loudly as ever. O my dear, precious, children. How precious they are to me: It seems they are all I have left to comfort me, now you are gone—& may they be spared to gladden my heart, with their loving presence. Vesper was pleased with the little paper you sent him. O, that I could know *to night* how you are. Try & get a discharge & come home, if you are able to come—but if you *cannot*, let me at least hear from you, & do the best you can. Be true to your self, & to your country; & pray our heavenly Father to hasten the day, when peace shall again smile upon this unhappy land, & give us back, those dear ones now languishing in sickness or toiling to subdue this great National Strife. It is getting late & I must close—The children are all in bed—they send much love to "dear Papa"—my teeth are feeling better. Good night, & may kind Angels guard you.

Ever yours

E. L. W.

Samuel to Ellen

Bridgport [sic]—Ala—Jan 17th 1864 [Sunday]

Dear Ellen; This is a pleasant Sabbath day, & I am wondering how, & where, you are spending it. It seems like spring, warm & so different from last week. I received your letter last Thursday: glad to hear you are well.

You ask if I have suitable clothing? We can draw every two weeks, what we need. It is four weeks tomorrow since I have done any work: I begin to feel quite well now, but rather weak. You ask if I am contented? You dont know me, if you think I can ever be contented away from my wife, & children. You are in my mind every hour I am awake &

---

18. I.e., in the morning.

this seperation is the hardest part of war, to me. I can stand every thing else, better.

We shall not draw pay now & dont know when we will; am very sorry—for I wanted to send some to you. Hope to hear from you soon. I sent 50 cts for stamps. Did you receive it? I want to hear from you every week—I read them over & over; If I could have them printed in book form, I would: they are very precious to me. I hope this war will soon close—Sometimes I think it will, but we cannot tell. Be a good boy my dear Vepy & Dallie, dont forget Papa. I must close now. good bye

From your ever loving husband.

S. W.

Samuel to Ellen

Bridgeport. Ala. Jan 23d 1864. [Saturday]

Dear Ellen. I thank you for the two letters I received *to day*. It made reading for all day. I am improving in health, though not able to do duty yet: but am around Camp & help the boys some, in cooking: have received nothing but kindness from Officers, or Soldiers. It is so warm here we get in the shade in the middle of the day for comfort. I find some noble boys here, & you must not worry about me to much—as I will let you know, if I have any serious attack of Camp disease[19]—Love to all—this is a short, poor letter, but it was most dark when I began to write, & I want to send it out to night.

Love to my precious little boys—& ever remembered Ellen—

From Samuel

---

19. The term refers generally to any illness associated with a military camp, typically caused by unsanitary conditions or a contagious disease.

Ellen to Samuel

Lincoln Jan 27th, 1864. [Wednesday]

My Dear Husband, I sent Vesper to the [Post] Office this morning
with my letter & he brought me *two* from you. And such good letters,
it has done my heart *good*, to read them: I cannot wait another week
to tell you how glad I am, to hear you are better. So I will write this to
send this afternoon & will send you some stamps. You ask if my health
is good? Yes, as good as usual, only people say I look *old*, I am so sober: besides I have lost a front tooth & when you come home, you must
not expect to find much of a *beauty*. How often do I find myself gazing
out of the window, at some imaginary object, & anxiously listening for
your well remembered footsteps. You say we will be happy when you *do*
come. Yes indeed! if our lives are all spared, & Heaven grant, they may
be. You speak of your knapsack being hard. O how I wish, I could send
you a pillow, but do not suppose I can.

It is a warm spring-like day to day: the snow is mostly gone in the
road. I am sorry, as it will be hard for our folks to get here from St
Johns; if they start next monday—Albert will go out & get them & I will
send out & get some grass seed to sow on the wheat.[20] Celia will lend
me money, until you send some. We do not suffer for anything. Wallace cuts my wood, & Albert draws it. They will make a "bee" this week
& get up a lot of it.[21] Since you went away, I have paid out 111,47. &
what I have sold from the place including what you have sent amounts
to 108,37. Have 7 or 8 dollars due us yet & 50 bushel turnips to sell—
which bring 20 cts per bushel. Our shoes, mine & the childrens cost
5,25. I have written this to let you see how we stand with the world.
Dont go to work until you get your full strength, & then be very careful. The children are both well & hearty. accept this hastily-written letter from your ever loving, & hopeful,

Wife & children.

---

20. Since wheat is not a perennial crop and does not regerminate, it appears that Ellen sowed a different crop as part of a rotation plan to replenish the soil. She later reports
"the grass is growing finely."

21. "Bee" refers to a gathering of acquaintances to jointly perform an activity for a
neighbor in need, such as harvesting a crop.

Samuel to Ellen

Bridgeport Ala Jan 29th 1864 [Friday]

Dear Wife, & Children—How are the dear ones to day, that are so constantly in my mind? I hope, well. This is beautiful weather nice warm moonlight nights, & such pleasant days. I suppose you are nearly freezing up in Mich. & perhaps hungry if I dont get pay soon. Have not done duty in five weeks—feel well—but dont get strong. Have no war news to write that I know of—I hear though that they are fighting at Knoxville, Tenn.[22] It is now Sunday morning. I am gaining strength slowly—hope soon to be on duty. This is a lovely day; tis useless to say I would like to be home with my family to day—but such is the *fact*. Heaven bless you all & preserve you from harm.

Your Absent Husband.

Ellen to Samuel

Lincoln, Feb 20nd 1864. [Tuesday]

My Dear Samuel. Again I take my pen to enjoy the privilege of a few moments sweet communion with you, through its silent medium. We are all still enjoying good health, & wish we might hear the same from you. Last week I wrote you two letters, & in one, sent you 8 postage stamps. I expected then to see our folks here before this time, but received a letter last week saying Mother was sick, & not able to come at present. To day Wallace is moving up to the County Seat. He has been appointed deputy County Clerk, & has rented a house just erected & intended for a Boot & Shoe store (just south of Mr Moshers[23] resi-

---

22. Skirmishes occurred on January 26–27 near Knoxville in the aftermath of unsuccessful attempts by Confederate general James Longstreet to defeat federal forces under Major General Ambrose E. Burnside in late 1863. *OR*, vol. 32, pt. 1, 2; Hess, *Knoxville Campaign*.

23. Likely Nelson Mosher (1806–1872), "one of the most prominent of the early settlers, coming to the county about 1857 and putting a small stock of goods at the center and staying there for a short time, then removing to the county seat, and who was elected as prosecuting attorney at the first county election and was afterward elected to several of the important offices of the county." Fancher, *Past and Present*, 319.

dence)—by a Mr Carter.[24] W[allace] occupies the lower floor, & Mr C[arter] the upper part; His rent is 50 cts per week including a garden spot; & Mr C[arter] boards with them, paying 3,00 per week for board.

Wallace has leased his farm (The Calkins place) at $50,00 per year & takes it in clearing. Arsene is well pleased with the change, from the old log house, to a new frame one. The neighbors here are usually well. I have been over to visit Mrs Holland[25] this afternoon. Last night Celia had a spelling school, & I & the children went up, with Amanda Caswell.[26] Geo. Drake[27] & Mr Kyes[28] brought us all home with horses, & sleigh—with *bells* & the children enjoyed it much. Celia came with us, & others of her young friends, & all stopped awhile to visit. I warmed a mince pie[29]—served some refreshments & then had some music from an Accordeon that Celia bought of Mr Williams[30] & presented to me. Of course, I was chief musician—C[elia] furnished the singing, then they bade us good night, & returned home except Amanda stayed with us over night. Albert & family are well—I expect him & hired man to morrow to cut me some wood. Wallace left a nice wood pile & he told A[lbert] he might have it, if he would chop as much for me. So I expect some nice wood now. I am sorry to have Wallace move away for he has been very kind to me, & we will miss him very much, but he will do far better there, & get his farm cleared without so much hard la-

---

24. "John Carter constructed a building," which John Kinney, who came to Mount Pleasant in 1863, "rented and utilized as a store" the next year, "the first regular *bona fide* store" in the town. *Portrait and Biographical Album*, 338–339.

25. Perhaps the mother of Alonzo D. and Lou Holland, mentioned previously. David Holland (1815–1887) of Shepherd, Isabella County, had two wives, one who died in 1854 and Mary (1826–1881). Find a Grave, https://www.findagrave.com/memorial/10869096/david-holland.

26. Apparently, a relation of David Caswell.

27. The Drake family lived in Coe Township, where a schoolhouse and district would bear their name and Lucy Drake would be a teacher. Fancher, *Past and Present*, 91, 143, 170.

28. Ransom Kyes was an early Euro-American inhabitant, purchasing (in 1855) and living on a two-hundred-acre parcel, later serving as sheriff. Fancher, *Past and Present*, 100, 321. He enlisted in the 10th Michigan Volunteer Cavalry in September 1864, age thirty-six, for one year and was discharged in June 1865. *Record of Service*, Vol. 40, 90. His gravestone has his name as "Keys." Find a Grave, https://www.findagrave.com/memorial/15172702/ransom-keys. Other Kyes family mentioned in these letters are Marion and Chauncey.

29. A pastry made typically with fruit, spices, and, perhaps, some type of meat, traditionally served at special occasions.

30. The 1860 Census lists William R. Williams, age forty-five, farmer, head of household, with Betsy, forty-three, and nine children, in Coe Township. A daughter, Everline, age eighteen, is a "school teacher." *Eighth United States Decennial Census*, Coe, Isabella, Mich., 19.

bor. Celia gives the best of satisfaction in her school. We went down to W[allace']s before they moved, & after dinner they went with us over to Alberts, where we found Fanchers folks; so we had a family re-union by *happen-stance*. All thought of *you*, & wished you were there. The children are teasing to go to bed, so I must close this rambling letter, with not much to write about, but little incidents of *forest life*. Good Night.

God bless & keep thee from all harm—

Write often, to your Ever faithful

Ellen—

Samuel to Ellen

Bridgeport, Ala—Feb 7th 1864. [Sunday]

Dearest Ellen—I will write a little to let you know how I am—but am sorry to say that I do not improve much. I have had a hard week of it with Diarrhea—have got it checked somewhat to day—& hope to soon be better—but it keeps me very weak. If our company starts on a march immediately—I presume I will be sent to the Hospital, but have managed to keep out of it—so far—I dont want to go there, & shall try hard, to keep with my Company. You must not worry—D[oug] Nelson[31] is here & is doing all he can for my comfort. He sends a fellow nearly 3 miles for fresh milk for me—makes me porrige[32]—bought me crackers, & tea & some cod-fish, & it has done me good. So I think I shall come out all right after a little. I have friends here that will do all they can for me. The rebels are having trouble—so many are deserting & coming into our lines—Well I must close for this time. I received two of your good letters to day: they do me more good than medicine.

Good bye—with love to my dear children & yourself—

From Samuel

---

31. Douglas Nelson of Isabella City enlisted in Company M on September 1, 1863, as sergeant, was commissioned second lieutenant on January 24, 1863, and promoted to first lieutenant in December, and resigned his commission on March 11, 1864, then honorably discharged. He was deputy clerk of the circuit court in 1862 and became president of the Mount Pleasant Exchange Savings Bank 1894–1900. *Record of Service*, vol. 43, 146–147; Robertson, *Michigan in the War*, 895; Fancher, *Past and Present*, 134; *Isabella County, Michigan*, 68.

32. Porridge is a dish of grain, such as oats, cooked in water or milk.

Ellen to Samuel

Lincoln Feb 9th 1864.

Tuesday Evening—
    My Dear Husband—
    It lacks only a few moments of nine—& my precious children are long
since in bed—my quiet room tells me that I am *alone*, that my companion is far, far away—Yet *not* alone, for an All-wise Providence watches
over us—& we are in his hands; & his tender care is over us all. It is a
very cold night, & I am obliged to keep the stove well filled with wood to
keep comfortable—so while my darlings are sleeping—I am keeping the
house as comfortable as possible—& to make the time pass pleasantly—I
am conversing—in imagination—with *you*—the absent one.
    It has been very pleasant the past week—last friday Althea came down
with her pony & cutter & took us home with her to attend the quarterly meeting, held at the Court House. This morning Wallace brought
us home, & fixed the chamber floor up for me—he furnished the lumber—Albert has just got back from St Johns with our folk's goods—but
they have not got here yet. Expect them soon—The children are well
with the exception of pretty hard colds—though Dallie has just gotten
over the chicken-pox, but was not much sick, except one day—he took
the disease from Charley Youngs children. Last Wednesday noon I got
word from Celia that I was to have a Surprise Party that evening—so,
I made readiness for them, as much as I could; with what I had to do
with. There was Mr & Mrs Atkins, Mr & Mrs Kyes, & sister—Mr & Mrs
Williams, D[r.] & Mrs Corbus,[33] Mrs Brickley, George Drake, & children enough with Celia to make up 15 besides myself & children. I got
supper about 10 o clock night; had to set two tables—I had raised biscuit & butter, pickles, berry sauce, apple pie, mince pie, tarts, cookies
& tea. It was all very nice? & if *you* had been present I should have enjoyed it much better than I did. They stayed until midnight, & thought
they had a very pleasant time. But you know *I* do not enjoy such parties
as well as many do, a good, religious meeting is more to my taste.
    Do not worry about us—we get along better than I expected I
could—Vesper is a good boy; he splits all the wood & brings it in, &

---

33. Wesley J. Corbus (1818–1893) "was the first physician" of Isabella County; his wife,
Christina, died in 1906. Fancher, *Past and Present*, 202, 325; Find a Grave, https://www
.findagrave.com/memorial/74136577/christiana-corbus.

brings most of the water; we have plenty in our well this winter—I received your letter last week, & glad to hear that you was feeling better. Wed' Morning—Celia came down last night. Came from a spelling school & got here just after I had retired. I must hurry & finish this so she can take it to the [Post] Office—as it is a bitterly cold morning & I dont want to send Vesper up. We are all well this morning & I sincerely hope you are. Be very careful of yourself—& dont try to work when you are not able to. Celia is ready to go to school & I must say—

Good Bye—

& Heaven bless you—

from Ellen.

Samuel to Ellen

Bridgeport Ala—Feb 13th 1864. [Saturday]

My Dear Wife, & Children. It is a great consolation to hear from you, so often—but how *much* rather I would like to *see* you. Am glad to know that you are well and trying to enjoy yourselves. I wish I could say that I was well, but I cannot yet: hope to be soon. I am able to be about, all the time, yet that terrible Chronic Diarhea sticks to me pretty hard. I received your letter this morning. I hope Wallace will do well, & I think he will, you will miss him—but he is not so very far away. I recd the stamps you sent & a nice letter from Vesper that I failed to mention in my last. I hope your folks will get there soon. The report is that this regiment is to be sent to Detroit to build fortifications this summer but I hardly believe it—yet I hope it is so. The weather here is nice & warm—roads are dry & dusty. I have no war news to write, except that the troops are going to the front which means business.[34] I have seen 4 regiments pass with banners unfurled & bands playing—since I have been writing this letter. Be good little boys—my children & take good care of mama. I must close hoping these few lines will find you well—Good bye

From your Absent Husband & father—

S. Woodworth,

Co M. 1st regiment Mich Vol.

Engineers & Mechanics.

---

34. The next major campaign, to capture Atlanta, would launch in May.

Ellen to Samuel

Lincoln, Feb 14th 1864. [Sunday]

(Sabbath Evening.)

My Dear Samuel. Another week has rolled away, bringing me tidings, again, from the dear Absent One: telling me that you are slowing [sic] improving in health, & strength, which is cheering to me—hoping you will speedily recover. How I should like to see your face this Evening: Only think, it is nearly five, *long*-months since you enlisted, to serve your Country; & I fear it will be many times five before she will cease to need your service—though, heaven knows—I hope not.

Every day is bringing its changes; & the war spirit manifests itself here, more strongly than ever. Mr Dunham[35] & Uncle Robbins,[36] H.O. Bigelow,[37] & several others have enlisted, 10 in all. There was two war meetings last week, one at Salt River[38] & one in Paynes[39] district. Fancher was their speaker, & to morrow night he will address them again, at Dunhams house. I intend to go, & then will write you the proceedings. After Albert had brought our folk's goods from St Johns & we were looking every day for them to arrive, we received a letter saying Pa & Ma were both sick & under the Drs care & wanted one of the boys to come home & see to them; so the next morning—early—Albert started for [New] York State.

Celia is here with us to night—she has only 4 weeks longer to teach. Last week the men all turned out & got up a nice pile of wood for Mrs McLane[40] & next Saturday, I hear—they intend serving me the same.

---

35. The first war meeting in Lincoln Township was held at the house of Azariah Dunham, who enlisted in the Fourth Cavalry on February 11, 1864, at Coe, for three years, age forty-four. Mustered February 27, 1864. Discharged on surgeon's certificate of disability at Grand Rapids, Michigan, July 28, 1864. Fancher, *Past and Present*, 313; *Record of Service*, vol. 34, 48.

36. William R. Robbins served in various public offices including the County Board of Supervisors and postmaster. Fancher, *Past and Present*, 85, 87, 90, 91, 307, 328.

37. Horace O. Bigelow, blacksmith and farmer, came to Coe Township in 1856 and acquired 320 acres. *Portrait and Biographical Album*, 287.

38. Location of a settlement and post office in Coe Township; it eventually became the town of Shepherd. Romig, *Michigan Place Names*, 510.

39. Perhaps Norman C. Payne of Chippewa, first supervisor of Chippewa Township and a member of the Board of Supervisors for Isabella County. *Isabella County, Michigan*, 18; *Portrait and Biographical Album*, 537.

40. Walter McLain's spouse.

The women go along to visit, & carry refreshments, & such a noisy, crowd—I never mingled with before. But war-widows must put up with anything—must swallow their pride—& accept thankfully the well-meant kindness; for we must be fed & clothed—& kept warm—and if war takes from us our own protectors—we must surely accept the donations of those left at home—or suffer. Yet I have great cause for thankfulness. My health is good, my children are all a fond mother could wish & though war causes sorrow, & trouble—I trust & pray we may meet again. If not may we be prepared to meet in that brighter & better world where there will be no more sorrow, or *parting*, no more tears shed. O my dear husband—shall it not be so?

Tuesday Afternoon—I will finish up my letter—as mail day is near at hand—It is the coldest day we have had since New Years. We just have to sit over the stove, & keep putting in wood to keep warm. Last night we went to the war meeting, but no one enlisted. Fancher & Althea came down & stayed with us over night. He paid me the ballance on the produce he bought—which amounted to seven dollars: that is all we have, in money—but it will last I trust—until we are better supplied.

O how it blusters, to day—I shall be glad when the cold weather is over: but we keep comfortable by staying indoors. Yesterday was quite mild, & we opened the potato pit[41]—as we had to have some to eat. I found a good many frozen, but perhaps inside farther they will be better. There are 30 bushel more of baga's & 20 of turnips yet to dispose of. Dr. Corbus, Mr Wilsey, & Brickley, will take them. Dont worry about *us* but take good care of your own-dear-self—& write often—

The Children send a kiss, & love—to dear Papa—

Faithfully yours

E. L. Woodworth

Samuel to Ellen

Bridgeport—Ala. Feb 21st 1864. [Sunday]

Dear Ellen—I recd three letters yesterday—one from you—one from Emily T____[42] & one from Celia. Am glad to hear that you are getting

---

41. A storage for potatoes.
42. Unknown.

along so well. I do not get strong yet, but able to be around—rode out about 6 miles into the country, & am gaining flesh. I should like to have been at your surprise party but was to far away. Yet I hope to be with you some-time, & the sooner the better, to suit me. I hear they are fighting at Knoxville but we dont get the particulars, I expect its lively times at the front.[43] I have not much to write that will interest you. Tell Celia that I thank her for writing, & will answer her letter when I feel a little stronger—O how much I do want to see you all again! Take good care of yourselves until I get home, & then I will take care of you. Now I must close hoping to hear good news from *home*. To my dear Wife & Children—

from Samuel Woodworth

Ellen to Samuel

Lincoln, Mich. Feb 22ond 1864. [Monday]

My Dear Samuel   I did not receive one line from you last week but I think the fault was in the mail's, & not you. So I flatter myself I will get the more this week, & I do hope to hear that you are enjoying good health again. I cannot say that we are all well now for I have got a felon[44] on the fore-finger of my left hand, & it is very painful. It has been coming over a week, & had no appearance of breaking. However, I manage to get along with Vesper's help & do my work—if it was on the other hand I could work better, but then I could not write to you so it is best as it is. Wed, 24th I will again resume my pen. I had written thus far when Celia & Emma[45] came down from the County Seat, so I laid by my writing. Our folks got here last friday, all safe—though Mothers health is poor, & Pa is not very strong. He has bought the Dr Burt place at the County Seat, & paid $600,00 for it. They will go directly to house-keeping. They are now at Fanchers, & Emma will stay with me awhile & do my work, for my finger is—or whole hand rather—very much swollen & I cannot use it. Pa came down & stayed last night

---

43. A skirmish was recorded on February 20 near Knoxville. *OR*, vol. 32, pt. 1, 3.

44. An infection of the soft tissue of the tip of a finger.

45. Emma A. Preston, born July 18, 1848, in New York, was a younger sister of Ellen's. She married Albert Fox in 1866 and died June 8, 1878, age twenty-nine. Find a Grave, https://www.findagrave.com/memorial/60542553/emma-a-fox.

& kept me company, for I have not slept much for two nights—but this morning I felt so anxious to get your letter that I came up to the [Post] Office with Celia when she came to school & I got a letter from you: But O sorrow! Must you stay there & die, & I not be with you! I know by your letter that you are in a bad situation, although you have put the best construction on what you tell me of your sickness. But O tell me the truth about it, & if you are able to come, get a furlough & come home.

If Doug Nelson is there, & so kind to you—tell him from me to use his influence to get you a discharge—& I will bless him with my last breath. I believe he can, if he will—& he surely will not *let* you, lie there & *die*.

Tomorrow the soldiers leave here for Corrunna.[46] [Jeremiah] Barnhart[47] has enlisted, & his wife goes with him to [New] York State. The enlistments are sufficient to fill our quota, so there will be no draft, at present. Last Saturday the men turned out, & got me up a splendid woodpile—about 15 cords all split up, at the door. There were 14 men & boys: Mr. Atkins, Keller,[48] Gibbs,[49] Williams, Brickley, D. Childs,[50] Mr. Wilsey & Amos—Charley Youngs—Eugene Corbus, Mr. Holland—Coonts[51]—the Hawley boys[52] & Wallace. Arsene came down & helped me & Mrs Wilsey & Mrs Corbus was all the women that came. I furnished dinner for them all. The sleighing is nearly gone, consequently the going is very bad. I am thinking of letting the sugar bush[53] to Alberts hired man.—Our folks like the woods very much & now if you was only home, I should be absolutely contented. I wish I knew if you needed money; if you do let me know, & I will send you some. I sold 8 dollars worth more of turnips last week to Spink[54]—& Mr Wilsey sent me an Order to draw $10,00 from the Treasury fund, for soldiers families—saying I *must* accept it: if I was to sensitive to accept provision,

---

46. The seat of Shiawassee County, Michigan.

47. Jeremiah Barnhart "enlisted in company C, Eighth Infantry, Feb. 17, 1864, at Coe, for 3 years, age 34. Mustered Feb. 27, 1864. Wounded in action at the Wilderness, Va., May, 1864. Discharged at Washington, D.C., July 10, 1865." *Record of Service*, vol. 8, 10.

48. The editor has been unable to identify this person.

49. The editor has been unable to identify this person.

50. Darwin Childs, son of Andrew F. Childs, who came to Isabella County in 1853. *Portrait and Biographical Album*, 458.

51. The editor has been unable to identify this person.

52. The editor has been unable to identify these people.

53. A forested area used for maple syrup.

54. The editor has been unable to identify this person.

I must accept that, provided to buy them with & when it was gone he would give me another order. He takes a fathers interest in my welfare & the neighbors are all very kind to us. I feel that I am not worthy of such kindness, yet when I consider that I have given my *husband* to Our Country, I feel that I am justly entitled to all the recompense they could possibly give. Hoping to hear from you soon & that you are feeling better I will paitiently [sic] wait another mail. Good bye & may kind heaven preserve thee & keep thee from harm—

Yours as Ever—

Ellen—

Samuel to Ellen

Bridgeport—Ala—Feb 28th 1864. [Sunday]

My Dear Ellen I received yours & Vepy's letter this morning. was very glad to hear of your good health. I expected to have drawn my pay so as to have sent you some money before this but have not—I hope to soon—Yet I think you should feel willing to accept what Orders the law sees fit to give you. You are entitled to it, & it is a false pride that keeps you from accepting it. There are Soldiers here who are worth their thousands—that their families draw from 4 to 15 dollars a month. Whoever takes their chances in this war, cannot receive too much pay— whether it come to the Soldier on the field, or the families left at home. I suppose you are anxious to hear how I am—I am not able to do duty yet—but have a fair appetite & am feeling pretty comfortable. If I am not able to work after I get my pay I will try & get a furlough—but it would cost me $20,00 or more to come—& I should so hate to come back to this kind of life again. I think we will all be home next fall— if not before. Keep up good courage, we will come out all right yet; and when I get home I think I shall be contented to stay there—How I would like to see the little hand that done that scribbling on Vepy's letter. My little Dallie boy—but I must not think of it—it wont do. We did expect to move away from this place before this but may stay some time yet. We are camped on the banks of the Tennessee river—a nice location, & I wash in the river every morning—I will send some money as soon as I get pay—I must close hoping to hear from you again soon.

Good bye—To E.—& the Children—

Samuel to Ellen

Bridgeport Ala March 7th 1864. [Monday]

My Dear Ellen, I received your letter to day & how *much* I prize such letters, you will never know. I am sorry to have you worry so about me. I am surely better, & have all the money I need—yet do not get our pay—expect to soon. Your hand was very painful, I am sorry to have you afflicted, with any thing so painful as a felon. I hope you are better ere this. Now that your folks are there to see to you, I dont know that I want to get a furlough; I should so hate to leave home again—but I feel in my heart that I shall be spared to come home, *some time*; it *must* be so.

How I would like to be there, & rig up my bush, & make some nice syrup—& then some of your biscuit & butter to eat with it—wouldn't it taste good?

Veppy my boy, how do you do; I will answer your nice letter before long—I do not forget you, or my little Dallie either. Take good care of mama—goodbye I must close this short letter: from *Sam*, to his dear—
—Wife & children.

Ellen to Samuel

Lincoln Mich—March 13th 1864. [Sunday]

Absent Husband. It seems a long time since I have heard from you because I received no letter last week. Wednesday the mail did not come in from St. Johns & I was much disappointed: but it came friday & I went up to the [post] office, quite sure I should get a letter, but was destined to disappointment again. I hope to get enough next week to make up for this, & if I can hear you are *well*, I will be satisfied. We are usually well here, I am doing my work alone again. My hand is so I can use it—But will never have the full use of my finger again. Dr. Corbus lanced it—it became so painful that the fourth night that I had been without sleep—I started toward morning & walked through the woods alone to his house—they were not up, but got up & made me a cup of tea & made me drink it—then gave me chloroform, but not enough to make me unconcious—then he cut it open & poulticed[55] it for me; & I

---

55. A medicinal paste applied to sores or lesions.

felt greatly relieved. Emma stayed with the Children. Last friday Ce-
lias school closed & Wallace came down & carried her, & Emma home.
I have not been up there yet to see them, the roads are so bad; but shall
when sugaring is over. We have had queer weather for sugar making.
The weather was warm a few days & many tapped their trees—we made
about 25 pounds & some syrup, then a cold rain storm came on, which
terminated in a freeze up; & it has not been sugar weather since. Our
hired man has made 75 new troughs, & got spouts made: built a sugar-
shanty & cut his wood, so when sugaring does come he will be ready
to attend to it.[56] Vesper works with him & seems to enjoy himself well.
He is strong, & hearty this spring, & grows fast. So does Dallie—he is
fat—as a pig, & is growing tall. Last night I dreamed of you—O how
much we would like to see you, but as I said before, if I can hear you
are *well*, I will be content. I hope your regiment *will* be sent to Detroit,
then I can come & see you, & bring you some things for your comfort.
We dont get any war news lately—so I know but little what is going on.
The week that our folks came I walked to Salt River, & back in a pretty
short time. They came here & of course are always used to having tea
to drink & as I had none, I felt worried over it & as none of our neighbors keep it, I put on my wraps & told ma I was going to get some tea
for dinner—she supposed I was going to the neighbors to borrow so
she said "all right" & I struck a bee-line for Salt River; bought a quarter of a pound for 50cts & got home in time to get dinner—Ma never
knew I had been to the store 3 miles away—she only remarked that "my
neighbors lived a good way off" or else I stayed to visit awhile." Monday Noon & a cold windy day. Dallie & I are alone; the boys are in the
woods to work. Have just been to dinner; shall I tell you what we had?
Boiled ham & potatoes, bread, butter & molasses, pumpkin pie & cold
water. I have baked 8 pies this forenoon. Mrs Hoag[57] gave me some
dried pumpkin, & Saturday they went away & left us to milk their cow,
so we got two milkings, & thought I would have a mess of pies—wish
I could send you one. Pa came down to see us yesterday—says he will
furnish me grass seed to sow the wheat—& when sugaring is over he
says I must come up & live with them so we wont be so lonely. They
are going to build a school house up there & if I go the children can at-

---

56. For information on this process, see "The History of Maple Syrup," Michigan Maple Syrup, https://www.michiganmaple.org/history/.

57. The spouse of enlistee James Hoag. Fancher, *Past and Present*, 314.

tend school. Wallace is getting fleshy, since he got into office—has all the business to do of the County Clerks office. Fancher is "Attorney & Cousellor at Law" & when I get there, I dont know just what I shall be: but shall try to be a good citizen, & true christian woman; & that is all we need aspire to in this world, & our duty to ourselves, our children our neighbors & our God, demand this much of us. & O my dear Husband, may we each live, that when we are called to leave this world of sorrow, we may be ready to put on the glorious crown of immortality, & chant the happy songs of the blessed. O blessed hope! How cheering the assurance, that this world of sorrow is not always to last, but that we can lift our eyes to that "beautiful beyond" & calmly say "Our Father not my will, but Thine be done."[58] Good bye; this letter is too long already—Ever remember with kindness—

Your Affectionate Wife, & Children.

Samuel to Ellen

March 13th 1864. Bridgeport Ala—[Sunday]

Dear Ellen, I have just received another of your precious letters, & when I compare them with mine, it makes me feel foolish. O, it does me *good*, to get such letters. I am gaining slowly—you must know—I walked down to town yesterday, & while there I was weighed—am not very heavy—112 pounds is all I weigh now. Twelve weeks ago I weighed 157. I walk with a cane, but feel pretty well. Do as you think best about leaving the place, & going to live with your folks. I will risk your own judgment in the matter: let the place if you go away—to Holland. Our pay-master is here & will pay to morrow—but only up to the 1st of January. I will send what I can to you: It is very pleasant here—the weather is fine. I hear that Doug Nelson has resigned, & starts for Detroit at 3 o clock this afternoon. I think I will send this by him with 20 dollars in it, to you. I shall keep enough by me to get what I need to eat. I have to be careful yet what I eat. I hope you will be careful of yourself—for I shall be home next fall to make you some work—yet I have learned to wait on myself. They say Soldiers are lazy after they get home—but I think if I once get there, I shall enjoy work on my own little place.

---

58. KJV, Luke 22:42.

I must close—give my love to all enquiring friends—& accept love for yourself & children.

from your Absent Husband.

Samuel W.

Ellen to Samuel

Lincoln. March 18th. 1864. [Friday]

Ever Dear Husband. To day is the first I have heard from you, since *two weeks ago last wednesday*—and you may believe I have felt very uneasy. Last weeks mail did not get here until friday, & then brought nothing for me: This week wednesday the mail failed again; but to day (friday) it came bringing me your long-looked-for letter, bearing date Feb 28th. I have sent one to you every week, so far. We are well & glad to hear that you are so much better. My hand is getting well—though not so I can sew any yet, & as to day is cold & blustering I thought I could pass away a leisure hour most agreeably to myself by writing a little to you—my absent husband. And when I commence to write there are so many things I want to say to you, I hardly know where to begin; so I will lay your letter beside me (that I have already read until I can repeat most of its contents,) & answer all your inquiries; for I have never kept any thing from you that you wished to know in regard to my affairs—& I never intend to. First you speak of the revival meetings here, & ask if I have taken an active part in them? Yes, my dear Samuel I have—though not, perhaps, as much as I ought. Yet I thank God that he has borne with me so long, & enabled me at last to speak of his goodness & acknowledge his merciful care & love, toward me, & mine. I have ever known my duty, but shrank from performing it looking to much at the cross, & to little at the crown, but I only blame myself—& wonder how I could, so long & willingly disregard the commands & requirements of our Heavenly Father. Our Saviour says "if we deny him before the world, he will deny us before our Father in heaven,"[59] and so long as we fail to confess him—just so long we deny him. But to day I bless his holy name—his presence is with me:—when I have felt bowed down with grief & my heart seemed bursting with sorrow, he has bade me

---

59. A paraphrase of KJV, Matthew 10:33.

look *up* & *live*. Live for him & his glorious cause. Live for my dear husband & children, & for humanity. And he has taken away the gloom, & filled my heart with his holy love & bade me rejoice, with exceeding joy. Yes Jesus is *mine*! and I am able to bear censure & rebuke, or whatever the world sees fit to cast upon me, knowing that his grace is sufficient; & that by & bye this earth-pilgrimage will be ended—this frail body beyond the reach of reproof—& the sweet assurance will be mine that I have not lived in vain. We are all created free moral agents—each one must act for themselves, one cannot live for another—& therefore cannot answer for another—consequently what we believe to be our duty—what sincere convictions of right we may have—or wrong—whatever our conscience prompts us to do, or points the way—the path of duty, we should most assuredly enter upon, in all sincerity & truth— ever looking to God for guidance; and he will never leave us—or forsake us: O my dear Husband let us ever do this & we shall never feel the need of a friend, a *Friend* that sticketh closer than a brother. I trust you will pardon me for writing so lengthy on this subject—for who can I speak so freely to as to you—altho we may not think alike, yet I hope the time is not far distant when we shall view in the same light a matter of so vast importance; and one that lies so near & dear to every christian heart.

Wednesday morning. I will now finish my letter that I began last friday. I am now at the County Seat—with our folks—came up monday— Fancher send his horse & cutter down for us to come & make a visit so I & the children left the hired man to keep house & started monday morning—had a pleasant sleigh-ride which the children greatly enjoyed; our pony was a speedy animal—Vesper says a regular 2-40 & we made good time, & laughed at the crooked paths we made over the snow—as he was headstrong & I am not the best of drivers—but we went safely & found our friends all well—They all join in sending love & best wishes to you. It is a very pleasant day & looks as though we might soon have spring. I am going back home to day & shall put this in the Chippewa P.O. I hope to find another letter from you, telling me you are now well—I will send you a few more stamps & if you do not get your pay—tell me immediately & I will divide what I have with you. I cannot think of your suffering for anything as long as we have a penny. I am going to move up here after sugaring & live in a part of Pa's house—& as the talk is now of organizing for a school here, I shall make application for it & earn something so as not to be wholly depen-

dent on you. Pa has gone to St Johns for his goods—took Alberts oxen
& wagon & started Monday morning, all alone. It is frozen & the roads
are much better than if he waits until it breaks up—The girls are laugh-
ing & talking with Dallie & Vesper is out playing with Mr Bentleys
boy;—they have moved into the court house[60]—& fitted up one part for
a shoe-shop. I think I have written all the news & must draw my letter
to a close—Ma's health is quite good—Celia is going to teach near Salt
River, & Emma in the Paine[61] district. They wish to be remembered to
you.

Good bye & accept love from your dear children &
Ever affectionate Wife—
E. L. W.

Samuel to Ellen

Bridgeport Ala—March 18th 1864. [Friday]

Dear Ellen—I will write a few lines—altho I sent a letter this week
by Doug Nelson & $20,00—I drew 48,00 but though[t] I would not
send more now. I am feeling some better, yet not well—& thought I
would keep enough by me so I could come home if I got worse—Our
company is quite small now—all that are able to work are detailed to
build block houses along the road, from here to Nashville.[62] 80 men
went from our company. It is a pleasant day but cold, raw wind. I suppose you are having maple sugar & syrup now, though if it is as cold
there as here you wont make much. You spoke of going home—I cant
advise you—only to do as you think best—I can trust you to do what
you like—but take good care of your-selves where ever you are—I am
on guard to day & have not time to write much—I brought two pails
of water this morning the first chores I have done in a long time—have

---

60. Isabella County's first courthouse was "a rough framed building" constructed by
David Ward, the landowner who platted Mount Pleasant and set aside a square for the
structure. Cumming, *This Place Mount Pleasant*, 37.

61. See n. 39 of this chapter.

62. These small forts proved efficacious in repelling attacks with a minimal defend-
ing force. Typically made of logs or heavy timbers, with "loop-hole" openings through
which to fire at the enemy, they were erected at critical points in the supply line. Hoffman,
Among the Enemy, 124. Mahan, *Treatise on Field Fortification*, 62–63.

just recd your letter of the 8th. I sent Vesper a soldiers hymn book this
week—am glad to hear that you are well—Love to all—especially my
 Dear children & their Mother—
 From Samuel.

Samuel to Ellen

Bridgeport, Ala. March 26th 1864. [Saturday]

Dearest Ellen—I received one more of your precious letters, so full
of hope & courage—it almost pays me for all I have suffered—& makes
me feel unworthy of so noble a woman.—First, I will say that I mean to
live, hence forth a christian life. I am glad for a great many things, that
I ever came here. I did not know or realize your noble worth, & good
counsel. Bring the children up in the fear of God, at the same time
teach them to love every thing that is just & true, or good. We may dif-
fer in our belief, but if we love & serve God & keep his commandments,
we surely shall not quarrel about religious creeds. My health is quite
good again. I have stood three days this week on guard, & feel better
to day, than I have in 14 weeks. I am so thankful, I cannot express my
thanks with my pen—but when I get *home* I can tell more to you than I
can write.

We have no late war news; but have had a stormy week. Monday, it
was cold & windy; tuesday it commenced to snow. Wednesday morning
snow was 15 inches deep: our tents had all they could stand under. To
day the weather is fine. Our Captain has just arrived:—there are some
hard rumors about D[oug] N[elson] probably there will be an investigation. I fear he isn't just what he ought to be:[63] but I must close with
love to my precious ones, at *home.*
 Samuel

---

63. As shown in the letters of April 5 and May 25, 1864, there apparently were questions
about Nelson's resignation.

Ellen to Samuel

Lincoln. March 28th 1864.

Monday Evening—Dear Husband—your welcome letter of the 7th inst came safely; & though brief it gladened my heart to hear that you were improving & had the means to make yourself comfortable—for I was fearful you was out of money—& where it was hard to get. How glad I am that you are getting better of that terrible disease Chronic Diarhea—so many have been carried to their graves by it.—Do use every precaution & not get down again. We are all usually well—since taking Kennedys medicine, Vesper has improved & both of our dear ones enjoy good health. He is in the bush this evening with the hired man—syruping down—& little Dallie is abed & asleep—so you see I am alone—yet not *alone*, for I feel the invisible presence of that great & good Being who has said "I am with you always, even unto the end of the world."[64] O how precious the promise; that he is ours, & we are his; heirs to a crown, to a kingdom—to a throne. O how rich: Dear Samuel now my soul is drawn toward you—how I want to see you, to tell so much better that I can write, all the thoughts of my poor heart. I trust the day is not far distant when we shall greet each other in a land of peace—free from the sound, or rumor of war: with families re-united—unsaddened by the loss of loved ones, will it not be a happy meeting?

Pa returned friday night with his goods—took him five days—but he had a large load, & the oxen are not swift travelers.

To day I have been sewing a little, the first in six weeks—so you see I have had rather of a tedious time with my finger. I have no news in particular to write—war news are meagre here in the woods & what we do get are unreliable. My page is nearly full & I must close—hoping to hear from you again wednesday. May Angels watch over you, & keep you from all harm is the prayer of your ever affectionate,

Ellen

---

64. KJV, Matthew 28:20.

Samuel to Ellen

Bridgeport Ala—March 31st 1864. [Thursday]

My Dear Wife & Children—Again I am writing to those that occupy most of my thoughts. How I would like to have had you take tea with me to night. Yesterday I was on guard, so to-day I had to sleep, or run about as I pleased—so I pleased to go to town, & I got 4 green apples, some ginger cake, one dried-apple pie, half a pound cheese, & our cook made some good biscuit. I baked one apple—made some tea & went to my tent to eat: but I was *alone*: my mind even left me & ran of[f] to Michigan, nor could I stop it till it got to that little log house in the woods & my dainty supper would not go down. I wished the boys had had the apples & you the tea & cheese, or you & the boys had been with me, I could have eaten a hearty meal for I have a good appetite. I am feeling better every day. Our company is nearly all gone, only a few left that are not able to work. With one soldier I occupy the whole tent where 10 have generally been all winter. I expect to go out where the rest of the boys are soon. It will suit me better than to stay here & stand guard every other day—it is not hard work—but I dont like to be out in the storm—or at night. You don't understand what guard duty is. We have to stay at our post, or rather, walk our beat 8 hours out of 24. On duty 2, & 4, off. My comrade is asleep & has been for a long time; with no one to speak to, I feel as though I was alone. The night is dark & still—only the rain beating on our tent, bringing a sense of lonliness. O how it rains—Good night to my dear family and I will finish my letter in the morning, & may God bless & protect you & keep you from all harm. Friday morning, April 1st. How is my little family, is the question I ask myself this morning: I hope, *well.* There has no one tried to April fool me this morning. My pipe was not stopped up & we didn't have any milk cup on the table without milk in it—as we have neither milk, or cup. It is a cloudy wet morning. I have been to the river—washed my towel & socks—my other clothes are all clean—3 good shirts, 2 pair pants, 2 [pair] drawers, my dress coat & over coat are but little worn— my boots I shall get mended to day. My eating outfit consists of 1 tin plate, tin cup & spoon, a little pail and knife—that is all I need; I will close & send some poetry that two soldiers copied for me who are un-

der arrest for desertion—& are kept here under guard—their home is in
Ingham Co.[65]

THE SOLDIERS LOVED ONES—

1st

When the bugle's blast is dying
In his tent the soldier's lying
Home afar his thoughts are hieing
To the land of liberty—
Thinks of those whom he left weeping
Dreams of them as he lies sleeping
Lord he leaves them in thy keeping
Loved ones—oft he thinks of thee.

2ond

When the revellie is beating
And the shades of night retreating
Home again his thoughts are flitting
To the cottage by the sea.
Through the fields again he's roaming
By the dark blue oceans foaming
Where the dear ones wait his coming
Loved ones, oft he thinks of thee.

3d

When the charge the bugle's sounding
When embattled hosts are shouting
Where the Eagle flag is floating
On the plains of Tennessee.
Missiles thick around him flying—
Scores of Comrades round him lying—
'Midst the wounded & the dying
Loved Ones, oft, he thinks of thee.

4th

Where in Vesper pray'rs engaging
When the morning drums awaking
When terrific strife is raging
Loved ones, oft he thinks of thee
Oh how warm will be that greeting
Blissful Happy be that meeting
Loved Ones now will cease their weeping
Home, he's come from Tennessee.

---

65. Ingham County, Michigan, location of the state capital.

Accept this from your Absent Husband hoping to be with you, ere long.

Ellen to Samuel

Lincoln. April 5th 1864. [Tuesday]

Another week has passed away & as usual I am seated by the table writing to my Absent Husband; who I would like to see so much. I received by last mail the letter you sent by D. Nelson containing the money—also another written by you one week later. I am glad you kept a part of the money by you—would rather do without ourselves than have you suffer for anything.

I had one dollar in the house when it came, & our store of provisions rather low, but providence would have provided—some way. Every thing is dear here this spring. Flour is $11,00 per barrel, Pork 16 & 18 cts per pound—potatoes 1,00 per bushel, butter 25 & 28 cts & sugar will be a scarce article if we dont get any more sugar weather. We have made about 100 pounds & about half of it is solid wax. It wouldnt cake & so I run it into a large crock & am going to keep it until you come home. It has hardly paid us to keep a man to work the bush as it has turned out, it would have been cheaper to have bought our sugar—but he has made 70 new troughs & got the bush in shape for another year.

Tell me what made D[oug] N[elson] resign. How very sick you must have been to lose so much flesh in so short a time. 45 pounds in 12 weeks! 15 pounds a month! how very thin & poor you must be. Do you really think you are getting *well*, now?

O join with me in your prayers—in an earnest petition to our dear Heavenly Father to restore you again to health, & to your little family. He *will*—O he must hear our prayers—We are all of us well. Vesper feels pleased of the hymn book you sent him—he & Dallie are very busy now days, with each a bow & arrow, that the hired man made them—Dallie says "the black birds have to *skedaddle*." Well it is time to close this rambling letter. May He who watches over all—preserve thee from harm is the prayer of—

Your Ellen.

Samuel to Ellen

Camp Cowan Station Tenn.[66] *April 10th 1864. [Sunday]*

Dear Ellen,
Again I will scribble a few lines to let you know where I am. I left camp & came out here, a week ago last friday, & have worked every day, until to day. We shall get through in a couple of days & then shall go somewhere's else to work. Our work is building block houses—This is a very pleasant place, & my health is so much improved, I enjoy myself & the good things we can get here to eat—especially fresh milk & warm corn bread, which you know, my passion for. I recd a letter from you, written at the County Seat, a *good, long* letter. If I could only write as you can but that is out of the question: and receiving one only makes me more anxious for another. It seems a long time to wait; for one to go there, & back. There are no news this time except it is a cold rainy day—& the tent is full—so I will close by repeating the wish so often expressed—'how I wish I was at home with my dear Wife & Children.
Sincerely yours,
Samuel Woodworth

Ellen to Samuel

Lincoln. Mich. April 12th 1864. [Tuesday]

My Dear Husband. The dearest, & most precious letter I *ever* received, I got last mail; and it was from your own hand my dear Samuel. O can you ever imagine how glad is my poor heart, & how it swells with thankfulness—and unutterable love toward the great Giver for answering my prayers in your behalf. Yes, dear Samuel I have long prayed fervently that you might become a christian—that your heart might be filled with Gods sweet grace, & your life be one of holiness: and the evidence has now come, in such meek & touching language, as is contained in your last precious letter, that my heart overflows with joy.—& when I read it I fell on my knees & praised God for his goodness, &

---

66. Near the town of Cowan, Tennessee, on the rail line southeast of Estill Springs, just north of a 2,200-foot tunnel that required guards.

kissed the blessed words in the exuberance of joy. Thirteen years ago to-morrow I became your wife. I was happy then because I loved you dearly—but I love you *better* now. Does it seem so long? That thirteen years of our wedded life has already passed & gone, & we have just begun to live! Just begun to realize for what we were created. Is it not so, dear S.—? How glad I am that you are better: be careful of yourself, for you are not past danger yet. I wrote you last week that your money came safely. I think Albert will work the place. I have got the wheat seeded—it is looking nicely—it took 3 pecks of grass-seed—at $3,00 per bushel. Our hired man is through & gone. I am going to send you a little cake of sugar, if you get it, I will send more. Eat it & think of us. The children are well & so am I. Accept a short letter, this time. Good bye.

Lovingly—Ellen—

Samuel to Ellen

Shell Mound, Tenn[67] *April 17th 1864 [Sunday]*

Loved ones at *Home.*

Another pleasant Sabbath day has dawned, & I am permitted to write a few lines to my dear little family. Yet I am sorry to say I have not always treated them as I should. I have done wrong so many times in actions more than deeds, & yet you have never complained nor upbraided me for it. You will forgive me wont you? How I would like to be with you to day; I think I could tell you some things that would interest you. We are now on the Tennessee river eight miles from Bridgeport building another block house. I am well now & enjoy myself the best I have in a long time. I hope you received the money I sent. I dont want you to feel as though you must teach to earn a living.—Do as you think best—but be careful of your health. I cannot eat hard tack—or bacon yet—or drink coffee—it dont agree with me. There are some good men in our company—yet there are others do not regard the Sabbath— every thing going on in the tent while I am writing, some reading, some playing cards—some doing one thing, some another. I have written every week to you, received a letter from you last monday & hope to get

---

67. Shellmound was a rail town on the south bank of the Tennessee River east of Bridgeport. *Atlas*, plate 32, map 5.

another to night. Love to you & my dear little boys, from your Absent Husband.

Ellen to Samuel

Lincoln, Mich April 18th 1864. [Monday]

My Dear Husband—It is a beautiful spring day & I have been very busy at work all the forenoon till now I am taking a short rest, & will improve it in writing to you. We are all usually well, & am so *glad* to hear that you are improving. How I would have enjoyed taking tea with you—yet the dainty feast would not have attracted me there so much, as the privilege of sitting face to face—& talking with my husband—once more. Yet I hope ere long to enjoy that privilege, & such hope cheers my heart, & whispers of a happy future, when we shall once more be united, to separate no more, till we part to meet again, in the mansion of the blest. O happy thought! How cheering is the promise, that we shall *there*, part no more; but shall be as the Angels in Heaven. What sweet words of comfort to the weary heart. Rest, above, *rest*, from all the cares & sorrows of life, & no more tears to shed. No more parting—but happiness—never ending, ever-enduring to all of Gods dear children.

> O life below; how brief, & poor, & sad:
> One heavy sigh!
> O life Above: how long, how fair & glad;
> An endless joy!
> O to be done with daily dying here,
> O to begin the living, in yon sphere.—[68]

You will be surprised to hear that I have taken the school at the County Seat—but I thought it better to be earning something myself & not be wholly dependent on you. I have not been up yet to agree on any terms, but expect to go this week before the school inspectors for examination. The school house is a new log-building, about 80 rods[69]

---

68. Bonar, *Hymns of Faith and Hope*, 74–75.

69. A unit of length used in surveying that equaled 16.5 feet; 80 rods was the equivalent of ¼ mile.

south & west of the Court House—built for a dwelling by Mr. Kinney—but will be used for school, while the new school house is being built.

Mr. Ferris,[70] Dr Meissler,[71] & Wallace, are the school officers—in Union township & Wallace is Justice of Peace; Pa is deputy Sheriff—Celia is expecting to teach in the Estee district[72] & Emma in Paynes.

Mother, & all the rest are usually well. I have bought 50 pounds sugar of Mr Holland & paid him 1 shilling per pound—as we only made about 100 pounds ourselves. I have to pay 6 dollars a hundred for flour to Pa & 15 cts per pound for pork. He is buying up Indian sugar & shipping it; he pays 10 cts.[73] Those verses you sent me were very nice & beautifully written: you said they were deserters; will they have to be shot? O I hope not. Marion Kyes[74] enlisted about two months ago, & now sleeps in a soldiers grave. He died in Baltimore—of quick consumption;[75] caused by taking a severe cold. Wednesday Morning. I am now at the County Seat—to Wallaces—staid here last night & am going to Mothers as soon as I finish this. Came up yesterday with Charley Youngs.—He & Albert came up to fish last night. We are all well. Dallie is just eating his breakfast & Aunt Nene is picking the bones out of his fish for him. Vesper staid with Willie last night to help him do the chores & they are coming up on foot to day. I hope it is as pleasant where you are.—Keep up good courage my dear Samuel for brighter days will dawn for us by & bye. Trust Him whose watchful care is ever over us; & accept the assurance of his love. Direct to Isabella City[76]—

Faithfully yours,

E.L.W.

---

70. Likely George A. Ferris (1835–1891), carpenter, farmer, and "squatter" on 160 acres in Union Township under the Homestead Act in 1862. *Portrait and Biographical Album*, 319; Find a Grave, https://www.findagrave.com/memorial/74757992/george-a-ferris.

71. Apparently Ernst G. H. Miessler, "a German missionary" who "wrote a dictionary in the Indian language." Fancher, *Past and Present*, 104; Find a Grave, https://www.findagrave.com/memorial/26706389/ernest-gustav_herman-miessler.

72. Perry H. Estee came to the County in 1854 and claimed land in section 18 of Coe Township.

73. Sugar making from maple sap was a traditional Ojibwe activity. See Thomas, "Historic American Indian Maple Sugar," 299; Keller, "America's Native Sweet," 117.

74. Marvin H. (or Myron Kyes) enlisted in company H, 8th Michigan Infantry, February 17, 1864, at Coe, age seventeen; died of disease at Baltimore, Maryland, March 31, 1864. *Record of Service*, vol. 8, 79.

75. Tuberculosis. Welsh, *Medical Histories of Union Generals*, 401.

76. The platted town formerly known as Indian Mills.

Samuel to Ellen

Camp Shell Mound. Tenn. April 24th 1864. [Sunday]

Dear Ellen. How do you & my little boys find yourselves this pleasant morning? I guess I would like to be with you & see for myself—I am feeling pretty well but have to be very careful what I eat.

Sunday Evening—I wrote so far this morning & was looking *out of the window* when I saw some Cattle. I left my writing & took a small pail & went & got it full of new milk, & had bread & milk for my dinner which I enjoyed very much. The boys wanted me to go up on the mountains into Georgia with them, so I went. We had a nice time; it is 20 miles from where we were to Lookout mountain, yet we could see it very plain.[77] O, Ellen how I did wish you was with me to view the beautiful scenery from those high rocks a mile above the river. It was a grand sight & you would have appreciated it, but I would give more to see my own little *home* & those that are so dear to me than I would to see the whole confederacy: It is getting dark & I must close for to night. Monday noon, Apr 25th. Dear Ellen I have just received another of your precious letters that tells me my dear ones are well: how much I think of them, & how can it be otherwise—The little cake of sugar looks sacred to me—I have tasted it, it is nice, *very nice*, & I thank you for it. I must close & go to work. I will bid you good bye & leave you in the care of Him who has said he would save to the uttermost. I feel we can trust Him. I will write more next time. To Ellen, Veppy, & Dallie.

Ellen to Samuel

Mt. Pleasant. Mich. April 24th 1864. [Sunday]

My Dear Samuel. It is a dark rainy evening. Celia & I have got the old folks & children to bed & thought we would improve an hour in writing to dear friends, before retiring: so we are now seated in their pleasant front chamber, by the stand, keeping time with our pens, to the constant patter of the rain against the window pane. All are usu-

---

77. Lookout Mountain is a major geographic feature south of Chattanooga, Tennessee, and the site of Civil War combat in late November 1863.

ally well except Mother is feeling rather poorly for a few days past, yet I hope to see her well soon. I came here last Tuesday & have not been down yet to move my things up here; but Pa will get a horse team & go down with me after them, this week. I think I shall like living up here, & shall feel quite contented if I can only know that you are well, & comfortable. I have taken the school, & will commence one week from tomorrow, so by the time that this reaches you, I shall be occupied in "teaching the young idea's how to shoot."[78] I was inspected yesterday at Mr Ferris's house by him, Dr Meissler & Wallace; had no difficulty in answering all the questions, & have my certificate for two years: I am to teach 4 months at 5 dollars a week. Our folks will board me for what I can help mornings & nights, & the children for a dollar apiece per week.—So I can lay by 12,00 a month, if I can stand it to do the work.

I have had good health this spring, so have the children. Vesper grows tall as he grows older & Dallie stout & chubby just as you used to be. Monday. It has rained nearly all day to day & being monday Celia & I have improved it in washing and house cleaning, & baked bread, pies & cake, besides.—

This place has grown considerable since you went away. There is now quite a little settlement here. Mr Bentley is going to build this summer & his brother in law Mr Lance[79] has built a new house east of the hotel. Mr Dunton[80] has a store. Mr Wood[81] is building next lot north of Pa, Mr Mosher has nearly finished his—& all are busy fencing their yards & setting out trees & shrubbery; & begins to look quite thriving. Wallace has bought a lot, got it cleared & enclosed, but does not expect to build this summer. Fancher has bought 2 more which makes him out 5 lots, all enclosed in one so he has a nice garden spot, & place for vegetables. Well it is nearly 10 o clock & all are wrapt in sweet slumber but me, & I must hasten to a close. How I would like to see you this evening— my mind is with you always & in silent earnest prayer, my thoughts are lifted to God—asking His care & guidance for you, & us, and my heart

78. A line from "Spring" by Scottish poet James Thomson (1700–1748; *The Seasons*, 1862, 33), which gained wide American popularity from 1800 to 1830 and again in the 1850s. Stevenson, "Transatlantic Travels," 124.

79. Perhaps George Lance; served on the schoolhouse building committee in 1864. Fancher, *Past and Present*, 146.

80. Henry Dunton; he was selling goods from his house before assisting John Kinney in establishing the first store. *Portrait and Biographical Album*, 339.

81. Unknown.

rejoices in the knowledge that you have given your heart to him, & will cling to the truths of the gospel. O how sweet it will be, when surrounded by dangers, & encompassed by foes on every hand, you can look to Jesus & feel that he is your *friend*, your guide & support; & he will never leave, or forsake us as long as we lean on him. Let us ever trust him.

Good Night—
Affectionately,
Ellen—

Samuel to Ellen

Shell Mound, Tenn. April 30th 1864. [Saturday]

Another rainy day finds me writing to you dear Ellen. My health is good; I feel quite natural once more. I received your & Wallace's letters yesterday of the 21st & was glad to hear that you were all well. I have not told you that the Small-pox had been in our Camp, for I knew you would worry for fear I would get it: it broke out here the first of March. We were all vaccinated, though it did not work on me. I have been with four different ones & cared for them while they were sick with it. (When I had the chicken-pox so very hard in [New] York State—Dr Peck told me then, I would never have the small-pox.) There has been 12 cases—3 have died: it is not so fatal here as measles. 6 have died of measles—I am quite well now & am very thankful for it.[82]

The boys tell me they did not think last winter I would live till this time: but I thank God for sparing my life & restoring me once more to health. We are getting a taste of hot weather here now—had a thunder shower last night—it makes me sweat to draw the cross cut-saw. I buy most of what I eat, instead of drawing rations—as the latter is sure to make me sick again. I have some money yet, & shall draw pay the middle of next month. I have loaned some 12,00 to boys that were sick; I could not see them suffer for little luxuries while I had a penny in my pocket. There are more than one that says "Sam is a good fellow." The

---

82. Smallpox was a highly contagious viral infection that could result in extensive scarring of skin, as well as death. See Terry Reimer, "Smallpox and Vaccination in the Civil War," National Museum of Civil War Medicine, November 9, 2004, https://www.civil warmed.org/surgeons-call/small_pox/.

soldier that wrote those verses was not shot; he was sent to the front, the other is sick in the Hospital. We have nearly finished this house; well it has stopped raining & I must go to work.

Sabbath, May 1st. at noon. O what a splendid day—and though it should be a day of rest—there is no rest for us to day: they are getting in a hurry & so we have to work. Would to God this war was over so that each one could be their own "boss." The road has been lined for the last 10 day with Soldiers going front. I thought I had seen Soldiers before but nothing like the throng that are crowding to the front.[83] It is pretty hard to be a christian, among what we have to contend with, & it seems now if I was at home I could live a christian life, yet I was with you a long time & did often very wrong, for which I am truly sorry for—& if I could write as easily as you I could express much that is in my mind. They are calling us to fall in for work, & I must close.

My love to all & accept a large share for yourself & my Precious children. Ever Yours. Samuel

---

83. The Atlanta Campaign of William T. Sherman. See Castel, *Decision in the West.*

The intact cover of Ellen
Preston Woodworth's journal.
Clarke Historical Library,
Mt. Pleasant, Mich.

Ellen and Samuel Woodworth, post–Civil
War. Clarke Historical Library.

The "drawing of the 'City'" of Mount Pleasant from the *Journal*,
as of Oct. 9, 1864. Clarke Historical Library.

VOLUNTEER ENLISTMENT.

STATE OF   TOWN OF *Coe*

MICHIGAN,   COUNTY OF *Isabella*

I, *Samuel Woodworth* born in *Java Wyoming Co* in the State of *New York* aged *Thirty one* years, and by occupation a *Carpenter* Do HEREBY ACKNOWLEDGE to have volunteered this *twenty second* day of *September* 1863 to serve as a **Soldier** in the 𝕬rmy of the 𝕌nited 𝕾tates of 𝕬merica, for the period of *THREE YEARS*, unless sooner discharged by proper authority: Do also agree to accept such bounty, pay, rations, and clothing, as are, or may be, established by law for volunteers. And I, *Samuel Woodworth* do solemnly swear, that I will bear true faith and allegiance to the **United States of America**, and that I will serve them honestly and faithfully against all their enemies or opposers whomsoever; and that I will observe and obey the orders of the President of the United States, and the orders of the officers appointed over me, according to the Rules and Articles of War.

Sworn and subscribed to, at *Coe*
this *23d* day of *September* 1863   *Samuel Woodworth*
BEFORE *P W Lester*
Notary Public

I CERTIFY, ON HONOR, That I have carefully examined the above named volunteer, agreeably to the General Regulations of the Army, and that in my opinion he is free from all bodily defects and mental infirmity, which would, in any way, disqualify him from performing the duties of a soldier.

J Samdu

EXAMINING SURGEON.

I CERTIFY, ON HONOR, That I have minutely inspected the Volunteer, *Samuel Woodworth* previously to his enlistment, and that he was entirely sober when enlisted; that, to the best of my judgment and belief, he is of lawful age; and that, in accepting him as duly qualified to perform the duties of an able-bodied soldier, I have strictly observed the Regulations which govern the recruiting service. This soldier has *blue* eyes *light* hair *light* complexion, is *five* feet *7* inches high.

1st Engineers & Mechanics
Regiment of *Michigan* Volunteers (Infantry.)
Sergt D Mc Nelson RECRUITING OFFICER.

Samuel Woodworth's certificate of enlistment, Sept. 23, 1863.
National Archives & Record Administration, Washington, D.C.

It is hereby certified that Ellen S. Woodworth has passed a satisfactory examination before us in the following branches viz: Orthography, Grammar, Reading, Geography, Writing & Arithmetic and is able to give instruction in the same. Has Moreover been found of good Moral character of good competent ability to teach a School &c. We have therefore licensed Her to teach in the Schools of this Township of Union in the County of Isabella for the Term of two years from date hereof.

Given under our hands this 23d day of Apr A 1864

W. W. Beston
A. G. Ferris
E. G. H. Missocus

School Inspectors
the Township of Union
County of Isabella, M.

Ellen Woodworth's teaching certificate, Apr. 23, 1864.
Clarke Historical Library.

Union army storage and transfer depot complex at Bridgeport, Ala.,
from Miller, *The Photographic History of the Civil War*, Volume Two.

Union army blockhouse on the Nashville & Chattanooga Railroad, 1864. Civil War photographs, 1861–1865, Library of Congress, Prints and Photographs Division. https://www.loc.gov/resource/cwpb.02147/

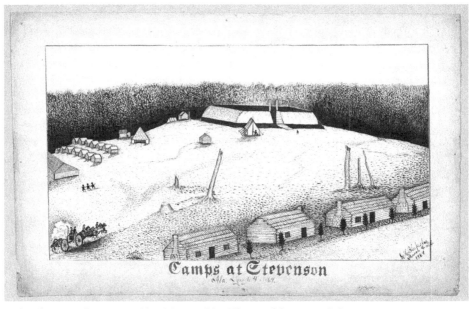

Union Camps at Stevenson, Ala., Mar. 4, 1864. Library of Congress, Prints and Photographs Division. https://www.loc.gov/resource/ppmsca.23042/

Nashville Hospital No. 15, where Samuel was a patient in January 1865. Courtesy of the Tennessee State Library & Archives.

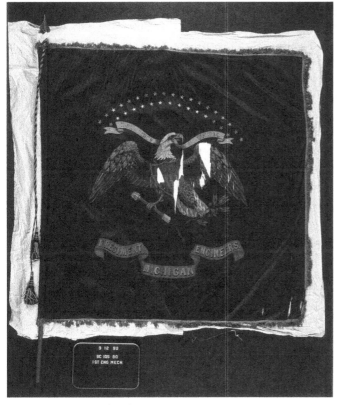

Regimental flag of the 1st Michigan Engineers & Mechanics. Courtesy of Michigan Save the Flags collection.

CHAPTER 3

May–August 1864

Ellen to Samuel

Mt. Pleasant Mich. May 3d 1864—[Tuesday]

Dear Husband; I will improve a leisure half hour, in writing to let you know that we are well, & hope you are the same. To day is the first day of school; it is now noon time, & while the scholars are eating their dinners, I must tell you how I have got along: well, for one half day, I have done nicely & think with a little practice I shall succeed admirably: Vesper is about as far advanced in learning as any of the boys in school, & behaves well; little Dallie has done firstrate though he forgets himself sometimes & speaks aloud. I wish you could hear him read; he speaks up very promptly & learns easily, especially for a five year old. The school house is perhaps a third of a mile from our folk's; just a pleasant walk for me to take nights & mornings, & if you only keep well, I believe I shall enjoy this summer pretty well. Mothers health is poor so I will have enough to do before & after school to keep me busy—Celia began her school this week, but Emma does not commence until the middle of the month. Pa is down on his farm now & Wallace is helping him & Arsene will stay with us nights or some of us with her while he is away. Fanchers folks are well, & are fixing up their place nicely. They keep an Indian girl to do their work, & she is very faithful. It is one o clock & I must ring the bell. (Recess.) I have heard all the classes read & will write a little more to you. It is quite cool to day, & a good fire is necessary to keep warm. We have a nice box stove & plenty of good wood, so we are all comfortable. It is quite healthy around here—no sickness that I know of—One of the Indian Mission School[1] teachers came over & staid one night with me last week.—She

---

1. The mission house was a multipurpose building used for religious and education activities, conducted in English and interpreted in Native language. Fancher, *Past and Present*, 98–99, 143.

has $400,00 a year & boards herself—a Miss Hines of Lansing, a lovely girl.[2] She boards at Elder Bradley[']s[3]—They are very nice people. I have become quite well acquainted with Mrs Bradley. I did not receive any letter last week—it seems an age to wait so long—to morrow is mail day & I *do hope* to hear from you again. From the latest news we hear that our army has met with defeat in two battles, one of Fort Pillow[4] & at some place in Arkansas.[5] It is so discouraging to hear that the Rebels are getting any advantage. I hope it may be the last victory they may ever know. Evening 8 o clock, I will try & finish my letter so as to send it out in the morning. Willie is up to see Vesper & they have been down to the river fishing—caught two since school—Now they are preparing for bed. Little Dallie has been asleep this long time, he gets tired through the day—playing so hard.—Arsene sits by me now—she says "O dear, how I do want to see Sam." Yes indeed I guess we would all like to see him if we could, but we know we cannot, so with hope— we look forward to the time when peace shall once more smile upon us, & we can welcome *home* those dear ones that are in memory so tenderly enshrined in our hearts; and for whom our daily prayers ascend to Him who watcheth over every creature & letteth not a sparrow fall to the ground without his notice, O what loving care for us. Can we help but thank him for it? To morrow is mail day—I can hardly wait till the mail comes in—so anxious to hear from you. Remember & direct to Isabella City now—as I will get them much quicker. Our folks all send love & best wishes—& now I must bid you good night. May Heavens rich blessings rest upon you, & kind Angels keep you from harm. Accept the love of your dear children & ever faithful

Ellen—

---

2. Maria Hines, from Lansing, taught at the mission school in this period. Fancher, *Past and Present*, 104.

3. Rev. George Bradley was a missionary to the local Indigenous population. Fancher, *Past and Present*, 99, 143.

4. On April 12, 1864, Confederate forces under command of Major General Nathan Bedford Forrest attacked and forced the surrender of the Union garrison at Fort Pillow on the Mississippi River north of Memphis, Tennessee. The battle became notorious for the massacre of African American soldiers during the surrender. Fuchs, *Unerring Fire*.

5. She likely means the Battle of Mansfield, Louisiana, on April 8, when Confederates under General Richard Taylor routed Union forces under General Nathaniel P. Banks. See Johnson, *Red River Campaign*.

Ellen to Samuel

May 8th 1864 (In school.) [Sunday]

Dear Samuel. I received a letter last friday, dated April 17th & was glad to hear from you again, in health. I had begun to be alarmed at your long silence (for it had been over two weeks,) but I suppose you are on the move & can not post your letters.

We are well & getting along nicely in School; only 15 scholars yet, but expect more when the roads are better.

Last Sabbath Elder Sheldon preached here in my school house, the first meeting we have had since I have been here. Wallace & wife—Emma, the children & I walked up & Pa got a horse & buggy & brought ma up—she is feeling better. We had quite a house full—they came from Chippewa & from the surrounding country. It seems good to live where the Sabbath is observed as a day of rest & worship—instead of hearing & seeing it continually profaned in visiting & playing—pounding & chopping—driving cattle &c. as it was down in our neighborhood. I do believe that is the most uncivilized, & unprincipled neighborhood there is in the woods—dont you? But I will forbear speaking farther. Vesper is learning nicely—Dallie reads in words of two letters. He is a stout little chub—wears a hat the same size Vesper does. I bought him a straw hat Saturday & had to pay *nine* shillings. Nothing very nice—but everything is getting dear—Flour is now 14 dollars a barrel, potatoes 1,50 per bushel (& small at that), pork 20 cts per pound—sugar 16 & 18 cts—butter 40 & every thing else accordingly. It is cheaper for me to do as I do than to keep house—but I have to *work*—This morning I got up between 4 & 5 o clock & went to washing—got two boilers full washed & ready to rinse, by 8 o clock—Emma got breakfast—then I got myself & the children ready for school, & swept out the school house before 9. We carry our dinner, & at night I get supper, do up the work, & find enough to keep me busy until bed time. Tuesday morning—I will try and finish my letter today so as to send out in the morning. It is quite chilly today—very different from yesterday. Last night after school Pa harnessed up Fanchers horse & Emma & I took the children & went down to the Village—(Indian Mills.) I bought Vesper some books (—geography & reader,) paid 1'20. O Samuel I wish you would come in to the School House & eat dinner with me. I have got some berry pie, cheese, biscuit, butter, & crackers. Vesper & Dallie have eaten theirs

& are out to play. How I would like to *see* you—O it does my heart so much good to know that you are living the life of a christian. May God in his Infinite mercy bestow his choicest blessings upon you & fill your soul with his sweet grace is the prayer of your ever affectionate

Ellen—

P.S.

Later—one word more & I will close. Albert says our wheat looks fine, he takes good care of things. To day Wallace is planting potatoes right across from the school house—for Mr Bently. On this street Mr Moshers house stands first, then Carters, (where Wallace lives)— next the little Sherman[6] house, then Wallaces lots. he will not build this summer—he paid 25 dollars a lot. Be a good boy.—Do not let the influence of wicked companions lead you astray. Shun the card table, as you would a *viper*—& ever let your life be devoted to God, your country, & your own little family. Good bye; write soon, & often.

Samuel to Ellen

May 15th 1864. [Sunday]

Shell Mound, Tenn.

My Dear Ellen—you must forgive me for not writing last week—this is the first time I have omitted writing you every week—but we are very busy. I have worked every day, & stood guard my turn, nights. Last Sunday we were mustered for pay & I had no time to write. To day we shall rest, if the Bushwhackers[7] will let us alone. I am all the one able to work that came from Isabella Co—all the rest in camp or in the invalid Corps.[8] I recd your letter, mailed the 5th saying you thought you would like teaching. I am afraid it will be to hard for you to teach, & work too. I would rather you would not do it—you cant stand so much a great while & it will be rather hard for my little Dall to stay at

---

6. Likely Henry Sherman, one of the first two Euro-American families in the county in 1854, at whose rural house the first Fourth of July celebration was held (*Portrait and Biographical Album*, 538), who sat on the first jury case in January 1862, and who erected the first schoolhouse in Mount Pleasant in 1864 (Fancher, *Past and Present*, 134, 146).

7. I.e., Confederate guerilla forces.

8. The "Invalid Corps" (1863; renamed "Veteran Reserve Corps" in 1864) was a Union military unit composed of soldiers who could only perform noncombat duty most often due to a war wound. Boatner, *Civil War Dictionary*, 870.

School all day, do be careful of yourselves. Dont think of improving the place—we will keep all the money we get till after this war is over—it will be worth something then. I received 4 months pay—68 dollars—I dont know how to send it but will risk some in this letter. Am not where I can express money. We have built one block house here, & are at work on another, two miles down the river.—We have cheering news from every quarter. I think this summer will close the war—It is not safe for me to keep money by me, for if I am taken prisoner, or caught, they will rob me of every cent;—but they wont get hold of me very easy—we go armed all the time, & sleep on our guns. 8 of our men have been caught & all killed but one, since we came here. They shot him & threw him off a ledge of rocks 30 feet,—but he crawled to camp. I saw him—his under jaw was broken & hung down on this breast, he belonged to the 28th N.Y.

I have one $50,00 bill I think I will risk in this letter.

Dont over-do—I know what there is to do at your fathers, & who will do it. I am glad to know that my children are good boys, I hope to see you all once more—but if not, we will meet again, if not here—in a far better world, I trust. Good bye—Love to all—hoping soon to hear from you again—

Ever, your true Husband.

Samuel to Ellen

Shell Mound, Tenn. May 15th 1864. [Sunday]

Dear Ellen. I will write this letter also to day to tell you that I have mailed one with $50,00 in to day & hope you will receive it soon. I am well at present, & hope you are, but I fear you have undertaken too much—to teach all day & go home & work until bed time: Dont try to do anything on the place—I think I will be home soon & then we can see to improving it ourselves—One dollar will be worth more after this war is over than two are now. I wrote all the news in my other letter so will say good bye. From your absent Husband—Samuel Woodworth

To Ellen, & the children.

Ellen to Samuel

Mt. Pleasant, Mich. May 17th 1864. [Tuesday]

Dear Husband—Again I sit down, to address a few lines to you, hoping they may find you well—I am very sorry to hear that there is so much sickness in your regiment, & such *dangerous* diseases, too, but I am glad that you can not have the small-pox: O how much there is to worry over—but do take care of your own health, if possible. What if you should get down again? No, no, it *must* not be, I hear that D. Nelson has returned home. I have not seen him & dont know that I care too. I have been down to Chippewa to night since school—(walked there, & back)—to get some things for mother. It is now after 9 o clock & all are asleep, but me. My health is very good—& the children are well, except Vesper has a swelling on the back of his neck. I let him stay home from school & to night he is resting well—Little Dallie is a hardy little fellow, & as solidly built, as you ever were. They are both *nice* boys *I* think. My school progresses nicely. I dont teach but five days a week, which is a dollar every day for teaching. It seems I am specially favored by Providence, every one is so kind to me, & so willing to help me along—I hope I may always find as many friends & be ever worthy of them. Pa is down on his farm again this week—Celia & Emma are both away now so our family is quite small. Mother has a hired girl this week to clean house, & put down carpets. Our folks keep a cow so the children have all the milk they want, & they are very fond of it. I am glad you can get milk occasionally. We hear that our Armies are winning great victories, but it must be at a fearful cost of precious lives[9]— Are *you* in great danger?

O my Father—care for the absent one, & protect him from all harm—O my husband, put your whole trust in Him, who alone, is able to save. We can do nothing ourselves. It is Jesus that can make us

9. Grant's Overland Campaign in Virginia had commenced with the Battle of the Wilderness on May 5, with fighting through May 21 in the Battle of Spotsylvania Courthouse, producing heavy casualties approaching thirty-five thousand killed, wounded, captured, or missing. Sherman's Atlanta Campaign had prompted skirmishes between May 1 and 13 before the Battle of Resaca on May 14–15 resulted in about four thousand Union losses, "of whom 600" were killed or mortally wounded. Trudeau, *Bloody Roads South*; *OR*, vol. 38, part I, 52; Castel, *Decision in the West*, 188.

happy—kneel at his feet & be willing to bear his cross—& he *will* guide you aright & keep you safe from harm—"God be with you till we meet again."

Yours faithfully—

E. L. W.

Samuel to Ellen

Shell Mound, Tenn—May 19th [Thursday]

It is raining to day, so I will write a few lines more to say I am well & in good spirits—on account of the good news from the front. O we will whip them out this Summer. I wrote last Sunday & sent you $50,00. I hope you will get it & let me know soon. I should like to visit your school some day—I am alone—that is, away from the Isabella boys. They are all in Camp sick—The cars are passing loaded with troops—a good many prisoners being brought through for a few days past. I want you to care for yourself especially—for if you get sick, what will be come of our little boys? You should not try to teach & do your own work, & your folks' besides. I wrote all the news in my other letters so will close by sending some verses I copied from an old Newspaper—

> Alas! Oh alas for the loved & dear
> Of those who sleep on a southern bier
> In vain for them are the lamps lit bright
> And the slippers & chair by the fire at night.
> In vain do their stricken spirits mourn
> For the brave & gallant, who never return.
> Father of Nations, O hasten we pray
> The rosy dawn of that glorious day
> When our beautiful Country united shall stand,
> The pride & delight of each nation & land,
> When strife between brothers, & country shall cease
> And the Soldier return to his fireside, in peace.

(Without a furlough.)

From your dutiful Husband, Samuel

Samuel to Ellen

Shell Mound, Tenn. May 22ond 1864. [Sunday]

Dearest Ellen, I have your letter of the 10th before me and have read it the third time. You never can know how precious they are to me. It has been eight long months since I enlisted; a longer time than I thought I would have to stay; but I did not know *then*, what I know *now*. Yet I *hope* to be home this fall. I have wrote three letters to you the past week, & have no news to write, but will tell you what chance I have to enjoy myself.

The weather is very warm, & the flies so thick I cant stay in the tent, only nights. There are eleven of us in one small tent—& you can imagine how comfortable it is for me, when I say they are the hardest set that I ever saw. They gamble all the spare time they have, & their language is to profane to repeat. This beautiful Sabbath day is not regarded at all by them & the wicked talk that I now hear would make your heart sick:—how little you know of war! There are boys here who were paid off two weeks ago, $50,00 or more that have lost every cent in gambling & have not to day a penny.—You told me to shun the card table—I can do that very easily—the hardest thing I have to contend against & guard is my *tongue*. They say I am a very still fellow: how little they know of my feelings. I am determined to be true to myself, my wife, my Country, & my God. It is a fixed purpose, & principle with me & will not easily be shaken. I intend to do *right*, thought I may not be called a *christian*. O, the horrors, of this war! The wounded Soldiers that I see brought in from the front; it makes ones heart bleed, with pity. It is awful! I do pray God it may soon end. I would rather stay here as hard as it is—the remainder of my life than to have either of my boys join the Army. Another phase of war is the destitution of the citizens, many of them coming to our Camp in a half starving condition & begging a little hard bread & bacon, or bacon fat—to keep them alive. The poor women & children suffer the most—but I will not attempt to describe it; but will pass to some other annoyances that the poor soldier has to contend with; mixed in with a disreputable set, our blankets become infested with vermin, & when I was sick I thought they (the gray backs) would carry me out of the tent; but I had my clothing boiled in lye to kill the nits, & now I am well I can at least keep myself comparatively free from them:[10] you would hardly know me now; my sickness caused most of my hair to fall out, & now I am nearly bald-headed. One more light affliction I will mention; I have some splen-did boils, or carbuncles;[11] have had from one, to three at a time, since about the middle of March,—have one now on my left ankle that is very painful; so that I can not wear my boot. I am as spotted as an ad-der, from the scars they leave, yet I feel well & am getting fleshy. I have thought I would keep it all from you—but now I am better, I had to tell you. I have wrote most of this, sitting on the bank of the river: This is a beautiful spot & I am at least free from the confusion in the tent. I have washed my clothes this morning (have to do it, or go dirty,) have bought me two cotton shirts, gave one dollar apiece. I hope to hear soon that you have received the money—shall worry about it until I hear. I have a mind not to send this—I did not intend to say a word to you about it, but have, & perhaps its all right.

Good bye, from

Your Ever loving Husband.—

Ellen to Samuel

Mt. Pleasant, Mich. May 25th 1864. [Wednesday]

Dear Samuel. I shall continue to write every week, if I *do not* hear from you; as I know you will be disappointed if you do not hear from us. Last week I received no letter, but news came through the papers that Soldiers were forbidden to write north for the space of *sixty days*.[12] I do not believe any Union Commander would issue so cruel a com-mand, just at this crisis, when such terrible battles are being fought, & the families of soldiers so doubly anxious to hear from their loved ones, on the battle field. Yet if such a decree is necessary—we must submit though the suspense be ever so hard to bear. Our health is good—(my-self & children) & Mother is better. I get along finely with my school—

---

10. "Gray backs" and "nits" refer to lice, an insect that spreads easily via human contact and feeds on human blood.

11. Carbuncles refer to a skin infection producing bumps. Welsh, *Medical Histories*, 400.

12. Ellen's anguish underscores the importance to her of their ability to enjoy regular correspondence. Mail delivery to the Army of the Potomac had been halted temporarily, an order that did not extend to Samuel's unit. Sodergren, *Army of the Potomac*, 50.

have no trouble, & like teaching as well as any employment I can engage in—have 17 scholars, the oldest boy 11 years old. Our darlings do nicely—little Dall rather inclined to be roguish in making faces to the girls, when he thinks my back is toward him; (same as his Pa used to be, I imagine, from what I have heard). It is now recess & the scholars are all out to play—D. H. Nelson has been to see me—came last Friday evening. He is looking better than I expected to see him—that is, *healthier*. He was very polite indeed, *very*; & extolled *you*, greatly: said he would rather have brought you home with him than any man in the regiment, although you exerted the greatest influence for *good* on your comrades, & was much needed there. I asked him why he resigned, & he said he received a *hurt* that rendered him unfit for military duty. We are having some pretty warm weather now & the musquetoes are very troublesome. Our folks think they can hardly stand such an annoyance, but they must get used to it if they live in the woods. I have got most through with one month of school—most $20,00 earned. I am making the dress that Pa bought for me when he was in St Johns—I talk of going to quarterly meeting next Saturday & I want to finish it to wear. The meeting is to be at the Pine River school house, between Salt River & Alma. I wish you were here to go with me for now that you too are walking in the "Light" we shall enjoy such meetings together. I am so *glad*, I can hardly express my thankfulness. O how sweet the thought that we shall meet—if not on earth—in that bright home above, where we shall part no more, *forever*. Blessed words; so full of hope & promise & they are for you, & me, & *all* that put their trust in God. O, let us ever trust him, ever seek to do his will, & walk worthy of his loving care. It is school time & I must close; remember me to the "boys in blue" from our way, & take good care of yourself—with love & best wishes from your absent friends.—

Afternoon recess—It is raining nicely now—we need it very much. Our folks are painting the house inside—some of the rooms are cream color, some nearly a slate color—& all are fresh & nice looking. I like living there & now that the girls are away—the work is not very hard. Wallaces folks well—he is doing off Mortons house,[13] Good bye—hoping to hear from you soon—Yours as ever—

Ellen

---

13. In 1863, the developer of Mount Pleasant, David Ward, "sold his land to Harvey and George Morton," who replatted it and built the first hotel in the town. *Isabella County, Michigan*, 7, 16.

Ellen to Samuel

Mt. Pleasant, Mich. May 30th 1864.

My Dear Husband—This pleasant monday morning finds me employing a few leisure moments in writing to you; but O how *much*
rather I would see you & talk with you. Last week I received two letters from you: one containing a *$50,00 green-back.* Thank you indeed—I
shall be very careful of it—you may be sure. I am glad to hear of your
continued health—but O dear, dont fall into the hands of those horrid
bushwhackers—what if it had been you that they had caught & treated
as they did that poor fellow that crawled back to Camp: Poor boy; &
yet somebody will perhaps mourn for him as sadly. We are hearing of
terrible battles in every weeks mail—& though our forces claim several
victories, it is at a fearful cost: "O when will Peace wreathe her chain
round us forever"[14]?

This week Wallace is making a change—he has rented Mr Morton's
property & will open a *Hotel.* I have let him take $40,00 of your money,
& took his note for it. I kept 10,00 to buy the children some clothes
with, as I do not expect to draw any money until school is half out. I
get along well—both in school & here at home with the old people on
one hand & the children to keep within bounds—on the other. They
bother Grandpa some-times in getting his things & not putting them
back where he keeps them; but they are not very mischievous. Our folks
are all well—The girls were both home Saturday. We did not go to quarterly meeting as we talked of—But Althea & I went over to Mr Bradleys
visiting, Saturday & sunday. I took Fanchers horse & buggy & carried
Celia part way to her school—as far as our place—& I stopped & looked
at our things, to see if they were safe—found every thing all right. The
wheat looks splendid, almost covers the stumps—& the grass is growing finely: but it seemed very lonely there—every thing reminded me of
you—your work on every hand.—I could not stay there long. Albert has
the Spring crops in on our place—potatoes, corn & sowed five bushel
of oats. (Tuesday noon) I will finish my letter while the scholars are
at play—Vesper did not come to day—he has a boil on his neck & last
night Fancher opened it, & it discharged freely—His neck was so lame
I let him stay at home. Little Dallie is here as keen as a brier; he dont

---

14. From the hymn, "When Shall We Meet Again?" See Boyden, *Eastern Harp*, 187.

get very tired in School, for I let the smallest children play out a good share of the time. Vesper has just come & feels better. I must close—will send you some more stamps soon & envelopes. Hoping to hear again this week from you: Accept love from the children

& your ever faithful,
Ellen

Samuel to Ellen

Shell Mound, Tenn. June, 3d 1864. [Friday]

Dear Wife; I will scribble a few lines to day while it is raining. We have just finished our third block-house here & shall leave to-morrow for Stevenson, Ala.[15] It will be a relief to me to get to our Company again. I hav'nt seen any one that I ever knew, in a long time, & I was never in the company of such a hard set of men before.

I received a letter from you yesterday, & glad to hear you are all, well; but I am still anxious about the money I sent you. I hope you will re-ceive it all right; I am well at present, with the exception of two large boils for comfort, one on the back of my neck, one on my leg, above my knee, but it wont do to mind trifles here. But the poor wounded Sol-diers that are carried through here—would cause your heart to bleed—three car loads went through yesterday, & more, or less, every day;—cut to pieces in all shapes—some with an arm gone—or leg—& mangled & torn with wounds & bruises—but why dwell on so painful a subject—O it looks cruel, & I hope it will be over soon. Be careful about letting Ves-per go near the river; keep him away if possible. There were 4 young fellows drowned here lately—went into the river to bathe; & could not swim.—Tell him, "Papa wants him to keep away from the water." But I must close now & go to work. Will try & write more next time. Love to all.

From Sam, to Ellen.

---

15. On the rail line west of Bridgeport.

Ellen to Samuel

Mt Pleasant—June 7th 1864. [Tuesday]

Dear Samuel. Another week has rolled around, & finds me as usual employing my "noon-day, hour" in writing to my Absent Husband. We are all enjoying excellent health, now, since Vesper has got well of his boils; he feels much better. He & Dallie are out to play, with the rest of the scholars; & I have nothing to disturb me here in the quiet old school-house, except an occasional musqueto finds his way into the room & makes an effort to divert my attention from my writing. It is quite cool to day, & last night we had a hard frost, so that to day, the vines & potato tops look as though they had been boiled. Mother mourns some about getting into this frosty region, but Pa takes it cool; He is now engaged in digging a well—has got down 15 feet & struck water: have to curb it all the way.[16] Ma is feeling quite well, for her now, & we get along nicely with the work; so dont worry for fear I will do too much.

Last night, after school Althea took her horse & buggy & carried me down to the Indian Mills; I traded a little & got Vesper a hat, & Dallie some cloth for pants: but if I can send out of the woods for my *necessaries*, I shall not buy much, here. Cheap print is now three shillings a yard—& cloth for children, 1,00 & 1,25 per yard. Provisions are on the rise—Flour 8 cts a pound, Pork 20, Tea $2,00 per pound, dried apples 25 cts—& Butter *way up*—yet our folks dont seem to mind it, & have their tea 3 times a day just as strong as though it only cost 50 cts instead of four times fifty.

Wallace does not have a great deal of custom yet but I think this fall, & winter—he will do well. I have just eaten a hand full of strawberries, the first of the season. The scholars found them in their rambles & brought them to the *"School Marm."* To day there are 18 scholars, but have had 24 some of the time: this is the sixth week of school, & I am glad to say that time passes more swiftly & pleasantly this summer to me than I ever expected it would. I feel at peace with all mankind & with my Creator; and I can trust all in his hands, feeling that he will or-

---

16. Curbing typically meant installing a structure around the mouth of a well, but it appears here to also mean installing a lining of a well to secure continuing access and preventing collapse.

der every thing for good to those that truly trust him. O blessed Name! How sweetly & soothingly it falls upon the ear, & lulls to rest the weary heart, & live worthy of his kind care & guidance, & his holy love.

I am so glad to hear that you are well—& happy. I often visit you in my dreams, & it seems you are always looking well, & in good spirits. O, how much we want to see you; and we look forward with bright anticipation to the time when you will again be with us. The children send love to "dear Papa." Little Dallie is very devotional, & every night his little prayers ascend for the safety of his papa & Gods dear blessing on us all. Who shall say that his baby-petitions are not heard, & answered? O may their lives be pure, & good, as they are now innocent—& as their years multiply, they may grow in knowledge & favor with Him; who entrusted them to our care, & will demand of us a faithful discharge of duty. Heaven bless our precious Lambs—& shelter them safely in His fold—

Tuesday Evening—I will finish my letter, to have it ready for the [post] office in the morning. I received yours, last mail & sent you some stamps, will send six more this time. I told you last week that the money came safely, & also what I done with it. I received a note from Albert yesterday saying the neighbors cattle were destroying our wheat. He said the fence was good, but the wheat was so tall that they reached it over the fence & got to crowding so that they pushed off the rails. I will see that the fence is made secure, & then if people dont take care of their cattle I will try & collect damage. Cha[u]nc[e]y Kyes has just married Amanda Stilwell. 6 weeks after he buried his wife (so much for *her* memory.)[17] Well I must close. Be a good boy, & ever remember,

Ellen

Samuel to Ellen

Stevenson. Ala—June 11th 1864. [Saturday]

Dear Ellen, I was very glad to get two letters yesterday, both from you—telling me you were well, & that you had received the $50,00 I sent. I am well, but there is much sickness in Camp. The small-pox

---

17. Amanda Caswell is previously mentioned; no such marriage is mentioned in Kyes's biographical sketch. *Portrait and Biographical Album*, 362–363.

stays with us yet—one or two come down with it every day—Our boys all yet in Hospital. The weather is wet, & warm; just the kind to produce sickness. The order has come to hold ourselves in readiness, to fall in to line at a moments warning, so I must stop writing.

Sunday morning—All quiet here yet. Forrest[18] did not make his appearance. To day is cool & nice, yet you would not think it was the Christian Sabbath, here in Camp. I am glad you can enjoy yourself so well; we have much to be thankful for; & if I am spared to return to my little family, & home, I think I shall appreciate it. Accept a short letter this time,

Good bye—Faithfully yours—Samuel

Ellen to Samuel

Mt. Pleasant. June 14th 1864. [Tuesday]

My Dear Samuel. I will try & write something to interest you again, but I write so often, there is little variety in my letters; yet I know you will be glad to hear that we are well, & enjoying ourselves as well as possible—under the circumstances. I get along well with my school— have not had to punish any yet—except I *slapped* one little boy, one day, for disobedience. This is the 7th week of school, have 24 scholars. Vesper & Dallie do nicely & are learning fast. I am sorry to hear of your afflictions & would bear some of them for you, if I could—though I might not have Job's patience. It seems very hard indeed that our poor sick soldiers should be troubled with *vermin*; that is far worse than the boils—& those are bad enough; & must be tedious to work with; but perhaps they will be beneficial to your health by cleansing your blood, & preventing any malignant disease. I do hope & pray that this present season may terminate this cruel warfare. I hear that John Stuart[19] is dead: fell mortally wounded, and his time of enlistment had nearly expired. How I pity his poor wife. She was counting the days—expecting, & waiting for his return. How many bitter tears she has shed: O

---

18. Confederate general Nathan Bedford Forrest, as discussed previously.

19. John N. Stuart (or Stewart) enlisted in Company C, 8th Michigan Infantry, August 16, 1861, at Alma, age twenty-seven; died June 1, 1864, at Washington, D.C., of wounds received in action at the Wilderness, May 12, 1864. *Record of Service*, vol. 8, 127. His wife's name is unknown to the author.

my God: may I never know such sorrow. O spare thy children, if possible—this bitter cup of anguish & permit us to be, once more a united & happy people—a prosperous & *purified Nation.* For this we will pray—Dear Samuel for this we will hope; that God in his own good time will restore our country—purged from the sin into which it has fallen.

Evening—9 o clock. I am sitting here alone—Our folks & the children are abed & asleep. I have a nice bedroom up stairs, with my bed, & a *trundle* bed; Vesper sleeps in the latter, but Dallie thinks he cant sleep away from his mama, so he sleeps with me. Since school, I have attended a tea-party to Mr Fanchers—Mr & Mrs Kinney[20]—Mrs Lance[21]—Pa & Ma & myself & children—Had a very nice supper. Already people are beginning to get quite fashionable—even in these wilds of Michigan, we get a glimpse occasionally of Aristocracy. Wallaces folks are doing well—have some travel, & keep boarders all the time. Last Saturday & Sunday was the Indian quarterly meeting, at Neibising:[22] the weather was beautiful so Sunday Celia, & Emma, Fancher & Althea & I all went up to meeting on horseback—Celia rode a colt of Mr Keyes[23] that had never been broken—Emma rode one about like it of Mr Frazers[24]—Fancher rode his—Althea rode an Indian pony & I had Mr Saunders[25] horse—a rather viscious old beast—then there were two other ladies from Emmas district, making 7 of us. Coming home we had the addition of Mr Babbitt[26] & two other gentlemen so it made quite a cav-

---

20. John Kinney (1837–1919) and Margaret M. Atkins (1838–1920). John would later serve as president of the Exchange Savings Bank of Mount Pleasant. Find a Grave, https://www.findagrave.com/memorial/74713271/john-kinney; *Isabella County, Michigan*, 68.

21. Mary Ann (Parmalee) Lance (1833–1905), wife of George A. Lance (1827–1882). Find a Grave, https://www.findagrave.com/memorial/75838613/mary-ann-lance; *Portrait and Biographical Album*, 504; Find a Grave, https://www.findagrave.com/memorial/75838611/george-lance.

22. Neibising, or Nippising, was a community north of Mount Pleasant in Isabella Township. According to an early twentieth-century guide, the name derives from a band of Ojibwe who, in that author's judgment, "readily accepted the Christian teachings of the missionaries." Hodge, *Handbook of American Indians*, 73–74. A church was built at "Ne-bee-sing" on the reservation as it then existed (*Portrait and Biographical Album*, 540), and a school (Fancher, *Past and Present*, 103–104).

23. Likely Kyes.

24. Likely John Fraser. Fancher, *Past and Present*, 268.

25. John Saunders. Fancher, *Past and Present*, 145–146; *Ninth United States Decennial Census*, Union Township, Isabella County, Mich., 7.

26. Likely Francis C. Babbitt (1812–1876), "one of the noted persons of the early settlement of Isabella," who platted out home lots in Isabella City with A. W. Fitch in 1861.

alcade. We had no accidents, winding through the woods, on the Indian trail—except the horse I rode was rather frisky & kicked up twice, when they rode too close to her heels—but she did not throw me; I had rather hard work to hold her though, so I changed with Fancher, & rode his horse home. We all enjoyed the ride very much, as well as the meeting. The mission house is a large square building packed full of our dusky *brothers*, & *sisters*—all listening attentively to the sermon, which was preached in English & interpreted in Indian. After service there was 15 or 20 indian babies sprinkled & two squaws—Elder Bradley officiating. There were some very intelligent looking Indians in the crowd & some very sweet singers. Altogether, it was quite a novelty to us, & we wished you had been with us.

Dallie & Pettie stayed with our folks & Vesper went Saturday down to visit Willie & stayed till Sunday night. He went over to our place—while there—& looked it over—Said the crops looked nice & he could not discover any mischief done them, by cattle. This week we have had some hard frosts—& some apprehend winter wheat injured by it. I hope not. I shall look for a letter from you tomorrow. I will send you some envelopes, this week—I sent stamps last week—It is ten oclock & I must close & go to bed: How I wish I knew where you were, at this present moment. I presume out on some lonely watch—or perchance calmly sleeping & dreaming of loved ones, far away. May holy Angels guard thy slumbers & keep thee from all harm—Good night—Ever.

your Ellen.

OUR WOODLAND HOME.

There's a cottage in the woodside,
Deeply shaded by the trees,
Which to me made sweetest music,
As they froliced in the breeze
There I've rested in the twilight,
There I've toiled from morn till night;
Till each shrub & fragrant blossom,
Had grown precious in my sight.
      There the birds that carol'd sweetly,
And the bees that sipped the flowers,
Were like friends, that came to greet me
In this cottage-home of *ours*:

Fancher, *Past and Present*, 324; *Isabella County, Michigan*, 7; Find a Grave, https://www.finda grave.com/memorial/82389316/francis-c-babbitt.

Yes, I loved the very insects,
As they sported round the door,
And the light, that glimmered faintly
Through the vines, upon the floor.
          There the house-hold band, but numbered
Only *four*, when all was told;
O, how dear was every member
Dearer far, to me, than gold.
But our little band was broken,—
Not by death, but change that comes,
Taking from our household treasures,
The most dear, & *needed* one.
          Now the cottage in the wood-side,
Looks so desolate and lone:
E'en the breeze that stirs the tree tops,
For the absent seem to moan—
And the shrubs and flowers seem weeping
For the faithful, tender care
Of the hand that used to tend them,
And the eye that watched them, there.
          But that hand has sadly left them,
And those eyes are dimmed with tears;
But 'tis only for a season;
I will *trust* that coming years,
Will restore the band now broken
To the dear and cherished home
There to rest—a happy household,
Never more from it to roam.

From E. to Samuel

Samuel to Ellen

Stevenson, Ala. June 19th 1864. [Sunday]

My Dear Wife—I will again commence a few lines to you hoping they may find you well. My health still remains good, although there is much sickness in camp; 38 being all that are able to work, out of a company of 147. This morning is warm & cloudy. I was glad to get your letter friday, telling me of your health, & prosperity. Dont worry over the crops; or try to get any pay if they are destroyed. It will cost more than it will come to; & cause you trouble beside. I dont expect to realize much profit from the place unless I am there to live on it, & see to things myself—We have good news from the front: Our men are driving them steadly, but we are losing thousands of our best men. The 4th Mich Cavalry passed through to the front, when we were at Shell Mound. They were a splendid regiment—900 strong, & now where are they! All but 150 are killed, & some of those are wounded & are here in the hospital.[27] I have got back into my old tent again, with our own Isabella boys, and I feel more at home, than I have in a long time. They are not able to work except around the tent, cooking &c.

Ellen, you say you feel at peace with all mankind? I hope it always may be so with you; but I cant say that I do; there are some rebs about here that need watching, & I cant say that I feel entirely at peace with them. But they are playing out; their course will soon be run. I hope to get just such a letter from you every week, as long as I stay away. I feel as though I was in the hands of that great and good Being, who will guide all things for the best. I am willing to trust *all* to him.

I must close & go out on inspection; Good bye for this time.

Yours as Ever

Sam

Ellen to Samuel

Mt Pleasant. June 20th 1864.

My Dear Sam I will commence early, this bright monday morning & write a little, along, so as to get a full letter by mail day. I hope it may be of some interest to you, altho I have so little variety to write about; my letters all posess a *sameness*, that seems to prevade all I write. We are all usually well, & feel very grateful for the continued good health granted us. If I, or either of the children should get sick it would be impossible for me to go on with my school & I should dislike very much to give it up, but it is time to call school & I must *adjourn* my writing.

Noon. I have eaten my dinner, & went out & fixed a board across a log for Dallie & another little boy to "teeter" as they call it, so as to keep

---

27. The eight-hundred-strong regiment marched east through Shell Mound in early May on the way to suffering "heavily" near Kingston, Georgia, on May 27, total casualties equaling thirty-six and "four good officers are severely wounded." Robertson, *Michigan in the War*, 663.

him quiet while I write. I think of going down to our place to night, after School, if Fancher is not using his horse, so I can have it to ride. I
want to see to our goods as I am going to let Jack Koonts's family live
there until he can get him a home somewhere—He says he will watch
the crops & take good care of things, & wants to stay all summer.[28] I
am afraid the crops will suffer for want of rain—it is very dry here—
not a drop of rain has fallen in over two weeks. Some people predict
a famine, & think the perilous times spoken of in the Bible are being
fulfilled: "It says famine & pestilence, & *wars*. Nation shall rise against
Nation &c."[29] I am sure there is *war* enough, & pestilence; as the small-
pox seems spreading over the country. We are taking the precaution
to vaccinate. The weather is very warm here; if it is as much warmer
where you are, as you are farther South, I dont know how you exist.
How I pity the poor Soldier: toiling through long heavy marches—with
no place but the hard damp earth to rest their wearied bodies, & tired
heads,—& then such poor fare hardly enough sometimes, to keep them
from starving; & surrounded by dangers on every hand. May God protect them, *one*, & *all*. A soldier looks dear to me; I love the uniform:
they have suffered & endured so much for our common good, & for
our Country's honor, that they inspire a reverence for the blue: Heaven
bless every true, & brave, & loyal, Soldier.

Tuesday—It is just as dry, & warm as ever: no signs of rain. I have
been down to our place—everything is suffering from drouth. Albert
is afraid he wont realize enough off our place to pay him for his labor.
I rode Fancher's horse down & expected to come back last night, as
he wanted to go away early this morning surveying (He is Civil Engi-
neer). But I was so tired I let Willie take the horse up last night, & Albert came up this morning with his Oxen & I rode with him. I walked
up to our place last night from Alberts, & back again, called on Mrs
Hoag. Mr Koonts had moved into our house but were gone away—it
didnt look much like our pleasant little *cottage home*, that I wrote you
about last week. I went out around the wheat, some places it is very
tall, others not. Then I went into the house lot, picked a few strawberries, looked into the well, found it dried up; went into the house &

---

28. Subsequent letters reveal the Koonts family soon moved away. The 1870 Census
(p. 30) reports John Koonts, age thirty-five, Ohio born, living in Paw Paw, Van Buren
County, Michigan, with his wife, children, and parents.

29. KJV, Matthew 24:7.

rested awhile & then went back to Alberts. This morning I milked one cow for Albert & Martha the other, while he done his other chores, so we could get to Mt P[leasant] in time for school—Met Willie & Vesper half way there, coming to meet us—so let him go on with Willie & have a playday until to morrow: Found little Dallie at school with the other scholars—he had brought my dinner—(the little darling)—Said he slept with Grandma last night: He is learning very fast, & now reads in reading—I hope to hear this week that you have gotten over having those painful boils. I received a letter last week that you were expecting to move: I am glad you are going to get away from those rough & wicked fellows you mentioned.

O, Samuel dont let such beings contaminate your [sic], or allow your good resolves to be shaken. Stand *firm*, amid trials and temptations. *Look*, to a dear Savior for strength: He is able, he is *willing*; his precious blood was shed for you, & me & cleanses from all sin:—And with your prayers, shall be mingled—those of your ever loving children, & devoted

Ellen

Samuel to Ellen

Stevenson, Ala. June 26th 1864. [Sunday]

Good Morning, My Dear Ellen—how do you get along this warm weather? I tell you, it takes the sweat out of us here—& yet they are talking of going on to Atlanta, Ga. I am feeling well, & getting fleshy. Have worked every day since the first of April. I received the envelopes you sent, last Thursday, also stamps—Am so glad to get your letters; they do me good—I would liked to have gone with you to Indian quarterly meeting, but it is my duty to be here, & every other man that is able. I would like to be near you, but I dont want the rebs to drive us that way—We have inspection, sunday morning. I dont know, as you know what that is so I will tell you. We have to take our Knapsacks, guns, haversacks, canteens, & clothes to be inspected by our Officers— they must be kept clean & in good order. This is the most quiet Sabbath I have ever seen in the Army: it is so hot that we get into the shade & keep still: after dinner I picked a few blackberries—they dont taste as good here as they do at home—they are sour. The boys are going to the river to swim & are calling for me.—Well I have had a good swim & feel cool & comfortable. I want you to continue to write every week. I have but little war news from the front—there are a good many prisoners passing through here for the past few days. How much I want to see you, & my dear little boys. They are calling me to supper & I will close.

   May God bless you & preserve you from all harm.

   Good bye to my dear Wife & Children.

Ellen to Samuel

Mt. Pleasant. June 28th 1864.

(Tuesday Evening.)

   My Dear Husband.

   Again I find myself addressing a few thoughts to you, hoping they may find you well. We are all usually well, & moving along in the same routine of duties, with a little variation this week, as I am having a weeks vacation—to extend till after the 4th of July. So I am unusually busy repairing the childrens clothing & making some new: doing some visiting &c—To day Althea & I have visited Miss Hines's Mission School. We found only about a dozen scholars of various ages—from 4 to 15—some of them quite intelligent looking, but *filthy* & disobedient. I would rather teach white children, at less remuneration. My school was half out last friday: have had no use for a *whip* & have had excellent discipline. Last mail I recd your letter, dated at Stevenson, Ala—am glad that you are with your own regiment again, though it seems you are as much in the midst of sickness & dangers. I hope you may not be disturbed by the enemy, or ever be taken into their loathsome prisons. How wretched I should be to hear you were a prisoner. I hope to hear again from you tomorrow: how anxiously we look forward to mail day—seven long days to intervene, between getting any news from the outside world. I am sorry you feel any prejudice toward Church organizations—especially the Methodist's, for they are the people of my choice, & if I ever unite with any, I must surely be a *methodist*: Not with any excitement, but with a calm & steady seaching of Scripture, & much prayer, a knowledge of Divine love, & an earnest desire to do my heavenly Fathers will; I am fully determined to choose the path of wisdom, & righteousness, & with Gods help to ever walk therein.

I have not yet joined, except on probation. If I conduct myself as becoming a christian, at the end of six months, I shall receive baptism, & be taken into the church—I expect to meet with trials, & temptations, with *opposition* & sin, as this is the lot of all, but if we are faithful to the light given us, we shall over come all obstacles, & win happiness in this life, & in the life to come, Life *everlasting.* Then should we not press onward to win the prize? Never letting our hearts grow faint, or weary, but struggle onward to win the golden crown, held out to us by a loving Saviours hand. How precious he is to me. What a *friend* to those who seek him with their whole heart! When my heart has felt o'er burdened with care & anxiety, he has whispered words of comfort, & bade me *hope.* Hope for happiness in this life, & a re-union with loved ones. O may I ever live worthy of the love & confidence of a dear husband— and loved children, whom, if seperated in this life I hope to meet & be united an *unbroken family,* in the mansions above. It is late & I must bid you Good night—May Holy Angels keep you from all harm. (Wednesday morning.) Good morning my dear Samuel what a splendid rain we are having this morning; the first we have had since the first sunday in June, & then not enough to lay the dust. So far, we have had a curious season—some of the time dry & warm—then the wind would shift to the north & a regular *freeze*, would follow. Night before last the frost cut down the corn again—(the second time this month,) and people are preparing to sow to millet, or buckwheat.[30] I expect our crops have shared the general distruction. I have not brought all of our household goods up yet; expect to get the remainder this week. Shall then keep house by myself in one part of Our folks' house—am getting somewhat tired of so much work, when all are at home. Ma does all she can but if we were by ourselves, hers would be easier for her, & I could do mine when I most felt like work.—Pa is down on his farm in Chippewa—doing his haying. It is a very light crop. Where will you be the fourth? I am talking of going to Salt River to a celebration. Mr Fancher will speak there, & we may all go down.

Next week I will be 31 years old. Will you think of me the 7th? The children are well & happy—they like living here. Dallie now lies on the carpet, singing one of his pretty tunes. He has a sweet voice. Vesper is

---

30. Millet was grown as a hardy cereal crop. Buckwheat had a similar purpose and was planted late in the season to bloom in cool weather.

still in bed; he likes to sleep mornings—(like this mama.) I must close this long letter. Write often, & take good care of yourself—

Good bye—

Affectionately,

E. L. Woodworth

Samuel to Ellen

Stevenson, Ala. July 3d 1864. [Sunday]

My Dear Ellen—I received another precious letter from you, yesterday, telling me you were well. I am glad you have good health.— dont *over do*, & get sick. I hope to hear that you have rain—It rains here nearly every day—I dont think that you really know what warm weather is, there. Some have died here from Sun-stroke.[31] It has been a busy time for us the past ten days—there has been quite a large force of Rebs across the river—firing at our pickets: we have been out on line of battle three nights, the past week—& could hear the bullets a little plainer than I cared about. Some of them went through the tops of our tents—but no one was hurt—The small-pox is with us yet—12 or 15 have had it here—only 2 have died since we came here. War news is scarce—nothing different since I last wrote. I hope there is a better time coming—where the good Book says the spear shall be made into a plow-share, & the sword into a pruning hook—& all nations shall be at peace—May that time soon come.[32] I think you felt rather lonely the night you went down to our place to see to things: I would liked to have met you there, & hope to see you there some time—My health is good—& the other boys improving. I would like your likenesses—shall send to Mother for yours & Dallie's if she will let me have them. Wish I had Vespers. I will close hoping to hear from you soon—Those verses were beautiful—I read them over & over—& visit in imagination our Woodland Cottage Home—God bless you all, & permit us safely to return to its loved shelter.

Ever your Samuel

---

31. Also known as "heat stroke," an illness brought on by excessive exposure to heat and sun where body temperature becomes too high.

32. KJV, Isaiah 2:34.

Ellen to Samuel

Mt Pleasant. July 6th 1864. [Wednesday]

Dear Husband—This is mail day again, & I have been so busy the past week that I have omitted writing till the last moment, but will have time to commence a letter & Ma says she will finish it. We are usually well—that is myself & children and are back again in school: Have helped celebrate the "*4th of Independence*," Saturday. I & the children got a ride down to Pas farm—staid at his house that night. Celia came over from her school, & Emma was there—(as her school is in that district). We had a good visit together: Sunday we all went to meeting to the Salt River School-house—& after meeting I & the children went home with Mr & Mrs Wilsey & stayed until monday then went with them to the celebration, which was held in the woods between Uncle Robbins house, & the School-house. The celebration was in the usual style—with speeches—plenty to eat, & Lemonade to drink. The children enjoyed it much. At night we rode home with Mr Paynes people—stayed over night, & he carried us home (to Mt P[leasant]) in the morning. So I have given you a *minute detail*, of how we spent the 4th. Tell us where you were, & what you were doing:

This morning we are having a warm rain; a nice growing time here now—but the showers came to late to benefit spring crops, a great deal. Mother will write all the news, if there are any to write: I will only say that Doug Nelson, & Nellie Babbitt[33] are married: & now it is time for me to close—hoping to hear from you *to day.*

Ever Thine—

E. L. Woodworth.

Well good morning Samuel—dont feel to much disappointed that Ellen could not fill the sheet; she will probably write more next time. My health is poor—it is quite a task for me to do much work, or wield the pen—Pa is well—is on his farm to work—but has had to divide his crops with Jack Frost & Madam Drouth till but little remains to him: but we will not complain of any trouble here if we can be spared the horrors

---

33. She was daughter of Abigail and F. C. Babbitt, who was the partner in business of Douglas H. Nelson. Fancher, *Past and Present*, 324; Find a Grave, https://www.findagrave .com/memorial/76299540/nellie-nelson.

of war. O Sam can it be possible that you are far away among that unfortunate throng? I was greatly disappointed in not seeing you when we came so far to be with our children. Ellen bears up bravely under all she has to undergo—there are but few women that takes their *loss*, as hard as she does having you away—She has just started off to school with her little group; she looks ten years younger than she did when we got here—Poor girl—she had nearly mourned her life away! but her time is now so completely monopolized, she cannot dwell so minutely on her trouble. She gets along finely with her school, & all seem to like her firstrate.

She intends to have her household goods brought here & live in a part of our house this winter, if you do not get back; it is not near as lonely for her as to live on your own place where every thing reminds her constantly of you—rest assured; her heart is *ever true*.

The children are well—Vesper wanted me to tell you that he was very glad of that paper you sent him; he enjoys himself well this summer, having so many boys to play with. Little Dall is as fat as a cub—he weighs over 40, Vesper 60 pounds & Ellen 105. Dall says he likes to go to school, but the School-marm *scolds* him more than she does when she is *Mama*, but I must close. May God protect you & bring you back to the embrace of your family.

Your ever affectionate

Mother Preston.

Samuel to Ellen

Stevenson. Ala. July 10th 1864. [Sunday]

Dear Wife, & Children. I would much like to be with you to day, but I am glad to have the privilege of writing to you, & hearing from you, so often. I am sorry to hear that the crops are so injured; I am afraid you will see hard times but we will hope for the best. I have been out & picked some blackberries, I had a few pounds of sugar, so I have made me some preserves; I wish you could taste of them you would say it was good. I try & enjoy myself as well as I can under the circumstances. I recd yours of the 29th yesterday: War news are more encouraging—2000 rebels passed through here yesterday & to-day that

Sherman captured near Atlanta.[34] I spent the 4th in the harness all day drilling, & shooting at a mark. The weather is very warm. I must close & go on dress parade—Love to All.

In haste, Sam—

Ellen to Samuel

Mt. Pleasant, July 12th 1864. [Tuesday]

My Dear Husband:

I will steal a few minutes while the children have recess, hoping to get time to write more than I did last week; we are all well & getting along very nicely. Time passes much more rapidly than it would if I had not something to keep me busy. The children are learning very fast. Vesper studies reading, writing, spelling, geography & mental arithmetic. Dallie reads in reading, & spells in words of four letters. It would amuse you to hear him speak to me in school; he never says Mama but imitates the other scholars, & says "please School Ma'm may I do this," (or what ever he wishes to ask.) I am now housekeeping by myself, & shall take the world easier.—It may cost me more to live, but it will be easier for me—I had grown thin under my labors—weighing only 105, the lightest I have been since we were married. My rooms are the upright part—the front one serving for parlor—dining room & kitchen; a large bedroom opening out of it—for sleeping room. Ma has gone down this week, to the farm to oversee the work—for Pa & his hired men. Celia's school will be out in 3 weeks then she will be at home—this week I & the children are alone. I have 7 weeks longer to teach, & they are asking me to prolong it one month more—which will take it to Oct—but I hardly think I can: I am getting tired.

(Afternoon 3 o clock) I have written all the time I could get at noon, & will pen a few more lines now—Wallace is helping Pa on the farm—Arsene not very well—but helps do her work—Fanchers folks well—are digging cellar for a new house. I have bought a barrel of flour of Mr Wilsey for 12 dollars, it is selling at the Mills for $16,00. I shall

---

34. Sherman was closing in on the city, but it did not surrender until September 2 after several battles.

live as economical as possible but provisions are all dear—Tea 2,40 per pound—potatoes 1,50 per bushel. I have some sugar of our own, & butter. Our folks will furnish us milk.—It is now after school—we have just had our supper, what think you we had? Well simply some boiled rice & sweetened cream, biscuit & butter, dutch cheese, & a cup of tea. Good enough for a queen, & not very expensive. Doug & his bride[35] returned last Saturday. Nellie look sweetly, but I fear her cup of happiness will have *bitter* dregs. We dont hear much war news lately. It seems they are trying to surround Richmond, cut of supplies & force a surrender, from hunger, instead of fighting.[36] O I hope ere long, that, not only the Rebel Capitol, but the whole Southern Confederacy will *collapse*. Then there will be a prospect of welcoming home those who are toiling far away, amid dangers & privations, for the restoration of our noble Union. Heaven bless our brave & gallant Soldiers. I am *proud* to be counted a Soldiers Wife: and when I think of the lonely hours I have passed since you went away, and still must pass—I feel that I too am doing something for our Country. I have given all I had to give, for the cause of Liberty & freedom; and should the happy hour come when we can welcome our brave Soldiers home, we can truly unite in the glad anthem of gratitude & praise that will burst from the national heart, & feel that we have *helped* hasten the happy era, & borne a share in this great & fearful struggle. God bless you, my dear Husband: Trust ever in the divine goodness of that Being who watches over the destiny of Nations, as well as the least of his creatures & letteth not a sparrow fall to the ground with out his notice. I received you[r] letter last week, & hope to hear again tomorrow. The children send much love to dear Papa—Take good care of yourself & do not let the constant contact with evil & wicked companions ever influence you to do wrong—Good night.

Believe me ever your affectionate—Ellen.

---

35. Douglas Nelson and Nellie Babbitt.

36. In mid-June, Union armies under Grant had encircled Richmond and Petersburg, its supply center a few miles to the south, but not until April 1865 would both cities fall into Union hands. Sodergren, *Army of the Potomac*, 66–67.

Samuel to Ellen

Stevenson, Ala. July 17th 1864. [Sunday]

What am I to write to you, my ever Dear Wife—that will interest you, the same thing, over & over again. I am well, & keep very busy. I received yesterday your letter—with your Mothers—I was glad to have her write me—I think you had a good time the 4th. How I would [have] enjoyed the trip with you:—Shall I ever be permitted to see my home & friends again? These are questions I ask myself often; O how long will this cruel war last? Sometimes I think I shall be home this fall, & then sometimes it seems impossible to ever get back & I almost wish I had never left you. Heaven forgive me if I do wrong: I want to hear from you often—& when I get any war news I will write it. D. N[elson] has done better than he deserves—I hope he will be kind to Nellie. Give my love to your Mother, & my precious boys—

and blessings crown you, my
Ever remembered Ellen.
S. Woodworth

Ellen to Samuel

Mt. Pleasant. July 19th 1864. [Tuesday]

My Dear Husband—
Another pleasant monday morning finds me in school, also the children—all well—except my head gets dizzy occasionally.—Saturday I went down to our place, & back again horseback—& it was rather hard on me—I wanted to pack the remainder of my things so Albert could bring them up this week. The horse rides hard, & I left him to Alberts & he & Martha went up with their team & got the goods & brought them to his place. I have been housekeeping one week—borrowed dishes of mother, till mine get here. The wheat is getting ripe—it will be a light crop owing to frost—The Spring crops dont amount to anything.

(At Noon). I have just eaten my dinner & sent the children out to play so I can write a little more to the dear Absent one. Albert has just gone by with my goods—so I will have something to keep me busy after school, this week, regulating & getting things in "style." Pa & Ma are going to the farm again this week & will stay through harvesting. Fanchers folks will stay in Ma's rooms while they move their house—& put up an upright. They will move it a little to the south. They are very kind to us—and have a noble little boy—a little curly headed fellow & he & Dallie think a world of each other: they play together all the time we are out of school. Vesper is a nice tall boy, & studies well in school; but I have to keep a strict & watchful eye over him, he is so fond of the water. He has disobeyed me two or three times, & went in swimming with the the [sic] other boys—when I had forbidden him. I had to punish him: It grieves me to have to be compelled to punish my children: but he needs a fathers advice—the want of which, makes my duty doubly vigilant: He never uses bad words, but he sometimes tries to deceive me—in regard to the water. But he is a dear boy & a great comfort to me—& help in taking care of Dallie—It costs quite a good deal to clothe them, everything is so dear—Factory cloth is now 80 cts per yard & print 40 & 50. (It is one o clock & I must call school.)

Afternoon recess—I feel better this afternoon, than I did this morning. I did not get a letter last week & to wait two long weeks in suspense—makes me nearly sick. The war news is discouraging—we hear that Baltimore & *Washington* are in the hands of the Enemy[37]—O will this wicked rebellion ever be put down? the North & South ever be united again in peace & fellowship, or must there always exist a wrangling, jealous hatred, as has always been between Great Brittain & the United States, How I long for peace to once more waft her sweet pinions over our land, to feel when I lie down at night, that our whole Country was bathed in peaceful slumbers & no bitter foe was lurking in their midst.

(Tuesday forenoon.) I will pass a leisure hour in writing as I felt so poorly this morning Althea said she would teach for me, & let me rest. So I am taking it easy in my quiet room at home. The children are in school, her little boy is with me. Fancher is helping Wallace draw in Morton's grain—he left all of his business for Wallace to see to. Albert is also helping them; Wallace has considerable custom. This morning I received a call from Doug Nelson & his bride. They were very cordial & sent a good deal of love to you—but I dont know as I can put it all

---

37. On July 11–12, 1864, Confederate troops under General Jubal Early threatened Washington, D.C., but withdrew before commencing a serious assault; neither Baltimore nor D.C. surrendered. See Cooling, *Jubal Early's Raid on Washington.*

in this little letter. They both wished me to call on them & I promised I would. Our children keep well—this morning when they started off to school with their dinner basket—they looked like two nice school boys, which they certainly are. Vesper went berrying last night & got enough to make a pie—but there are but few berries this year. The sad news came this week that Mr Goodsell[38] was dead: He was wounded some time ago—Poor Mrs Goodsell! I called on her about 4 weeks ago & she could talk of nothing but her husband—She knew he was wounded—but thought he was getting better.[39] How hard for her to give him up. O may I never know such sorrow as hers. (Wed' morning.) I am feeling better to day, am just going to school—I do hope to hear from you to day. Good bye my dear Boy—& may the dear Saviour preserve you from all harm—is the earnest prayer of

Your ever faithful

Ellen.

Samuel to Ellen

Stevenson Ala—July 26th 1864.

Dear Ellen—This pleasant Sabbath morning[40] finds me writing a few lines to dear friends far away—We are having nice cool weather, now days; & good news from every quarter. The Rebs are deserting by thousands. Some 2500 have left & come into our lines, within the past week. I saw 800 of them yesterday; & there is a lot more of them here this morning: They tell of seeing hard times, & their looks show it: They are poor, ragged, & hungry: Sherman has got Atlanta with a lot of prisoners;[41] I feel encouraged to believe that fighting is about done, here. I received your letter yesterday saying you were living by yourself—I think it will be easier for you. I wouldn't advise you to engage to teach an-

---

38. Andrew J. Goodsell enlisted in company H, 8th Michigan Infantry, February 19, 1864, at Union, for three years, age thirty-eight. He was wounded at the Battle of Cold Harbor, June 3, 1864, and died in hospital at Baltimore, Maryland, July 2, 1864. *Record of Service*, vol. 8, 58.

39. Louisa Goodsell, born about 1830. They had three children. *Seventh United States Decennial Census*, Isabella Township, Isabella County, Mich., 15.

40. Samuel may have misdated his letter; July 26, 1864, was a Tuesday.

41. Sherman's capture of Atlanta occurred on September 2.

other month; it is to hard for you: If I earn enough, I want you to use it to live on.

Our pay is due again, but dont know how soon we will get it. My health is good, haven't had the asthma since last fall. We are living better now than ever—we got ripe apples, potatoes, & vegetables of all kinds: I have been & picked 4 quarts of blackberries & Dove[42] has made some pies, so we shall live on the top shelf for awhile. I have not had a cross word from any comrade, or an Officer yet. There are but few here that can say that. Send me a few stamps if you have them—Tell Veppy to be a good boy & keep away from the water. Love to all.

Ever yours,
S. W.

Ellen to Samuel

Mt. Pleasant. July 26th 1864. [Tuesday]

Ever dear Husband—Again I sit down to pen a few lines to you, hoping they will find you well. I am feeling a good deal better than when I last wrote. I went home with Dr Meisslers children last Friday & stayed over night. Mr Meissler gave me a bottle of german medicine that is helping me. My stomach was out of order & that was the cause of my bad feelings. I am glad to hear that you are feeling well & enjoying yourself among the blackberries. I would really like some of your preserves, for that is something we don't have,—yet I would rather you would have them, it is so few luxuries our dear Soldiers get. It seems you are getting nearer to danger—I did not expect you were so exposed to the enemy's guns.—We can only trust all to that *One*, who is *able* to shield us from all harm. Our precious Saviour! Praise his name forever: How glad am I that I have found him, precious, to my Soul. O my dear Husband— *do* you rest wholly upon the Atoning blood of a crucified redeemer? If not, go at once to the foot of the cross, ask *Him* to give you this price-less inheritance. But I trust you already know what it is—that this all-important subject has been your theme—& the prayers of your wife shall ever supplicate for you, through all the dangers of this dark, & bloody war. It is now 10 o clock at night—all are wrapped in peaceful slumber,

42. William Dove enlisted the same day and place as Samuel. *Record of Service*, vol. 43, 59.

while I sit writing to him who fills my thoughts through the long days, & weeks & months that have passed, & are passing, in his absence. I suppose you will want to hear about the crops. Wallace & Pa have been down & helped Albert cut the wheat & put it up. They had over 900 bundles, bound, & the rest they mowed for fodder—the hay hardly pays for cutting. The wheat I shall have threshed for our own use. The barrel of flour I bargained for of Mr Wilsey, he thought I had concluded not to take, because he didn't get the word I sent him, & he let other parties have it. It is now selling, for—(at the mills) 16 & 20 dollars a barrel—according to quality—& I cant afford it. Since school I have been down to the mills—Althea carried me down. I went to Babbitts Store & bought me some shoes—paid $3,00 the second pair of fine shoes that I have had since we came from [New] York State. I bought a quarter pound of tea & had to pay 56 cts (18 shillings per pound.) It costs more to live here than if I had stayed on our place as I have to dress better—being in school—but I have got $80,00 most earned & that will help some, when if I had staid at home I wouldn't have earned anything. The children are both well. Tomorrow is mail day again; hope I will get good news from you. I received two letters from you last mail: wasn't I glad? Be cautious of the enemy—take care of your health & excuse a short letter this time, for it is late & I must be up early in the morning.

Good Night—Truly yours—

Ellen.

Samuel to Ellen

Stevenson, Ala—July 31st 1864. [Sunday]

Dear Wife, & Children, I received a good long letter from you last night: How I would like to be with you to day, instead of writing. I see by your letters, you sometimes get a little discouraged; I dont wonder at it, yet I hope you will not fret over the cost of living—that is the least of my trouble: if you can only get enough to make yourselves comfortable I will be satisfied—it is all I ask, & will please me better than for you to try to earn so much—& neglect your health. Tell Doug & Nellie, I wish them much joy: he said he should write to me as soon as he got home—but I have not yet heard from him. I am well, & as I have no news to write except there is great excitement at present here about being mustered out this fall—many think we will—I dare not hope to much so I will write now to Vesper.—Good morning my dear boy—I want to ask you some questions, & I want you to write to me & answer them;—Are you as good a boy as you was when I was there? Do you do all that Mama tells you too, & just as she tells you? I hope you do. Do you always speak the truth? O I would rather lose my right arm than to have my Veppy tell a lie! You are getting to be a large boy & can be a great help to your Mama, & I want you to watch over Dallie that he does nothing he ought not to. Dont ever go away unless your Mama knows where you are, & gives permission. Do you ever say bad, or wicked words? No, I hope not: Do you ever go into the water; if so, does Mama know where you are? Now Veppy, if you have ever done any of these things I want you to write & tell me, & promise to never do so again. Your Mama knows what is right for you to do—Your Papa thinks a great deal about you, & wants you to remember what he writes you. I hope to live to get home & be with you again—Now Veppy write, & tell me all I ask—Little Dallie you cannot write yet, but you must not forget Papa, will you? Be good little boys—take good care of Mama until I come.

Good bye—from Papa—far away.

Samuel to Ellen

Stevenson Ala—August 4th 1864. [Thursday]

Dear Ellen as to day is a day of rest I though I would improve a part of it in writing to loved ones, *far away*.

To day is a lovely day—but yesterday we had a fearful storm, which lasted nearly all night: It thundered, rained & blew the hardest I ever saw it: & this morning we were a wet set of boys. Our tents were blown down & we were at the mercy of the elements, but are all right this morning. I am well, & I do hope to hear the same from you. I received your stamps. I had but 1 left. I see I was sadly fooled about the fighting being nearly done near Atlanta. We cant believe much that we hear in Camp. I shall finish this Sunday—I hope to hear from you before then. I wrote to Veppy last Sunday. There is a good deal of talk about our regiment being mustered out with the old regiment. Some are sure we will, I think it very doubtful—If we are we shall be home about the

1st of Nov. I dont think we will get pay again until Sept. We have quiet times here now but we have to get to business in the early morning—We are called at 4 o clock—go to work at 5, & work till half-past 6 at night. (Saturday Evening). I have received your letter of the 26th so glad to hear that your health is improved—am very glad of your counsel—it is good; I will try & heed it. I wrote to you once, of my resolves—I meant what I said. It has been my study since to do my Saviours will; but I cannot express my thoughts in writing; but Dear Ellen, if I live to see you again, I shall respect your feelings—though I may not see every thing just as you do—I shall never be as thoughtless & wayward as I used to be. How I want to see you & those precious children.—Little Dallie, Papa has not forgotten his little boy—he wants to see you very much. I wrote to Veppy last week—you must be good children.

Ellen there are some large boxes of mine over to Hollands—they will do to put your wheat in—Write often—I must bid you good night—from Sam—to his Wife & children.

Ellen to Samuel

Mt Pleasant. August 9th 1864.

(Tuesday Afternoon.)

Dear Samuel Emma is visiting my school to day & while she is hearing the classes in spelling I will write to you. It is very warm weather & the heat is oppressive. I get along well, & time is winging its way so that my school is most out; unless I teach another month, which would make me out $100,00. But I hardly feel able to do it. Five years ago such an amount of money would have seemed like quite a sum: but now every thing is so high, it dont go far. To day noon, Emma & I had quite a treat; we went up to Mr Cases & had some beautiful honey to eat. They sent for us last Saturday to come, but I had company & could not go. Hannah Stuart, & Eliza Estee came up horse back, to see me. Poor Mrs Stuart—she was dressed in deep mourning, & looks very sad indeed. Sunday we all went to hear Mr Goodsells funeral sermon preached—Ma rode with Fancher's folks & I rode with Mr Bradley's. Elder's Sheldon & Bradley preached the funeral sermon—& afterwards Mrs Goodsell had her little babe sprinkled. She takes his death very hard—Seats were made in the grove opposite her house to accomodate the large crowd that came to pay their respect to his memory. Since school, Vesper has been berrying, & I have baked a couple of pies. What few berries escaped the drouth—the Squaws get, so if we buy of them we have to pay 10 & 12 cts per quart. I should enjoy a few of your ripe apples—something we dont see here in the woods. There is considerable going on here for a little place—to help pass away time. We are beginning the study of German. Mr Meissler teaches it. Althea & I joined the class (free to me.) So tomorrow after school is our German lesson—Thursday evening prayer meeting—Friday evening a "Social" & Saturday a *select* Tea party given by Mrs I.E. Arnold:[43] The invitations are limited & include Mrs Babbitt,[44] Mrs. D. Nelson, Mrs Fancher & "your humble servant." The children are enjoying good health, & send love & a kiss to Papa. O when will peace be restored to our distracted Country? and those who are so bravely defending her in this hour of peril be restored to home & friends again? Only He who hears the ravens cry & knoweth all, can bring peace & happiness to the now lonely fireside's: and my faith is strong that he will overrule the sorrow, & bring joy & comfort to the true & faithful. I received your letter last week & will send you some stamps in this. It is getting late & I must close.

Good night—& may guardian Angels keep thee from harm.
Ellen.

Ellen to Samuel

Mt Pleasant, Aug 15th 1864. [Monday]

Dearest Husband—Again I find myself writing to my absent one: It is monday noon—& a very pleasant, though warm day. I am here in my old school house—have just finished my dinner & sent the scholars out to play. Shall I tell you what we had? boiled eggs, bread & but-

---

43. Susan E. (Foy) Arnold, second wife of Irving E. Arnold, businessman in Mount Pleasant. His son, Dexter, was the first Euro-American birth in the village, in 1862. *Portrait and Biographical Album*, 269, 319, 381, 388, 414.

44. Abigail (Fitch) Babbitt (1817–1893), brought "the first flowers cultivated in Isabella County." I. E. Arnold "built four schoolhouses for the United States government for the use of the Indians" in 1858–1859. Find a Grave, https://www.findagrave.com/memorial/82389244/abigail-mason-babbitt; *Portrait and Biographical Album*, 539; Fancher, *Past and Present*, 143.

ter, & cucumbers. What are you eating for your dinner? I wish I knew,
& just where you were eating it: Shall we ever eat together again? Yes—
Oh yes; it *must* be so. I cannot have it otherwise. Your last letter speaks
of a possibility of your being mustered out of service *this fall*! O dare I
hope, for it: If it can be so my cup of happiness will overflow. We are
yet all spared in health, children well & happy. Mr Bentley is building a
house across the street from the Court House. Fancher is having a nice
house put up—Albert & Wallace are at work for him this week—Mr.
Joslyn does the carpenter work.

I did not go to Mrs Arnolds Saturday—I had company & had to stay
home—Mrs Hoag & Martha came up to see me. I have company most
every Saturday—but as it is all the spare day I have—I have to make it my
washing—ironing, & baking day—whether I have company, or not. Pa is
getting ready for a 10 acre logging bee next thursday. Celia is his housekeeper & will cook for them. Ma & Emma are here at home, now. I wish
you could come & visit my school this afternoon. The girls have visited
it & pronounce me a "cute School ma'm," what do you think about it?
(Afternoon recess.) I will write on so as to have my letter ready for mail
day. To morrow after school Althea & I intend calling on Mrs Babbitt,
& Nellie. She & Doug rode up Saturday horseback & called at the gate.
She is a lovely girl, & far his superior. (Monday Evening). All in bed but
myself, & I ought to be but I was hindered from writing much this afternoon, so will converse awhile with you before retiring. I wish you could
look in some evening when the children are preparing for bed—& see the
sweet simplicity of childish faith exemplified, in our dear little Dallie: he
hardly waits to get his good-night kiss, before you see him go quietly by
himself—kneel down, close his eyes & put up his little hands together, &
then repeat his little prayer with such earnestness, such trustfulness, that
God will take care of us all & bless his dear Papa & keep him from all
harm. Oh! it seems that angels might bow, to listen to such childish in-
nocence—such sweet simplicity. Vesper does the same only he is so much
older, that he frequently sits up till I get ready to retire, & then joins me
in our evening devotions. He is a good boy lately, since that time I wrote
you about, I have had no occasion to punish him. He dont go to the water since without permission. How good you talked to him in his letter; I
read it to him, & it brought tears to his eyes as well as mine; I shall have
him answer it soon. He is a tall fine looking boy, & if he lives, I trust will
make a good & useful man—He helps me in the house a good deal—
picks up wood—& picks what berries he can.

(Tuesday afternoon, recess.) I guess you will think it takes me a long time to write a letter, but I have to write as I can catch spare moments. This noon I went down to the river bank—back of the school house with the scholars & they all enjoyed it much. To night I am going down to the mills to get some little presents for the scholars, as I have only 8 days more to teach, & ere this reaches you I shall be out of school.

I hope to get good news from you to morrow. Excuse this scribbling at the bottom of the page: they are german letters, & I will let you see how well I can write—

Good bye, Ever thine Ellen L. Woodworth.

Mount Pleasant, Mich.

Samuel to Ellen

Stevenson Ala—August 17th 1864. [Wednesday]

I have you now—my own dear Wife & little Dall, boy: came last night from Java & you can never know how glad I was to see those much loved faces—so familiar—it seems as though you must speak to me. And while I look at them, my eyes fill with tears & I ask myself "shall I ever hear those sweet voices again?" I miss Veppy, I wish I had his picture too. I received your ever welcome letter, also 3 others from Java— Mother, Melvin, & Vira.[45] I did not write sunday; I did not have time. We lost some mules & I & 5 others were sent out on horseback to find them. We scoured the country—had a good time; found where they were making Cider, had what we wanted to drink—& all the apples & peaches we could eat; we got a lot of green corn & went back to camp.

I am glad you have got the wheat cared for—dont dispose of any. I fear you will get so attached to "City life" you wont want to go back into the woods to live with me, when I get home. The prospect is not very good for me to get home this fall. We are having very hot weather, & many are sick—I am well with the exception of a sore on my leg that has been there since April—it discharges a good deal—Last week I caught cold in it & for a couple of days it was very painful. I bathed it in cold water & got the inflamation out of it & it is better now. They

---

45. In the 1860 Census, Vira A., was ten years old and living with her parents. *Eighth United States Decennial Census,* Java, Wyoming, N.Y., 855.

are calling me to work & I must close. Hoping to hear again soon from those who are ever in my thoughts.

Good bye for this time—from Sam

Samuel to Ellen

Stevenson Ala. August 21st 1864. [Sunday]

Dear Ones at Home—This is a dark & rainy day, & a very lonesome day to me, & many others.

We had a sad duty to perform to day; Sargeant Muir[46] was killed last night, by the falling of a stick of timber: We were raising a block house. He was a noble fellow;—he staid in the tent with me last winter when I was sick & done all a brother could for me; he was buried to day at 2 o clock: O how many more lives will it take to put this rebellion down? Things look dark to me sometimes I tell you. There are a large part of our company sick on account of the hot weather. I received your letter containing stamps—I was just out. I have money, but there are no stamps for sale. I was glad to hear you were well. By the time this reaches you, your school will be out, your time seems pretty well taken up. I hope you will now take a holiday, & rest up—dont try to teach any more. I am well except my leg, or shin, it is a bad sore & has bothered me all summer. I guess it will get well some time. We have done a good deal of heavy work here, & I hear we are to leave here soon.

Ellen when you are away from your children, & all of your friends, as long as I have been you can tell my feelings then, & not until then, & not much prospects of seeing them for two years to come. I tell you my courage almost forsakes me: and if it was not for you, dearest Ellen, & those helpless little boys, how gladly would I lay my life down. I could leave this world of trouble, without one regret. O, if you was with me to cheer me, what would I not give. I feel rather down hearted to day—I ought not to write it to you—but it is a sad day to me.

The war news are not very encouraging, at present. But God is just & will do all things right. You will tell me to look to Jesus: Dont I? If

---

46. William F. Muir enlisted in Company M, 1st Michigan Engineers and Mechanics, November 8, 1863, at Hamtramck, age twenty-three. He was killed "while raising timber for block house" at Stevenson, Alabama, August 20, 1864. *Record of Service*, vol. 43, 144.

you could see me on my knees, & see the repentant tears running down my cheeks, you would say bless God.—It is my earnest desire to live a christian life. I know you pray for me—I can feel the influence—of your prayers—May God bless you & protect my little children from all harm—

My love to all—Good bye—from Sam, to Ellen.

Ellen to Samuel

Mt Pleasant. Aug 28th 1864. [Sunday]

Dear Husband—I will fulfill my promise of writing to you every week altho I have nothing new to write. I did not receive any letter last week—perhaps I will get two this, but I had much rather they would come weekly—it is such a long time to wait *two whole weeks*. The talk is now about the draft which is to take place the 5th of next month. Everyone is anxious to avoid it, & yet some, *must* go, out of every town, to make up the quota. I am thankful I have not *that* trouble, yet if Albert or Wallace should be drawn, it would cause us all trouble. O if this war could only be settled up in an honorable way—without fighting it out, how glad we would all be. Sunday we all attended the Indian Camp Meeting & stayed in the evening until nearly midnight. It was held about 1 1/4 miles beyond the Indian Mills. There were fully 500 persons on the ground: two thirds of the number being Indians. All passed of quietly, & orderly; & the spirit of the Lord seemed to rest upon many of our dusky brethren. Three days more will finish my school & then I shall be free. I will let Vesper write some, & then I will finish.

My Dear Papa—It has been a long time since I wrote to you, but I have been very busy, going to school & helping Ma at home. I was glad to get your letter & I will try & answer your questions. I did, once, go in swimming when Ma told me not to, but I will never do so again. I have been trying to do better, and I think I am as good a boy, as I was when you went away. We are all well, and I hope you are the same. I never swear, nor ever mean to tell a lie. I hope you will write to me again. From

Vesper Le grande Woodworth, to
My Dear Papa.

(Tuesday Afternoon) two o clock—It has just began to rain, very moderate, & looks as though we might have quite a rain. Every thing needs it, badly. I never remember seeing it so dry, the whole season through. I bought a little flour last night at 8 cts a pound; a little fresh beef at 10 cts. Eggs can be bought for 25, & 30 cts per dozen—but no potatoes at any price. Yet we shall fare as well as other people— You must excuse Vespers letter—he wrote it all by himself in school, & I think he composes pretty well for a boy of his age. Well I must attend to my school—good bye until you hear from us again. Faithfully thine—E. L. W.

Ellen to Samuel

Lincoln. Sept 3d 1864. [Saturday]

My Dear Husband—I received two letters from you last mail & their contents have been a source of both sorrow & rejoicing with me. Sorrow, because you feel so lonely, & unsatisfied with a Soldiers life, & a seperation from your family, which we all keenly feel: But dear Samuel keep up good *courage*, look on the brightest side; although the day may be long a-dawning; yet I do believe that the day will come when you will come home & enjoy the society of those who feel the seperation as truly as you do. We have a strong *hope*, & that sustains us. That *hope* tells us to look beyond these dark & troublous days of strife & contention, when wickedness, and Rebellion shall be *conquered*; & peace reign triumphantly in our land. Then my Dear Husband, we can *welcome home* the absent ones, in joy, & gladness. You now realize some thing of the anguish that wrung my soul when you enlisted; but heaven forbid that you should ever feel the *intensity* of grief that filled my heart at that time. It wasn't because I lacked Patriotism; for I felt & knew that your Country needed you, & every other such brave heart as yours; but O, how much *we* needed you too; Yet God has given me strength to pass through it; & bid me look to Him for support, and in so doing I have been blessed;—& I feel that He will care for *you*. I feel that his strong arm is about you, & that you will be permitted to pass through this great National Struggle *unharmed*; & return to us in safety. And the great *joy* that your letters brought me is because you too are seeking comfort from that great never-failing Source. Now dear Samuel you are on the right path—first conviction—a *true genuine* repentance—then we

may expect Gods love & forgiveness: & we must seek for it until we find
it. But we cannot expect to change our own hearts—from a sinful to a
spiritual state—by merely reforming in our actions or moral natures—
(this as a natural consequence will follow after we have received God's
pardon.) O how thankful I am that you are thus seeking! and may his
love ever fill your soul to overflowing. Yes, you have our daily prayers,
asking protection & care for dear Papa.

It is sunday to day—cold, & cloudy—& we are at Alberts. I & the children came down friday night, (walked down.) So, you may know that
we are all well. The machine came that day & yesterday threshed our
wheat. It is a very small crop—only 25 bushel in all. I shall keep it for
our use. It is worth 3,00 per bushel—I shall have it hauled up to the
County seat & store it in Wallaces barn—Some people barely got their
seed—Mrs Goodsell had 8 bushel of from two acres—& others just cut
theirs for fodder. We will go home tommorrow. Hoping to hear from
you this week.

All send love—Bye-bye, Ellen—

Sept 5th. I will add another page before sending what I wrote down
to Alberts—We staid there until Monday forenoon, & as A[lbert] had
no place to store it, I hired Mr Parker to get the boxes from Hollands
& take the wheat up for me—paid him $2,00. It is stored in Wallaces
barn—I gave the straw for threshing. Our place stands empty again. Mr
Koonts has moved away—O how lonely it looks there. I can never live
there again, unless you are there: I feel so sorry about your sore leg—
how hard to have to keep to work—night & day.—I am afraid you will
have a fever sore. I dont believe cold water is just the right thing for it.
You need some cooling salve[47] to heal it up, & something to cleanse
your blood: See the Doctor about it before it runs to long. Vesper is not
feeling quite well to day. He worked to hard helping them thresh: &
took cold, has some fever—I have given him a dose of pills—& he feels
better this after noon—so he has got his Geography out, to find where
the last battles are being fought. Dallie is well, & has got some large illustrations of battle scenes spread out on the floor, & trying to find his
papa among the Soldiers. He has decided that one of them looks like
you, & thinks it really is his papa. I hear that a photographer is coming
here—if so I will get all of our pictures taken & send you; but you must

---

47. An ointment that would promote healing of the skin.

promise not to have the *blues* over them; but look at them & think the
time will soon come, when you will have us all on your hands again to
look after, & keep straight; & resolve to enjoy your *freedom* while you
have a chance. For you know I am a regular *Zantippe*,[48] sometimes.

(Evening.) Vesper is feeling still better—he sits by me reading, while
I am writing. Little Dallie is abed & asleep—he has been busy to day
picking up chips—waiting on Vesper—& running over to amuse Pet
(who is not feeling well—) & his little legs get tired; at night; so he goes
early to bed. To day is the day of the draft; but it will be several days
before we get the returns; as it does not take place here. Write often:
good bye from you dear children, and Ellen.

Samuel to Ellen

Stevenson Ala—Sept 4th 1864. [Sunday]

Once again, Dearest Ellen—I am permitted to write a few lines to
those I *would so like to see*. We are having lively times now days—the
Rebs are all around us—We are doing picket duty. They have torn up
the track in different places all the way to Nashville.—They are reported
30,000 strong. There has no trains passed since wednesday, so we have
no mail this week, nor dont know when we shall get any—We can hold
this place as long as we have any thing to eat, & our ammunition lasts.

They say we have 20 days provisions, on hand. Our boys are after
them, & I guess they will be glad to get back to Georgia. We dont feel
in any particular danger; Sherman has got Atlanta now, for certain.[49] I
cant tell when this will reach you—it will have to go in a round about
way. (Sunday Evening). I will continue to write—you may get it. My
health is good but I have a bad leg: The Doctor thinks he can cure it if
I will keep still a couple of weeks—I guess I shall be obliged to, but I
hate to. I got so sick of that last winter: You dont know any thing *there*,
about *hot* weather, & I hope we have seen the worst of it. Political matters are creating quite an excitement—I think Uncle Abraham is losing

---

48. The wife of Greek philosopher Socrates, whose name had become proverbial for a
bad-tempered spouse.

49. On September 1 and 2, the Confederate army abandoned its defense of Atlanta and
Union forces moved in. The disruption of communications mentioned in this letter occurred because of Confederate raiding, not a full-scale campaign. *OR*, vol. 38, pt. 5, 763,
777; Hoffman, *My Brave Mechanics*, 210–211.

friends among the Soldiers—he may be all right but he will lose votes by the course he is taking.

We shall be shut out from the world here a week or so before the trains can run—it may be more, or less. We dont know how much damage there is done yet. I hear that our men are driving, & whipping them badly; You say you would like to have me step in some evening & see the boys prepare for bed? You are right; I would, & I shall the first opportunity I have. I can see my little family kneeling, and asking our Heavenly Father to protect one that is far away; amid dangers & temptations: I feel that your prayers have been mercifully answered; and I hope to be worthy of them. Words fail to express my gratitude to you my dear Wife. I must close & go a mile & a half and stay in a fort to night; & help support the battery in case of an attack. Ten of us staid there last night. I want to hear from you, & O, those little boys—how much I think of them: Give my love to all, & accept a large share for yourself. From your Absent Husband—Samuel

Samuel to Ellen

Stevenson, Ala. Sept 10th 1864. [Saturday]

Dear Ellen, I will write a few lines, to assure you that we are all right, yet: We have had to keep a sharp lookout for a few days past: The Rebs came within two miles of here, & we did expect to have to fight: but they concluded to let us alone: it was well for them that they did for they would have got something to remember if they had come within the reach of our guns. Wheeler got across the River; he lost all of his artillery & 2500 of his men.[50] John Morgan[51] was killed, & his staff taken prisoners. Sherman has whipped Hood,[52] & taken 14000 prison-

---

50. Confederate general Joseph Wheeler, cavalry commander. He conducted a raid across the Tennessee River against the Nashville & Chattanooga Railroad in late August–early September, requiring Woodworth and his comrades to stand "on full alert and [be] prepared for the worst." The mission failed "because Union repair crews quickly restore[d] damaged sections of the railways attacked." Hoffman, *My Brave Mechanics*, 210–211; Fredriksen, *Civil War Almanac*, 495.

51. Confederate general John Hunt Morgan, cavalry commander, was killed on September 4 in East Tennessee. Fredriksen, *Civil War Almanac*, 734–736.

52. Confederate general John Bell Hood, commander of the Army of Tennessee. Fredriksen, *Civil War Almanac*, 687–689.

ers, so you see the rebel army is about distroyed; that is, the Cumberland Army. They did not do much damage; the cars are running again. I hope to get a letter from you to day. I received yours & Vespers, last night. I think he writes well—& that he is, & will be, a good boy. I want him to write often. Cant little Dall print a few words & send to me? I have kept still this week on account of my leg, & it is getting better. My general health is good, & we have a plenty to eat. How I wish you had some of the peaches that are rotting here on the trees; they grow all over the country. I should like to live here on some of these plantations & I dont know but what I shall yet. We haven't been paid yet but expect it next week. I will put a ring in here that one of the Soldiers made for me—it isn't much of a present, but you will wear it & think of me, wont you? I was on guard last night: it was a pleasant night, & where do you suppose my thoughts were? I will leave that for you to guess. Ellen this is my birthday, you will think of it, wont you? Good bye for this time—with love to all—

From, Sam—

Ellen to Samuel

Mt Pleasant. Sept, 12th 1864.

(Monday afternoon)

Dear Samuel. I will pen a few lines, while sitting still to let the sick ones sleep: The children & myself are usually well, but Ma is very sick with Billous Fever.[53] She was taken nearly a week ago but got so much better Saturday that she insisted on my going to a two-days meeting that I had made calculations to attend.—Sunday she was taken worse, & only sleeps under the influence of opiates. I did not get home until last night. It was held at the Gulick School-house.[54] I & Dallie walked up Saturday as far as Mrs Lovelands[55] & stayed over night with her, af-

---

53. Bilious fever referred to several conditions, sometimes associated with malaria or typhoid, but also related to migraine or other nondisease sources, with symptoms such as headache, abdominal pain, and constipation. Welsh, *Medical Histories*, 399, 406.

54. In Union Township, "the first school was a log building built in 1855 and taught by Elizabeth Gulick." *Isabella County, Michigan*, 20; Fancher, *Past and Present*, 143.

55. Likely Sarah E. (Baker) Loveland, wife of Samuel. Find a Grave, https://www.findagrave.com/memorial/94971924/sarah-e-loveland.

ter attending the afternoon meeting. Sunday morning I was baptized (by immersion,) & united with the M.E. Church. I was baptized in the Chippewa river—by Father Wilcox[56]—a grand, & good old man—& it seemed to me the woods & surrounding scenery was never so lovely, or the water so beautiful—& the song of birds so full of praise, as then; Little Dallie stood on the bank, (among those that went from Church)—& looked quietly on. How I wished you had been there to be baptized with me; & while I thought of you I wondered if you, too, were praising God for his goodness. O, I hope you have found him— ere this—precious to your soul—& are now, able to go on your way rejoicing. Saturday was your 32ond birth-day—how did you celebrate it? If you had been here, I should have made you a birth-day cake. I hope you are better of that sore—but am afraid you suffer more than you admit. I wish I could come & doctor it up for you—Ah, if wishes could avail any thing, I should have flown *southward* many, many times in the past twelve months. But *patience* must be the watchword—ever trusting for the dawning of that happy day when we shall be re-united in *our own humble, & happy home.* Fanchers folks, & Emma are also on the sick list—with chills & Fever—yesterday Emma took 12 ague pills, & she may break it.[57] Celia is well & the main stay of the family—at present. Pa is well—is now on his way after the Dr—(Corbus.) I got a grist of our wheat ground, it makes good flour—& pretty good weight.

(Wednesday morning). Mother feels some better—I took care of her alone last night. O how it did rain in the night—& thunder & lighten—I thought of my Soldier Boy & wondered if he was exposed to such drenching rains: O *when*, shall I see your face again? But He, who watcheth over all, *will* take care of you, & bring you safely to the happy, *welcome home.*

As Ever—Ellen—

---

56. Unknown.

57. "Ague" was a term used for common feverous conditions; quinine was typically prescribed as a remedy, Billings, *Hardtack and Coffee*, 176, 213, perhaps here in pill form.

Ellen to Samuel

Mt Pleasant Mich. Sept 18th 1864. [Sunday]

Dear Sam I will commence another letter hoping I may be fortunate enough to get one this week, as I received none—last mail, & I was most sadly disappointed. All the sick are improving: We are well— Dallie is as fat as a *pumpkin*: he now sits by me in his little chair, while Vesper has the bible open on *his* lap, studying his sabbath school lesson—in the large rocking chair. What are you doing this quiet Sabbath day? Spending it profitably to both Soul, & body—I hope. (Tuesday noon). You see I did not make much progress writing Sunday, but have some good news to communicate, by waiting. Wallaces folks are feeling very rich—they have a nice Boy-baby weighing 10 1/2 pounds—I have been there most of the time, & shall go up by & by to dress—"Tombolin"[58]—Dallie has gone up to see his little *new* cousin: while Vesper is out with the boys gathering Butternuts. Dallie wished he had worn his new pants that had deep pockets in—so he could have put that little baby in & brought it home.—The Draft has not come off yet—has been postponed—so many are enlisting—Brickley has enlisted, & starts this morning for his regiment the 12th Mich. He enlisted out of the woods & came home in Soldiers uniform. He enlisted for 1 year, & receives $450, town, & $100, County bounty besides his wages.—& whatever State bounty he may receive. Pa is down on his farm to day; is so attached to it he can hardly stay home over night: has a family living there that he boards with. His wheat turned out better than ours—he had between 80 & 90 bushel & sells it for $3,00 per bush[el]. He had 16 tons of hay & sold it for $35.00 per ton. Oats sell of 1 dollar a bushel. War news are encouraging if *reliable*: We hear that Grant has whipped Beauregard to death, cut his army all up & captured fort Darling which gives our gunboats free access to Richmond, & that will have to succumb, next.[59] And now people think that fighting will soon be a thing of the *past*. O, I hope it may be so; & "welcome *Home*" be the glad re-

---

58. Perhaps "a figure of folk ballads popular in New England throughout the 1800s." Gencarella, *Wicked Weird & Wily Yankees*, 245–247.

59. Fort Darling was a Confederate post located at Drewry's Bluff, commanding a bend in the James River near Richmond and thus blocking Union vessels from ascending to the capital. The report of its capture was false, and the "lull" around Richmond and Petersburg continued. General P. G. T. Beauregard was not involved in this fighting, as he

frain. Till then—may kind Heaven protect you Mr Dear Husband & fill your Soul with that peace that passeth understanding. If you need money—let me know. I will send you to day, 8 stamps. Children, & I send each a kiss to Papa.

E. L. W.

Samuel to Ellen

Stevenson Ala Sept 22ond 1864. [Thursday]

Dear Ellen—Through the kind care, & protection of a merciful Providence, I am permitted this great pleasure of writing to those that I dearly love: altho I review my past life with sorrow—it is with feelings far different from what they were one year ago—*Then* I would as soon have lost my head, as had you join the *Methodist* Church: but if I had been taught differently when young, I should not have felt so, & would not have had to look back on 12 years of my life with shame for the treatment I have shown you. Forgive me Ellen—& do what ever you think is *right*. It is my whole study to know, & do my duty as a Christian & a Soldier & if my life is spared I will try to atone in part—for my past conduct. I want our children to be educated, if possible—different from what I was. I was a head strong—way ward boy—& knew no control. I now realize the need of the education I refused to take, & which would have been so much better for me. I am well aware that I did not realize what I was doing when I enlisted—& it was cruel in me to leave you as I did but I feel it, not only *my duty*—but every other man that is able to do military duty, to be here. You say I will never feel the anguish & anxiety that you have. I think you *guess* at that. I have the satisfaction of knowing it was my own doings—which is not a great deal—certainly: but I have had time for reflection, & my aim is to do right: It has been my study for the last six months to learn what I ought to do—and it is from you my dear Ellen—that I have learned a great deal. I have peace of mind, that I never knew before. I feel that I have a friend with me—something to sustain me—and when all others forsake me—He will prove true. Yes, we have his word for it, & we can rely on that.

was providing defense of Petersburg to the south. Long and Long, *Civil War Day by Day*, 569, 575.

My health is good & my leg most well. I shall take as good care of myself as possible. We have harder storms here than I ever saw there. I received stamps to day—was glad of them. Well Vesper how do you get along & my little Dall boy? Your Mama says you are good boys—that is what I always want to hear. I hope to live to see you. May a kind providence protect & guide you aright is the wish of your father—

Good by for this time—with much love to all—

S. W.

Ellen to Samuel

Sept 26th 1864. Mt Pleasant. Mich. [Monday]

Dear Samuel Another week has rolled around, reminding me that the same duties must be performed, as in weeks past; and the first duty, is to write to you. We are all usually well. There has been a good deal of excitement in anticipation of the draft, & several enlisted, for fear of being drafted.[60] We shall hear more particulars of the draft by this weeks mail. I received two letters from you last week, one of them containing a ring, which is now on my finger—I think it very pretty & it exactly fits me. Celia sits by me & says "tell Sam to send me a ring just like it." I have been up to see Arsene—found her sitting up holding her *boy*. She feels very proud of him. They are talking of naming him Wallace Worth Preston, quite a pretty name. I have been trying my hand—in trade—& with your approval & help, I think we shall come out all right. There is a new house just north of Pa's with two lots—30 dollars worth of fruit & shrubbery—a good well—The house consists of a good sized upright & wing—piazza in front—house finished on outside except painting—board fence around the premises, & the price of all $425,00. I can pay $100,00 now & make the rest in payments to Pa—I shall earn all I can & save all I can, & with what you are able to send home I think we can pay for it. If I dont teach this winter I can keep a few boarders—or rent a part of it, to a small family. I shall move in next week & I think the rise of property here will be good interest on our means invested here,

---

60. Conscription spurred enlistments since those drafted into service, rather than enlisted voluntarily, were accused of cowardice. Long and Long, *Civil War Day by Day,* 707–708.

& when you come we can sell & build us a good home on the farm—
Lots that were bought here last year for $25,00 now sell for $60,00.

I want to hear how your leg is—I fear you have no soft cloth to wrap
it up in—I have a soft linen table cloth, cant I send it to you by mail? I
hear to night that the draft has come off & that from this county Charly
Youngs—Billy Myers[61]—William Payne—Mace Foutch & 3 others that
we do not know—Mr Payne has just gone by horseback on the jump—
to hire a substitute up among the Indians. Wallace has sold his farm
to Mr Cole & will buy Pa's. It is a cold rainy day: The equinoxal storm
is just setting in.[62] Cold weather will soon be upon us. I had such a
splendid dream last night—I thought we lived on the banks of a beautiful broad river & I saw a large steamer moving along up the river toward where we lived, & soon I perceived that it bore a Rebel flag. I was
much alarmed & thought our last hour had come, & I thought every
one else was frightened too: but presently a larger & handsomer vessel—all white—came sailing up from the other direction, & as she came
nearer I saw the *Union* flag waving high above it. She came steadily
along & just as the rebels were getting ready to blow up our house, the
Union Vessel captured them & took them all prisoners! then we all re-
joiced & as there were many Soldiers, & not much to eat we all went
to cooking & carrying victuals to them. I carried a lot of fried cakes &
passed them around among the poor Soldiers; & I can see now how ea-
gerly they watched me & how thankful they looked & how happy we all
felt because our *Union was saved.* I beg of you to be careful of yourself,
& be willing to keep still, if necessary—in order to get your leg well:
spend your time in writing to me one week, & see if you cant fill a sheet
of foolscap—like this. Put in all the particulars if its only where you
sleep—who with, who you eat with, talk with—what you talk about—
think about—what you do evenings, where you sit, what you sit on,
how you look, how you feel—& how you are treated; any thing concerning you is of great interest to me. Tell me about every thing: How
do you enjoy your mind? Do you still find the Saviour precious to your
Soul? If so, how great is your happiness; how sweet your enjoyment: If
not, O, keep seeking till you find Him; let not your heart get faint—do

---

61. Joseph Myers, from Shepherd, was drafted and mustered as a private in the 23rd
Michigan Infantry on September 22, 1864. He joined the regiment at Johnsonville, Tennessee, on November 12. *Record of Service*, vol. 23, 76.

62. The fall equinox, in September when the sun crosses from north to south in the sky.

not get discouraged: The Christians life is a continual warfare: fighting to over come evil; Fighting for an incorruptible crown of glory! for a seat at the right hand of God. The promise is to the faithful: Then let us not get weary—let us *never* get faint. Fix your eye on the rich prize that awaits us. Look at the blessings that will attend us in this life, & ask Jesus to ever keep us faithful, so that should we be called to leave this world—at any time—we can say—

> Farewell Mortality, Jesus is mine.
> Welcome eternity, Jesus is *mine.*
> Welcome, O loved, and blest—
> Welcome, sweet scenes of rest,
> Welcome my Saviour's breast,
> Jesus is *mine.*[63]

Faithfully Yours—
Ellen L. Woodworth.

Ellen to Samuel

Mt Pleasant. Mich. Oct 2ond 1864. [Sunday]

Ever dear Husband—I received your welcome letter of the 24th ult & this beautiful Sabbath afternoon will devote to answering it. I have been down to the mills this forenoon to attend the funeral services of Henry Sheldon: He was a Soldier & died in hospital.[64] The meeting was held in the Indian Council house—Thomas Campbell[65] preached from the words—"Ye have fought a good fight"[66] &c. Celia & Emma, the children & I went. The children rode down but walked home with us. You say in your letter, "you cannot write as I do." O, Samuel dont say that again—If I have ever written any thing that has caused your heart

---

63. A hymn by Jane Catharine Bonar in *Songs for the Wilderness* (1855), 35–36; see Julian, *Dictionary of Hymnology*, 162.

64. Henry P. Sheldon, age nineteen, enlisted in Company C, 8th Michigan Infantry, on February 17, 1864, at Coe. Died May 18, 1864, at Fredericksburg, of wounds received in action on May 12, 1864. *Record of Service*, vol. 8, 120.

65. John T. Campbell, farmer, born around 1833, lived in Coe Township according to the 1860 Census. His twenty-one-year-old spouse, Sarah E. Campbell, and thirty-year-old brother, Thomas Campbell, also resided there. *Eighth Decennial United States Census*, Coe, Isabella, Mich., 16.

66. KJV, 2 Timothy 4:7.

to rejoice, as your last letter has mine, I am glad, indeed. When I read it, I wept for *joy*. Tears, bursting from an overflowing heart in thanksgiving, that at last, my husband had found that Pearl of greatest price. The life-long prayer of my heart is now answered. *Now* I have a christian Husband—a *praying* husband. One that will join with me in guiding the minds of our children aright, & by precept & example, teach them the way to live—That shall fit them for eternity. What can I render to my Heavenly Father for all his mercies? While many are languishing on beds of sickness, he keeps us in health. He watches over, & guards us from every harm. He has heard, & answered my prayers. He has watched over & protected you from dangers on every hand, & now he has put a new song into your mouth—new love into your heart, that the world can never give, or take away. Praise his name forever.

Tuesday, Oct. 4th. I & children well—Althea & Pettie sick with Ague. Mother not well—Pa getting ready to go out to St Johns for a load of stuff for himself. Wallace has sold his farm for $600, & bought Pa's for 1300; will move onto it next month.[67] Albert's children are sick with bloody dysentery; Willie & Dalton are quite sick—Mr Payne hired Caswells son-in-law as a substitute & gives him $800[68]; Every thing in the provision line getting dearer—butter is now 50 cts a pound—fresh pork 20 cts & other things accordingly. I expect to move into the house I have bargained for this week—Good bye for this time,

With love from all.—Yours as ever—

Ellen—

Samuel to Ellen

Stevenson Ala—Oct 5th 1864. [Wednesday]

Dear Ones at Home—I omitted writing last week—I did not get any mail until this morning: for the past ten days the cars have not been running: One train left here last friday at noon, got out 8 miles,

---

67. In 1870, William and Mary Preston were living adjacent to Wallace and Arsenath Preston in Union Township. *Ninth United States Decennial Census*; Isabella County, Michigan; p. 1.

68. Perhaps Norman C. Payne, first supervisor of Chippewa Township and a member of the Board of Supervisors for Isabella County, who had been drafted and was seeking to fulfill his obligation by obtaining someone (a "substitute") to take his place.

& found the track torn up. They were surrounded—3 of them shot, & all the rest taken prisoners except two that escaped, & came back. We have but a few men here now—barely enough to guard the place. I have been very busy—we work days and do picket duty at night; the most of the time. Rations are getting low—we have no meat & for three days we had each a small loaf of bread each day & coffee twice a day. To day we expect our full amount of rations again. I began to feel very anxious to hear from you—but the letter I received to day pays me for waiting—so full of hope and good news it cheers me on. I needed something of the kind just at this present time, for I was nearly played out. I have not had my clothes dry—two hours at a time in over a week—it has rained nearly all the time. We dont get our pay yet & dont know when we shall. Am glad to hear good news from Wallaces folks—tell her to be careful of herself, & baby. I am glad to hear of the enlistments there—it is a shame for men to desert their Country in this time of greatest need. We do not get news here—on account of not receiving newspapers for two weeks—but think we will, in a few days. I dont expect now to get home this fall unless the war comes to a close. If you & the boys keep good health I can stand it altho I do dread to stay out another cold, dreary winter. It has been a year now since I have slept under a roof & many nights in the open air yet my health is good except my leg is sore yet—I have used it pretty hard lately: but I have not felt the asthma in 8 months. You say you hope my Sabbaths are spent profitably to both Soul & body? That is what I intend to do, not only Sundays but every other day. Love to the children—& excuse a short letter this time for want of time to write. Good bye—

from your Husband—S. W.

Samuel to Ellen

Stevenson Ala—Oct 9th 1864. [Sunday]

To my Dear Wife, & Children. Another pleasant Sabbath morning has dawned upon us, & we have the blessed privilege of resting, which we all stand in need of—we have had busy times & bad weather for the past two weeks. I received a letter friday from you & will try & answer a part of the questions you asked. Am glad to hear you are getting along so nicely, but somewhat surprised at your buying so expensive a place at present, but I will do all I can to help you pay for it. The rumor is in Camp again this morning that we are to be mustered out, & are not to receive any more pay until we go out—If I get what is coming to me I can get home with about $150, perhaps more. I soon shall have six months pay due, at 18 dollars a month; there is $75, government bounty coming to me yet. If we have good luck & our health, we can pay for it: but it is very uncertain where I shall be—I am as liable to be in some rebel prison, or a rebel bullet may put a stop to me earning any more, but we will hope for the best; Dont stint yourself or the boys—nor ever let them cry for bread—and now for the questions—1st where do I sleep? Sometimes on the ground—or on a bunk in my tent; last night in the open air with my head leaning against a stump, about a mile from camp only I didn't sleep—as I was on picket duty—it was a cold night, & hard frost. Sometimes I sleep in a fort or in a blockhouse. I have sat on most every thing but a chair, but have not sat on one, or slept in a bed, since I left Detroit. My leg does not get well, but my health is good—but I must close for this time—hoping to hear from you soon—Good bye & may Heavens choicest blessings be showered on my ever dear wife and children—

Samuel Woodworth.

Ellen to Samuel

Mt Pleasant Oct 9th 1864—

Sabbath Afternoon—Dear Husband—Here I am sitting cosy & comfortable in our own, "new home." Last night is the first we have slept here—though I commenced moving thursday. There is a large front room (which will be our living room this winter), a large bed-room, pantry, kitchen, small bed-room & wood-room below. They are not done off inside yet, but I shall have them ceiled & papered this winter, & then they will be comfortable. We are having a taste of cold weather now—yesterday was very cold, & this morning the ground was white with snow, but it soon disappeared, beneath the mild rays of an October sun. Vesper is now getting supper, while I am writing; he has put over the kettles—got the potatoes ready—& is urging me to do the rest so he can eat & get in his night-wood.

Well supper is over—Shall I tell you what we had? Potatoes & *soda-*

gravy—squash—bread & butter—sugar & tea, with good appetites for relish. It is now evening. I have just read the 58th chapter of Isaiah—knelt with my precious children in prayer—kissed them good night—& tucked them warmly in their snug little bed—so while they are sweetly sleeping, I will spend a few moments more in writing to the dearest friend I have on earth; "the object of my waking thoughts, the idol of my dreams,"[69] and though seperated so far, I feel that are hearts now centre on one theme—that will elevate & purify our thoughts, & fill our hearts with love, joy & happiness. That theme, is the religion of the meek & lowly Saviour—

Monday Evening—Pa has just got home from St Johns—He bought considerable stuff for Fanchers folks—& himself. He paid $18.50 for three common delaine dress patterns: for Ma, Celia, & Emma—I sent for half a pound of tea & some Kerosene oil. Couldn't afford myself a new dress just now—though perhaps I need one, & several other things if I would allow myself to think so. We are to have a nice addition to our village, which will add to the beauty & value of our place—& that is, the erection of a church—Mr Bradley has been over & selected the lots, which Mr Mortons Uncle has donated: they lie next to Pa's on the east, so we will be close to meeting. I will make a drawing of the "City" so you can see where the church is to be. This dotted mark is the main street, running north & south [see illustration].

This is the size & extent of our village at present—but it will increase in size—this winter & the coming Spring. The children are pleased to live here, as they can play in the yard without trespassing & Dallie says he can *Sing* without waking up Grandma. Grandpa brought them some apples to night & they are enjoying them; Next week is Indian payment[70] & a photographer is expected here. I will get our pictures & send you. It is now tuesday evening & I will try & finish my letter. The clock is just striking nine. Children sleeping in quiet rest, & in the stillness of my cosy room, by the cheerful fire, I will finish up this lengthy letter; The question that comes to me, is where is my absent one? Is he

---

69. Perhaps from Beazley, *Roue*, 58.

70. Article 2 of the 1855 treaty required the U.S. government to make certain payments to the Ojibwe in annual installments. A total of over $200,000 was due to be paid to the Odawas and Ojibwe from 1865 on, and the payments during 1863–1864 were made in currency (i.e., paper dollars), not coin, as the treaty required. *Statutes at Large*, vol. XI, 634; *Report of the Commissioner*, 453–454.

sleeping beneath his tent or out on the lonely watch: perchance resting wearily on his hard knapsack—with no covering but the stars above
him. (O Father, hasten the day when our brave Soldier boys, now struggling with hardships & sorrow—may return to brighten the homes that
so anxiously await them.) Keep a brave heart—my Boy—for the day
will dawn, ere long—when Slavery—& rebellion will be wiped out—and
the heroes of this war come proudly marching home. Then will joy &
gladness take the place of heart-aches, & tears—& toil & trials be forgotten. Till then good-bye & the blessed Saviour keep thee from all harm
is the prayer of your—Ellen

Samuel to Ellen

Stevenson Ala—Oct 15th 1864. [Saturday]

Dear Ellen—I am having a few days of rest, & will write again to you
altho I have not heard from you since I wrote. I am doctoring my leg,
& riging up for winter—that is getting new clothes & blankets. I wrote
Sunday that we did not expect to get paid off at present but monday
morning the pay-master came & gave us 4 months pay—but he thinks
we will go home by Dec 1st & I will not send any until I see how matters
turn. we hear all sorts of rumors, only to have it contradicted. The 58th
New York regiment came here last tuesday & we are relieved from Infantry duty. Our work is done here & we are under marching orders—
but may stay here some time yet. The weather is nice & cool here now,
wouldn't I like to be at home to day with my nice little family—in our
own new house! I think if we can pay for it it will be a good investment—& if we have our health—we will. It is much pleasanter for you,
& the children, to be by yourselves—and also for Grandpas folks—It
will be pretty expensive for you to keep boarders—but do as you think
best. Sunday—Oct 16th. Are you well this morning Dear Ellen? I wish
I could see & ask you that question & various others—O how much I
would like to be there to day. It is a nice quiet day here in camp—and I
feel that I am doing my duty to my God, & my country—& that is a satisfaction that I was a stranger to—one year ago. I have come to the conclusion that it is a just war—I have had an opportunity to learn something of the horrid institution of Slavery. O how wicked; how cruel! I
have conversed with a great many, from all parts of the south that have

come into our lines for protection—& it has drawn tears from my eyes to listen to their sad story.

There are some very inteligent Negroes—when I get home I will tell you some of their sad history. You will now call me an abolishionist; all right; When I know I am wrong, I give up willingly. I had my likeness taken last night—it is not very well done—I will send it to you—also Celia a ring. They are made of guta-percha[71] & ornamented with silver; & are durable—Do not praise me in your letters—I am a weak & changable mortal, surrounded with temptation—yet I mean to be firm in my pursuit for the right—& with the help of a great & merciful God, I will be a true Christian. I know I have your prayers; they have been supplicating long, & ardently for me, & you will receive your reward. That Heavens choicest blessings may rest upon my devoted family—& guide them in the path of duty is the wish of your Absent Husband.

To Ellen: from Samuel

Ellen to Samuel

Mt Pleasant. Oct 18th 1864. [Tuesday]

Dearest Husband—Why did I not get one word from you last week? To day I have heard the report that your regiment had been taken *prisoners*, and if I thought it true I should go wild—but I dont believe it—I think the reason your letters are delayed, is because they dont always reach St Johns in time for Mondays mail—so they must lay over there, a whole week—which causes sad disappointment. We are all well—That is the children & I, with the exception of colds. We have had some bad weather—though for a few days it has been lovely—October weather—warm & hazy—with beautiful moonlight evenings—just such as I used to listen for the welcome sound of Fannys fleet footsteps & the iron-axle buggy—to say nothing of the little driver.—Those were happy years—dear Samuel; how I love to recall them. Yet I believe there are happier ones in store for us.—

We now have a firmer foundation to build upon—a faith that sustains us, & centers our hopes & joys on a risen Redeemer—who has gone

---

71. A latex substance derived from a tree native to the southern hemisphere.

to prepare a bright home for his children—& yet who is ever present with us to guide & direct us if we but put our trust in Him. Dear Samuel may we ever be found walking in this perfect trust, & faith. I have no news to write this week, I wrote it all last week. Vesper is getting quite a wood-pile—he chops very handy—has now just commenced on a large beech log that Grandpa drew up for him. Dallie is as busy as a bee—from morning till night—about something. He wants me to tell his Papa to come home, & not stay away so long—I tell him papa will come as soon as the war is over, but that he has to help build railroads & bridges, so that all the Soldiers can ride home—after they have made the naughty men, South—behave themselves. To night I am invited to a Social to Mr Arnolds—dont know as I shall attend—yet it is a great treat for the few there are to go. Refreshments are served—the conversation is both religious & political—closing with singing & prayer—How I wish we had a melodeon[72]—Our children have such sweet voices, & such a musical talent. When you come home we will talk about buying one, wont we? Every body here thinks the last draft has been made, that will be necessary, & that fighting will cease, when it is known positively who will be our next president, whether it will be "honest Abe" or little Mac.[73] For my part, it makes but little difference to me which is elected, if it but be the one best fitted to close this terrible war, and restore peace to our suffering country—Keep up good courage my dear Samuel for surely a kind providence watches over those that put their trust in Him; & the day may not be far distant, when you, & I, & our little ones, will be gathered again around our happy fireside. Be true to God, to yourself, & your Country, & all will be well with you. You may have trials to endure—but the promise is to those who stand firm & steadfast, to the end. I do hope to hear from you to morrow. The Children send much love to you. Excuse a short letter this week, & I will do better next time. Write often—& as lengthy as possible.

(Good bye, & Heaven bless you.) Ever Yours—E. L. W.

> Like the shadow on the dial—lingers still our parting kiss—
> Life has no severer trial—death no pang to equal this;
> But within our little cottage, one fond heart will love thee still—

---

72. A small keyboard-operated musical instrument similar to an organ.

73. General George B. McClellan, the Democratic Party candidate against Lincoln in November 1864.

Ever praying God to keep thee; keep thee safe from every ill:
Other skies will bend above thee, other hearts may seek thy shrine,
But no other heart will love thee, with the *constancy* of mine.[74]

E. L. W.

Samuel to Ellen

Stevenson, Ala. Oct 21st 1864. [Friday]

Dear Ellen—It is ten o clock—but I must write a few lines to you—to
let you know how I am, as we have orders to go early in the morning
to Atlanta, Ga. My health is good at present. I will send some money
in this, though I have not given up all hope of getting home this fall.
I hear that Sherman has whipped Hood again & taken 4000 prisoners[75]—I think it is so for 1500 passed through here to day.—As bad as
I want to come home, I would like the satisfaction of helping wind up
this war—we can whip them, & they know it, and if we have to stay
this winter, I am glad to go South. It is 200 miles from here. I received
your letter of the 12th; never fear of writing too long ones—I never
tire of reading your letters.—I was reading my testament when the Orderly brought the letter to me.—I carry it in my pocket, & when I have
a spare moment I read it—I want to understand my whole duty. I long
to be with you, that I may learn of you. I will put 20 dollars in this, &
if I do not come—will send more. It costs me something to live—I cant
eat the old hard-tack—some of it full of worms—nor stinking bacon—as
soon as I try to eat it, it makes me sick; & so I buy my own food—soft
bread, & cheese—milk & some corn cake, when I could get them. (Saturday after dinner.) Our Knapsacks were all packed ready to start—
when a dispatch came for us to stay here—till further orders: it isn't
the first time we have been fooled—Our Colonel is bound we shall be

---

74. From "We Part For Ever", Morris, *Poems by George P. Morris*, 218–219. Ellen modified
the verses to fit their situation and in a more hopeful light.

75. After abandoning Atlanta to Sherman, Hood moved his forces to threaten the
Union supply line. Sherman responded by sending troops north, which, on October 16,
encountered Hood's rear guard at Ship's Gap, Georgia, between Resaca and LaFayette.
The results: "had some skirmishing and captured a number of prisoners;" "most of the
rebel infantry fell into our hands." *OR*, vol. 39, pt. 1, 603, 742. Woodworth's estimate was
too high.

mustered out this fall—Vesper & Dallie be good boys—always speak the truth. May Heaven bless & protect my Dear Wife & Children is the prayer of your absent Husband

& Father—Samuel Woodworth.

Ellen to Samuel

Mt Pleasant—Oct 24th 1864. [Monday]

I received two letters from you last mail—was very glad to hear you was well,—but from your letter I infer you are in more danger from the enemy—which is a source of great anxiety to me. You say you are liable to be in some Rebel prison! why are you left so unguarded? You surely have not apprehended such danger before—or else you have kept it from me. How can I bear the thought that you must ever languish in their vile prisons—subject to the treatment that our Soldiers have to endure at their hands: No! no: It cannot, it *must* not be so, & I will not dwell on such a supposition—for I believe a watchful eye—is over my Absent One—& will shield him in the hour of danger. We are all usually well—but I have a patient now in my care—that is very sick of Lung-fever.[76] A lumber-man taken sick in Camp & no friends to care for him—His overseer brought him to town & hired me to take him in & care for him. He is a Canadian—22 years old—Poor boy, I feel sorry for him, & do all I can for him—the doctor comes every other day & he takes his medicine without a murmur—he has been here since last friday—to day he sleeps most of the time—he is *very sick*. His name is Michael Holuhan. Lester[77] talks of coming west again—Land is very high now—a good many coming in in search of farms—Wallace was offered 200, more than he paid Pa for his—already—but did not take it. (Wednesday Morning, Oct. 26th). Our poor sufferer Michael has left this world of sorrow, & his body now lies ready for burial—he died last night—very quietly. We done all we could for his comfort, & I done

---

76. Perhaps pneumonia.

77. Lester Woodworth, younger brother of Samuel, born 1838 in Java Center, New York, died July 28, 1909, Java Village, New York, age seventy-one. Find a Grave, https://www.findagrave.com/memorial/63857302/lester-woodworth. In the 1860 Census, he was living in the home of his parents, Charles and Nancy Woodworth, along with Arsenath, nineteen, and Vira A., ten. *Eighth United States Decennial Census*, Java, Wyoming, N.Y., 855.

for him, as I would for a brother,—or as I would wish a friend of mine
cared for—if they were among strangers. The doctor & Pa stayed with
him last night—so I & the children staid with Mother—& did not see
him die. I talked with him in the evening & asked him if he was ready
& willing to go. He said "One year more & I will willingly go, but now
I want to see Mother." Poor boy; he will meet his mother only at the
judgment day, & then I hope, to dwell with her in the mansions of the
blest. The children are well—I am some tired, but shall get rested in a
few days—I have but little news to write—& my head is somewhat con-
fused, so will not write as lengthy as usual—The funeral will be tomorrow. Do not worry for fear the children will suffer for anything: They
wont, as long as we are spared to them; & surely not, while *I live*. The
Artist did not come—so I cannot send their pictures. We dont get much
war news—Probably wont until after Election. If I was a *man*, I should
vote for Abraham Lincoln, by all means, for I never could favor the
Rebels enough to help elect a man of their choice. Their hopes are built
on the election of McLellan.[78]

Good bye for this time—Ever yours—E. L. W.

Samuel to Ellen

Stevenson Ala—Oct 24th 1864. [Monday]

Dear Wife—I will write a few words & send you $10,00 more. I sent
20,00 Saturday. I will also send my likeness—I am going out on the
road—to work a few days. I shall send more money the next time I
write. I am well & hope this will find you the same, & that you will receive the money safely. Good bye for this time—I must go—remember
me as your absent & ever true Husband—Samuel Woodworth.

Nov 3d/64. Again I seat myself to pen a few lines to the dearest
friend I have on earth. I am sorry to have you worry so about me—
if you don't get my letters regular.—The Rebs are doing all they can to
stop communication: they have burned a number of trains lately be-

---

78. The Democratic Party platform called for peace negotiations with the Confederacy
without an end to slavery. In contrast, Lincoln sought to prosecute the war to victory and
emancipation. Rafuse, *McClellan's War*; Perret, *Lincoln's War*.

tween here & Louisville; & I fear they have got some of my letters that contained money. We have not had any mail in two weeks. I have been out on the road about ten miles from here: we finished & came to camp to day. I have not wrote since a week last monday. I hope to hear to-morrow from you. We are having hard fighting all around us—but I guess it will stop; for Sherman has sent 10 or 12000 Soldiers here this week & they will guard the road now for awhile.[79] I have sent $30,00 & have 20 more to send—but will wait till I hear you have received what I have sent. My health is good. I feel the best I have in a long time. I am glad to hear Vesper is so good to his mama—& so industrious at the wood pile. I would be very glad to get you a Melodeon, but think we can not afford one until we get the place paid for; then if I come home I will see what I can do about it. It is 12 o clock night & I must close—good night. Friday the 4th. This is a cold rainy morning, yet I am contented & I might say happy. I have much to be thankful for,—how dark & dreary such days used to be to me: How could I have lived so long in sin & wickedness? how blind I was, to all that was pure, & good. I feel as though I have a Friend, who is with me at all times, & who will sustain me in a trying hour. I know not how soon my time will come to meet my God, & give an account of my conduct here.—I have sinned against Him, but I will do so no more. I have no desire to turn again from the path of truth: my mind is constantly seeking to know my duty, & the desire of my heart is to do right. I will look to Jesus for help; for He hath said "Look unto me & be saved." How precious those words—how soothing to an aching heart. O how I wish I could express my feelings to you, Ellen. But you know the joy of a soul freed from sin: my prayer is that we may always be found in the path of duty. May heaven bless you my dear Wife & children, is the prayer of your Absent Husband.

S. W.

---

79. After unsuccessfully seeking to bring Hood to battle, Sherman would decide to abandon his supply line from Atlanta to Nashville and strike out in a "March to the Sea" across Georgia and South Carolina. He would provide for a defense of Nashville and Chattanooga, hoping that Hood would attack Union forces entrenched there. Fredriksen, *Civil War Almanac*, 689, 771–772.

Ellen to Samuel

Mt. Pleasant Nov 7th 1864. [Monday]

My Dear Husband—Again I take my pen to inform you of what is transpiring in this northern Country, & also to let you know that I received two letters last week—one containing 20, & the other 10 dollars, also your likeness—which looks just like you: Our own Papa-Sam. The children have to show it to every body that comes in; & you may be sure we all look at it, *some.* We are all well—I have one boarder so I have a little more to do—than when I & the children are alone. He is the Editor & Proprietor of our paper (that is to be) & his name is Church.[80] You needn't be at all jealous, because I have got a literary companion here, for he is a little wrinkled up old man, nearly bald-headed & wears spectacles: is very quiet, says but little, & occupies the chamber. So now I have given you a fair discription of my boarder. I entertained the club Social last week—(each one contributes toward refreshments.) The house was full, & every thing passed off pleasantly. There were present Mr & Mrs Arnold—Mr & Mrs Kinney—Mr & Mrs Fancher, Wallace & Arsene—Young Mr Bradl[e]y & Miss Hines—Mary Mosher—Miss Gulick,[81] Old Mrs Bradl[e]y, Mrs Williams, Mrs Nellie Nelson, Albert, Celia & Emma, & my *Editor*, besides a good quantity of children. Our supper consisted of Bread & butter, crackers & cheese—cookies & several kinds of cake—with coffee, cream & sugar. The next one will be held at the house of I.E. Arnolds at the "Mills." Yesterday our new Circuit Preacher, preached in the Court House. His name is *Garlick*.[82] After sermon he called here, & took tea. To day I have been very busy baking, & doing all sorts of house-work. To morrow is Election, & there may be some here to dinner. Last friday I attended a *select* Tea-party, given by Mrs Arnold in honor of Mr Mosher's wife & daughter who have just come in to the woods—Mrs A[rnold] sent her horse & buggy for

---

80. "O. B. Church started a weekly paper called the *Northern Pioneer*"; its first issue was dated November 30, 1864. Church also acted as notary public. Fancher, *Past and Present,* 191; Cumming, *This Place Mount Pleasant,* 27–28.

81. Likely Martha Ellen Gulick (1847–1923). Find a Grave, https://www.findagrave .com/memorial/72992558/martha-ellen-bellingar.

82. Likely L. M. Garlick of the Methodist Episcopal Church. Ellis, *History of Shiawassee and Clinton,* 412, 505.

me & Mrs Fancher, & after tea Mr Arnold brought us home. Mrs Babbitt, & Nellie—Mrs Mosher & her daughter—Althea & myself—were all
that were invited—a very stylish, & aristocratic affair. Our place here is
fast changing hands—from the original owners—Dr Corbus has bought
two lots north of me & intends building before long. How I wish you
were here to night, Vesper & Dallie have just gone to bed—& I can hear
the sound of their innocent voices repeating their evening prayer—the
last words of which come distinctly to my ear—as I am writing—God
bless papa & mama, & pardon all our sins, & make us good little boys,
Amen. Surely God will hear their little prayers & watch over the Absent
one, & bring him safely to his little ones, to join with them—ere long—
in their evening devotions. You say you have not given up all hope of
coming home this fall! I have not either—yet I dare not hope too much
for the chances are—if you are able to work—you will be kept as long as
any body. The fire is out & I must bid you good night—& finish this in
the morning.

　　Tuesday Evening—I did not get to write this morning—The Election
is now over & this town elected their Union ticket[83]—Mr Bentley is now
Treasurer insted of Mosher—Wallace is Register of deeds—Milton Bradley, County Clerk—but as you have a ticket you will see who are on it. It
is a warm rainy day—the air feels like summer, but I expect it is only the
precursor of cold winter, weather. I cant help but dread it—as I have no
one to get up cold mornings & build fires as I used to have—recollect if
you come home this winter, you will have that to do—now hadn't you
rather stay where you are? We have received glorious War news—if true.
Grant has captured half of Lee's army; and Sheridan is sweeping all before him.[84] Three *Cheers* for the *red, white,* & *blue*. To morrow is Vespers
10th birthday.—Ten years ago comes vividly to my recollection. How little we then realized what changes ten years would bring! And yet—to
us—it might have been far worse—for our lives have all been spared—
mercifully preserved mid the changes time has wrought—and I trust we
both have found the narrow path that leads up the shining way, to a
home in glory! to the Mansion of the blest: O let us ever persue it with

---

83. The National Union Party, comprising Republicans and War Democrats, won the
national election as well, reelecting Abraham Lincoln. Waugh, *Reelecting Lincoln.*

84. The report as to Grant was untrue; Major General Philip A. Sheridan had, on October 19, defeated the main Confederate force at Cedar Creek in the Shenandoah Valley of
Virginia, rendering it no longer a threat. Frederiksen, *Civil War Almanac,* 767, 769.

watchfulness & prayer that our feet stumble not, or turn aside into the path of the tempter. To-morrow is mail day again—with hopes of hearing again from my dear Husband. I will send you a copy of our paper as soon as published—It is to be called the "Northern Pioneer." Let me beg of you to keep money enough, *always* to provide decent food for yourself.—*Shame* on a government that will allow the brave Soldiers, to eat wormy Bread, & putrid Bacon! I would rather never receive a penny from you—dont deprive yourself of anything that you need. Remember me to all your comrades that are with you, & write *every week*, if *possible*. Good Night.

Accept the love of your affectionate Children, & devoted Ellen—

Samuel to Ellen

Stevenson. Ala—Nov 8th 1864. [Tuesday]

Dearest Ellen—It is now 10 o clock but I am not sleepy, so I will write the news—I had the pleasure of seeing Charley Youngs & Jo Myers[85]— as they were passing through here. Wasn't I glad to see them—& didn't they shake me though? Charley said he would give much to stay with me—they looked hard—they had been to Altanta & were on their way back to Nashville. They dont like to board with "Uncle Sam" & they see the need of money—I let Charley have $10,00. He said his wife would make it right with you. I was glad that I could help them. We had a great deal to say, & a short time to say it in, but when he spoke of you my eyes filled with tears: what is it that chokes me at such times? O it is a mystery to me how I could voluntarily have left my precious family in the woods; & when he told me how sad & lonely you appeared, & how pale & poor you looked last winter, the tears came fast, & freely. Can you forgive me, my noble, uncomplaining Wife? If my life is spared I will be more considerate, & if possible, to make our "woodland Home" pleasant, it shall be: I have those pretty verses nearly learned by heart—I thank you for them. I fear your care for others will tax your

---

85. Joseph Myers from Shepherd was drafted and mustered in as private to the 23rd Michigan Infantry on September 22, 1864. He joined the regiment at Johnsonville, Tennessee, on November 12. *Record of Service*, vol. 23, 76.

strength. I know it is living up to the golden rule to feed the hungry & care for the destitute—and the poor Stranger that you cared for needed a friend & his Mother will bless you, & God will reward you for such acts of kindness.

But do not take to much upon your slender shoulders—I should be wild with grief to hear you were sick—or those dear children. There is not an hour in the day, that I do not ask God to sustain you, & protect you & those precious boys from harm, & lead them in the path of truth. It is late & I must close. We have had our Election here to day— Two-thirds of the votes were for Lincoln. I did not vote. Thursday 10th. I will finish my letter & start it onward so it wont lay over in St Johns. This is one of the finest days I ever saw—so clear & cool; but we have had two days of cold rain. I hope to hear that you have got the money I sent. My health is good. The old regiment has gone home & we are left[86]—The Captain says I shall have a furlough—I dont know as I want one—coming back again will be harder than staying here. Little boys remember your papa—dont forget me will you? I think of you often, & hope to live to see you. Good bye for this time.

Sam.

Ellen to Samuel

Mt Pleasant. Mich—Nov 13th 1864. [Sunday]

My Dear Husband. Another week has rolled around, & this pleasant Sabbath eve finds me writing again to the Absent one. We are all well, & are anxious to hear the same from you. Last week the Detroit mail did not come in, consequently I did not get any letter from you. You will probably know by this time whether the prospects are more favorable for your getting discharged. I dont like to live in such suspense—hoping—yet not daring to hope for fear of disappointment. I have rented the wing part of my house to our new County Clerk—Milton Bradley. They are nice people & have two little children. He gives me a dollar a week rent—for the winter & will move in this week. Then I

---

86. The three-year terms of 1861 enlistees in the regiment had ended, and they were officially mustered out on October 31, journeying home by rail in the succeeding days. Hoffman, *Among the Enemy*, 141–143.

have 4,50 a week for boarding Mr Church. I make our expenses as light as possible—but yet it costs a good deal to live, everything is so dear. I have to pay Pa 1,25 per week for fire wood, he furnishes it all split up ready to burn. I have had an application to teach the Gulick School this winter. He offered me a house to live in & $26,00 a month. Then I could rent this part of my house for a dollar a week to Mr Church—& the 2,00 for the house & 6,50 a week for teaching would enable me to make another payment on my house in the Spring. There is nothing certain about us having a Post Office established here at the County Seat—this winter & if there is I might not be appointed Post Mistress— though that has been the talk. Wallace moves this week down onto his farm. He has taken their school to teach this winter, & Emma will board with them & attend school. Their little boy Worth is a nice baby, & very pretty. Fancher goes to Detroit next week to buy new furni- ture for their parlor—& talks of a new Piano. Celia is at home now & is to teach the school that I taught last summer. She gets six dollars a week, & boards at home. Mothers health is better now. I have had Martha Gulick helping me to day & getting my goods all placed in my part of the house. We have scoured the pantry—cleaned the win- dows & doors—chamber, & stairs & room below—baked bread—four mince pies—cookies—& ironed a basket of clothes—got 3 meals &c.— how is that for being smart? We have had a little snow & some quite cold weather; & now the ground is frozen hard.

(Wednesday Morning). I must finish my letter & send it out this morning. I do hope the mailbags will contain half a dozen letters for me to day. I hardly know what to decide, about teaching this winter. I must let the Director know this afternoon. I dislike to move up there, with my children—& only for earning the money—I would not think of it. You will think I am "covetous of gain" I am afraid, No, not that, but I want to do what I can.[87] I have been making the children some nice red flannel shirts. Vesper has just put his on this morning, & thinks it pretty nice. I had to pay a dollar a yard but that is cheaper than factory cotton cloth at 80 cts. Another of those Lumbermen died at the Mills, & was buried yesterday. They have an epidemic among them called

---

87. The quoted phrase may derive from Niccolò Machiavelli, *Il Principe* ("The Prince"), first published in 1532, and mentioned in early American political thought; alternatively, the issue of coveting, i.e., to yearn or lust for something, is a biblical subject.

"Diphtheria of the Lungs" the same that Michael[88] died with, which proves often fatal. There are 300 men now in the pineries, lumbering, but my time is up & I must close. Good bye & may Heaven protect you in all your wanderings, & bring you safely home is the prayer of your—
Ellen

Samuel to Ellen

Stevenson. Ala—Nov 16th 1864. [Wednesday]

Again I seat myself to pen a few lines to my precious wife & children. I would like to be at home this cold rainy day. O, wouldn't I? Yes indeed! It seems as though sometimes I *must* come home, but Abraham has a firm hold of me, so I shall have to stay; yet he clothes me well, & feeds us—such as it is. It is the sleeping that troubles me most. I worked a couple of days in the wet & took cold in my leg: it commenced swelling, & became very painful. The Doctor poulticed it, & it has broken out from the knee to the foot. The Captain & Lieutenant[89] staid with me & bathed it in salt & water. The Captain says I shall not work any more till he knows it is well, & sound. I have to lay it upon a stool while I write, & it is quite comfortable. I think it will be some time before I can work, but may be not. I cannot walk much or sit with my foot on the ground, but when kept up, it does not pain so very much. I spend my time in reading: we get all kinds of reading matter, but there is none so acceptable as that, that comes from you. I look for a letter soon from you. I want to hear if the money reached you. Do not worry about me. I have told you full as bad as it is. The Captain said if I wanted a furlough he would get me one; I told him I did not, at present. I must insist on your being more careful of your health. Think of the responsibility resting upon you—who would care for those little boys if you were sick? The idea has become so impressed on my mind that it is with a trembling

---

88. Michael Houlahan, who had died in her home in October 1864.

89. Presumably First Lieutenant Daniel M. Moore of Rome Township, who entered service September 27, 1861, Company D, 1st Engineers and Mechanics; promoted to first lieutenant, September 1, 1863, and captain, November 3, 1864; and Second Lieutenant Caleb A. Ensign of Jonesville, who entered service October 22, 1862, Battery C, 1st Light Artillery; commissioned second lieutenant, 1st Engineers and Mechanics, December 8, 1863, and first lieutenant, Mar. 11, 1864. Robertson, *Michigan in the War*, 891, 823.

hand I open a letter that comes from Isabella. O, heed what I say. I must close for to day & eat my supper, it is ready for me. The Captains Cook has just sent me a nice pumpkin pie. Every one is very kind to me; I do not deserve such kindness.

Thursday Morning—This is a nice morning. Every thing is very quiet about here now. Our Company are all out on detail, except 8, or 10 that are doing light duty here. There is not much war news. Sherman is destroying every thing south of Chatanooga: he will start on a big raid soon: They say he is bound for the Sea-coast, our regiment are with him, all except Co. M. & L. They will see hard times I fear. except my leg—I feel well. I walked down to the Cooks shanty this morning. I will try & spend my time as pleasantly & profitably as possible. I feel our Saviour, Jesus Christ will sustain me, if I am true to my trust. Other refuge have I none—hangs my helpless soul on Thee.

Good bye—From your affectionate Husband—S. W.

Ellen to Samuel

Mt Pleasant. Nov 21st 1864. [Monday]

My Dear Sam   I received your letter last Friday, after waiting two long weeks without hearing from you—the roads are in such condition the mail could not get through, until friday; but I have your welcome letter, telling me you are well, & I feel much better about you. We are all well; I wrote you last week that I thought of taking a winter school—but I have not. I was so undecided I failed to let them know in time & they have hired another teacher. Mr. Gulick told me, he would have given me a dollar a week more than he pays her & built fires—if he had known I would teach. Well I feel it is all for the best—though I would have liked to be earning more than I am. Mr Bradleys family now live here & I find them very agreeable neighbors; and my boarder makes my fire every morning so I find it quite comfortable, & pleasant, so far.—Lester & his wife have come to try their fortune in the woods—once more. They got here last Wednesday noon; staid with me that day & the next went down to Wallaces.—Lel calculates to work in the Lumber Camp & Marie will stay with Arsene. They have a little boy about Worth's age. I dont know which has changed—Lester, or I; but it seems to me he is much more rough in his language—& less refined than he used to be, & besides that he is a decided *Copperhead*.[90] So different from my dear Husband: O how I love to peruse your precious letters, & linger over them drinking in the sweet expressions of purity, & heavenly love, they contain. What a source of comfort it is to me to know that my husband is daily growing in grace—every day rising higher above the dross of worldliness, & sin. & becoming more & more a devoted follower of Christ.

> O, how happy are they whom the Savior obey,
> And have laid up their treasure above;
> Tongue can *never* express the sweet comfort, & peace
> Of a soul in its earliest love.[91]

Is it not so? O happy day, when we can bow together before the throne of grace in praises to God for all his goodness to us. I am also glad to see that your views on the question of Slavery, and the justness of the course pursued by our leaders in this war, is changing—from what your belief was formerly. There are none so blind as those that *wont* see; is an old adage—and Lester & Albert are of that type—But if any one will listen to reason and look for the *right*, they will not be governed by party spirit, when truth, & *Justice* tells them they are in error. Last friday, a sad accident occurred down to Salt River—Mr Kuntz (the man that lived on our place) took his gun for the purpose of hunting & went as far as Wessels store—he stepped in said good morning—& at the same time set his gun by his side, when by some means it went off—the ball passing in just below his cheek & penetrated the brain. He never spoke again—but breathed a couple of hours, & expired.— He leaves a Wife & two little ones, in poverty. Poor woman—my heart aches for her. Tell me something of the boys that enlisted with you: what kind of soldier is Alonzo.—You recollect the *Sabbath* evening he came to our house & wanted you to play cards? O, Sam—you did not realize then how badly I felt, & how *wicked* such things seemed, to me, and why I shed tears, when I thought you were going to play, & that you should be drawn in to such company: They were not tears of anger, but of sorrow: and now you realize how distasteful such things are. O

---

90. Term for one who favored ending the war without emancipation or victory over the rebellion.

91. From the hymn "O How Happy Are They!" by Charles Wesley (1707–1788) in *Hymns and Sacred Poems*, 123.

how differently the holy spirit & the word of God, lead us to see things from what we do when living in a state of unbelief, & sin.

(Tuesday Evening). It is very cold to night, & trying hard to snow, though we have none yet, to speak of. Albert came up to night & brought me a chicken for Thanksgiving which is day after tomorrow. He is feeling pretty sober for there was another draft made last week & he has heard that he was one of the number drawn—though he has not yet been notified. O I hope not, for his family's sake—How could they spare him?

I suppose Uncle Abraham is elected, sure enough, & I do hope to hear that the Rebels are now willing to give up, beaten—and not prolong this war another four years in the vain hope of electing a President to suit them. I am tired to night & must go to bed. I have done my washing & cleaning to day—besides my house work. The children are in bed & asleep, long ago. I have got them new warm stockings & mittens for winter & am making Vesper a coat, out of your old black frock coat. The children are well & grow fast. They talk of their Papa, a good deal—everyday. The clock is striking 10. & I must be up early in the morning—Good Night—& think often of your

Affectionate Wife,

E. L. Woodworth.

Samuel to Ellen

Stevenson. Ala. Nov 24th 1864. [Friday]

Again, Dearest Ellen, I seat myself—with pleasure to write a few lines to you: I am well except my ankle & that is improving. I am excused from duty yet; The Doctor think the sores on my leg are of a scrofulous nature[92] & very hard to cure—he says he can heal them up, but exposure or hard marching, will cause them to break out again. We have marching orders again—we are ordered to Nashville from thence out on the northwestern road to build Block-houses, this winter.[93] I, for one would rather went farther south, on some accounts I have been here so

---

92. I.e., a swollen or ulcerous condition. *Lexicon Medicum*, 274-275.

93. On November 21, Hood's army left Florence, Alabama, en route to Nashville. Long, *Civil War Day by Day*, 598.

long, I have got some what attached to this place. It seems like home to me: not my dear home in the woods, O, no, there is no place so dear to *me*, as that. Home, *Sweet home*, there is no place on earth, like it. Will I ever have the blessed privilege of seeing my home, & dear friends again? I do believe I shall; and this hope cheers me to look forward to a bright, & happy future. We are talking of having a grand Thanksgiving supper to-night, if we do I will tell you tomorrow what we had. (Nov 25th) Good morning: How do you find yourself this morning? well; & happy, I hope. We had our Thanksgiving Supper, and it was a *grand* one. We had Oysters, warm biscuit, & butter, crackers, custard-pie & a good cup of *tea*; & we enjoyed it hugely. O there are better days a com-ing—by & bye.—I did not get any letter from this mornings mail, & feel disappointed. Do you imagine there is any danger of my being jealous of your literary boarder? no, I guess not, but I do begrudge him, his new home. Take good care of yourself & children—and remember me as your best earthly-friend, at all times. Good bye—From your ever true (Sam.)

Ellen to Samuel

Mt Pleasant. Mich. Nov 29th 1864. [Tuesday]

Ever Remembered Husband—This evening finds me—as usual—sit-ting pen in hand—thinking of the absent one—& trying to trace a few scattering thoughts on paper—for your perusal. We are all well, and the children now both stand beside me—Vesper with his slate & pen-cil—and Dallie with a book—asking questions on various subjects. To day has been warm, & windy; yesterday & last night very rainy—& has cleared of pleasant; but we can't expect it to last long. I am glad you had an opportunity of seeing some of your friends from this way. It must have been a pleasant surprise on both sides. The money you let him have has been paid, what was coming to me—I was owing them for wheat, & should have paid it before he went away if I had seen him—I have paid up all we owe—& 10,00 on the Robbins note—there remains $10,45 which I shall pay soon—& then our last debt is paid except for the place—& I have paid $100,00 on it. Pa will give us all the time we want, at 7 per cent interest.

I received a letter from you last week, saying the Old recruits had been discharged & you were retained! I expected it, & yet I had *hoped* you might come. Sometimes I think I will write to you to come home on a furlough—but when I think of the parting again, it seems I could not go through with it. O Father in Heaven, hasten the day when wars shall cease, & we be permitted to welcome our loved ones to our hearts & homes again—O hasten that happy period & Thy great Name shall have all the praise, forever, & ever. Yet teach us still to say, not my will, but Thine, be done. It is nine o'clock, the children are now in bed & Mr Church has just come in from his Office: & Lester has been here this evening & wrote a letter to Melvin. He is working for Mr Kinney—gets 36 dollars a month. His Wife is at Wallaces now but I expect her here to stay awhile—as Lel is homesick without them. Our first paper has just been issued & I will send you a copy this week—To morrow our school begins. The children are anxious to go, & I am glad Celia is the teacher, she will take such good care of them. I shall send Dallie only when the weather is pleasant. Albert's children—that is—Mary & Willie—will also attend—Mary live[s] with Grandma & Willie at Fanchers—(Wednesday Morning). I have just fixed the children off to school, & will set down & finish my letter. Last Sabbath Brother Garlick preached in the Court-House, & we are now to have preaching every Sabbath. Elder Bradley, & his son Milton will preach between his appointments. How I wish you were here to attend, & join our class meetings. My heart would rejoice to hear you make a public profession & speak of Gods goodness—of what he has done for you. O for the time when we can bow together & seek Gods blessing upon ourselves & children. Remember us ever in your prayers—that I may ever do my duty. It is getting time to send my letter & I must close—Dont expose your precious life unnecessarily—& write often. What little war news we get is favorable. Soldiers expect to come marching home—by Spring. The war ended—& peace *once more* established in our now unhappy Country—God grant it may be so. Excuse a short letter this time I have written in a hurry & poorly, at that. Friend[s] all send love. Accept the same from your devoted Wife.

Ellen L. Woodworth.

CHAPTER 4

September 1864–May 1865

"OUR NATION IS PURGED FROM SIN"

Samuel to Ellen

Elk River. Tenn. Dec 4th 1864. [Sunday]

Dear Ellen—I seat myself to pen a few lines, not knowing how soon, or how long before it may reach you. We left Stevenson last monday night & got here tuesday. The Rebels are all around us—have torn the track up both sides of us, & burned the water-tank one mile from this place. We have not had any mail since coming here, nor dont know when we will, but hope soon to hear from you. They are having hard fighting between here & Nashville. We hear that the Rebels are being badly whipped and are running in every direction, & have lost 8000 men.[1] If the report is true the cars will be through in a few days. I hope they will for we have been two days with out any thing to eat, except what we took from the citizens: but our boys like foraging though it hardly seems right. They have "captured" fresh pork & beef & mutton; they got 25 bushels of corn & took it to the mill, & now we are living on the top shelf—& are all enjoying ourselves first-rate. Night before last, the Bushwhackers chased our boys to camp—when it got dark, our boys went back to see them: they went about a mile & laid down to await results: they did not have long to wait before they heard them coming on the jump: They came within ten feet before our boys halted them, & told them to surrender; there was about 30 or over of them & they didn't seem inclined to do so. There were only 13 of our men, but they could not see them as they lay on the ground; our boys fired kill-

---

1. At the November 30 Battle of Franklin in Tennessee, Hood attacked the Union forces under Major General John M. Schofield. The outcome, a bloody Confederate defeat, resulted in deaths of six rebel generals in the frontal assault on an entrenched federal line. Schofield withdrew into the defenses of Nashville; Hood slowly pursued. See McDonough and Connelly, *Five Tragic Hours.*

ing 3, & wounding two of their number & killed 2 horses. Our boys got
7 guns & one mule & came back to well satisfied. The Rebs were awfully
frightened. (Wed. 7th). We are still ignorant of what is going on outside of our Camp. I am well except my leg & that is better. I do want
to hear from home, & I know you will be anxious to hear from me—
but "what cant be cured, must be endured." How little I thought last
fall when I left here, that I should come back this winter & camp on the
same ground again, but here I am, & I will try & content myself. I think
sometimes that I will have to serve three years; & if I do, I dont know
as it makes any difference where I am. We are called into line of battle
about every night. The Bushwhackers fire on our pickets—I have not
had my clothes off since we came here, but lay with my gun by my side,
ready to fall in at a moments warning. I dont know where our Isabella
boys are. I saw them last at a place 8 miles from here. There is only 60
of our men here—things look rather dark at present, but I guess every
thing will be all right in a few days. Please excuse this poorly written
letter, & remember it is from your "awkward" but ever true Husband.
   Sam.—To Ellen.

Ellen to Samuel

Mt Pleasant. Dec 4th 1864. [Sunday]

My Dear Husband—
This Sabbath Evening I commence another letter to you, *hoping* it
may find you much better than when last you wrote. How I wish I
could come & take care of you, but I cant & so I write this to have you
come home, if you are able to, & can get a furlough of 30 days—& perhaps they will extend it to sixty. By that time we can heal up that poor
sore leg. Lel says it wont cost you any thing on the train. I dont know,
I am sure—but if it does, or dont, we want to see you; O, so much—
though it will be very, *very* hard to part with you again—But if you stay
there & keep getting worse, we may *never* see you. We are all well. I
have been to meeting to day—there was quite a congregation, for this
place—about 50, & 20 to class meeting.
   After meeting the minister stopped for supper to Mr Bradleys & Mr
Church, the children & I took tea with them. This evening Fanchers

folks, Mr Bradleys & we, all met to Grandpas & sung till 8 o clock, and now I am writing to you, while the children are preparing for bed.

(Tuesday Evening). Lester said he would write some—so I have waited for him & he has filled one page of my letter, which you will be glad to receive. We are having a slight snow storm, & it begins to look wintry: but we have a comfortable house to live in, to what we did last winter, so I dont dread cold weather as I did then. Vesper goes to school every day; but I dont send Dallie much, for he gets into the snow; & then I want him for company. He is a bright eyed, chubby little fellow & is a great deal of company for me. He & Vesper think a great deal of each other & you may be sure, that I think a great deal of them. I have not felt quite as well for a few weeks, but yet I am not sick. I am glad that I did not undertake to teach this winter, I dont think I could have went through with my school, & done my work, as I did last summer—You know I am never very strong, but sometimes I get terribly ambitious. I shall have plenty of time to rest this winter & if it wasnt for my anxiety about you, I should have but little to worry me. Yet, while you are in the land of dangers & suffering my mind must carry a weight of anxiety—& my nervous system be called into constant action. I have written to have you come home—for I think it is for the best. If you come we will some of us meet you at any place you may designate either St Johns or St Louis.[2] There is an express, or stage running now from St Johns to Alma. Dont take up with any hard fare—but look out for yourself, & keep clear of those cruel, & hated guerrillas. I can hardly wait the slow motion of the mails. I want to hear from you so—there is one thing certain: if you dont get cured before long—you will lose your limb, if not your life. But, I will leave you in the hands of a merciful Father, & pray him to keep you from all harm. Good bye for this time—

Ever your loving wife & children—

Ellen, Vesper, & Dallie.

---

2. A town near Alma, south of Mount Pleasant.

Ellen to Samuel

Mt Pleasant. Mich. Dec 20th 1864. [Tuesday]

Absent Husband: Once again I sit down to pen a message to you far away—in a distant-unfriendly land. We are all well, & if I could hear as much from you, how very glad I would be: it has been two weeks since I received any tidings of you.—I wrote two or three weeks ago to have you come home on furlough, & it has seemed the past few days as though you were coming—so much so that I sat up Saturday night till past 12 o clock watching for you—but I had to give up the idea & retire. Yet every day, I look for you, & a step at night on the piazza brings to my heart an extra beating. Why am I so apprehensive? is it because you are in danger—or sick—or something worse? No none can give me a reply. Pa started for St Johns this morning to meet Mr Fancher, & bring in his furniture. He will have a rough time, as it is a cold, raw day—Wallaces baby has been sick—though better now,—and Althea & I went down last Thursday to see them, & stayed over night. We left all of our children to Grandpa's. Going down we ran the cutter on to a stump & had a fine tip-over. She was driving & did not see it. I was not hurt at all but she plunged way over me & struck her head on a log—& was dazed for a few moments. I ran on & caught the horse—gathered up the robes & blankets, & we were all right again. My boarder went out of the woods on business & has not returned, consequently, we have no paper published this week—To day I have been over caring for Mother, most all day. She has had a hard chill & to night has fever—She is not well, much of the time, & as Celia is teaching, & Emma away, it is quite hard for her to do the work. We hear very encouraging news from the seat of War—Hood has been twice beaten in Tenn[3]—& Sherman is doing good work at Savanna, Ga,[4] but you probably know more about it, than we do. O that victory, may follow upon victory until our Nation is purged from sin, & our brave & noble Soldiers permitted to return to their Homes. But now, duty lies in aiding the Government—& in protecting

---

3. On December 15–16, the Army of the Cumberland under Major General George H. Thomas struck Hood's Army of Tennessee "a devastating blow," ending its effectiveness as a fighting force. Long, *Civil War Day by Day*, 610–611.

4. On December 12, communication had been made from Sherman to the federal naval forces near Savannah, advising the War Department that Union land forces were investing the Confederate defenses of the port city. Long, *Civil War Day by Day*, 609.

our Country from the foe: and we must lay aside every selfish wish, & submit to wait patiently the will of Providence knowing that in God's own good time He will work all things aright, trusting him for guidance & protection, through every dark hour of sorrow, & danger. The children are quite well—Vesper attends School regularly—Dallie stays with me & reads at home, and he enjoys being with his Mama. Our folks call him babyish. He is not; but he is a very affectionate child, & clings to those that love him, & pet him. Next monday is his 5th Birthday: he says he must have a birth-day cake—& send his Papa a piece. Christmas & New-years are close at hand. Where will you spend them? I wish it might be with us—perhaps it is not for the best.

I hope surely to hear from you tomorrow. I feel greater anxiety now that your leg is so bad. Mrs Bradley said she dreamed you came in, last night—& she can see just how you looked—thinks she would surely know you—though she has never seen you. The children send much love, & kisses to Papa—& accept the same from me: and be assured that our greatest earthly joy will be to welcome you home again—no more to roam.

Faithfully—yours,

Ellen L. Woodworth.

Samuel to Ellen

Elk River—Tenn. Dec 23d 1864. [Friday]

Dear Ellen—You are anxious to hear from me, I have no doubt. It has been four weeks since I have heard from you, yet we are all right. We expect to get mail to day. There has been hard fighting all around us, & if reports are true the Rebels are badly punished. I have not had my clothes off, since we came here. We have slept on our guns—ready to fight at any moment: Our Pickets have been shot at most every night—& altogether we have seen hard times. We could not get a load of wood, without being fired at—& the coldest weather I have seen since I came here. We have lost only 3 of our men—1 killed, & two taken prisoners. I think we have been very fortunate. I could not take the care of my leg that it required, & have suffered quite severely with it. The Captain says I must go to the Hospital: I hate to leave my Company— but I think I shall be obliged to—and shall go in a few days—if the cars run.—We are looking for them all the time, Two trains came down from Murfreesborough[5] last night: they said the cars would be through from Nashville—to-day. We have lived on Johnny Cake,[6] & parched corn, as long as I care too. I tell you we have had to keep close—& a sharp look out.—Dont give yourself any uneasiness if you do not hear very regularly from me. You had better not write until you know where I am. I will let you know as soon as possible. I fear you are having a cold time there now. O, I do hope my dear family are well & happy. I cannot be with you either this Christmas or New Years—but think of me as one that *would*, if it were *possible*.

(Saturday Morning). The mail came last night. It brought me five letters & a paper. 3 of them from my precious wife, 1 from my dear Mother, & 1 from sister Vira.—The paper is good but the letters far better. I have much to think of & a good deal to say but I cannot write it. I will answer Lesters letter soon.[7] He is mistaken about its not costing me any thing: I should have to pay half fare both ways. I cannot deny but that I see some lonely hours—& at times I feel almost willing to leave this world of sin & suffering: But why need I complain? I have a *Friend*, with me whose loving voice cheers me on, & whispers continually in my ear, words of hope, & love: and bide me look to our Father in heaven: he can sustain us, & I will trust myself in his hands, & none other. O it is sweet to know that Jesus, is our friend. May we ever be worthy of such a friend is the prayer of my heart. I must close—I wrote 3 weeks ago & the letter is here yet—I dont know when they will go—Perhaps to day—or to morrow—Be of good cheer. From your Husband.

Samuel Woodworth.

(Co. M. 1st Mich Engineers, & Mechanics)

---

5. A town southeast of Nashville, Tennessee, and site of a large fortified Union base.

6. A fried or baked flatbread made of cornmeal, originating with Native Americans.

7. Though he and wife, Maria, came to Isabella County, they returned to New York to live. In the 1870 Census they are recorded in Wethersfield, Wyoming, New York, with children Charles, six, Riley, four, and Rupert, seven months. *Eighth Decennial United States Census*, Wethersfield, Wyoming, N.Y., 371B.

Ellen to Samuel

Mt Pleasant Dec 27th 1864. [Tuesday]

Dearest Husband—Another long week has passed, & no tidings of you! Three weeks of suspense—what can be the reason—Are you sick, or a prisoner—or—O what! Not dead! No, no. My Heavenly Father will preserve your life—He has kept you *so* far—and I will trust his Mercy. But tomorrow is mail day again—I shall—I *must* hear from you tomorrow. We are all well, & I have written every week to you, since you left home. Ma is better & yesterday She & I went down to Alberts, & staid all night. I went over to our Old place.—Dallie went with me—he thought he never could live there any more—without Papa was there. It does look very desolate there. I had not been there since threshing time, & the neighbors had improved the opportunity to let down the fences so their cattle could have the benefit of the new seeded ground—& fall feed. Such a lawless, set of people, I never wish to live among. But there is no remedy for it—only when you get home we will sell our place here & build us a nice house on the farm, where we can take care of what belongs to us—ourselves. Wont that be a happy day? The children are looking forward to it, as hopefully, as I am. I have no boarder now but have considerable sewing to do. Fancher got home from Detroit last thursday night, be brought Althea a new Organ—paid $160,00. I am going to take lessons on it & get so I can play by the time you get home. I have a new mantle to make & a gingham dress—the boy some pants, Vesper a coat, & myself some under clothes. What do you do for mittens & socks this cold weather? Do you have comfortable clothing & a warm place to sleep? How much I want to see you, & *talk* with you: I got sadly disappointed last Friday. I was at Fanchers, & Althea looked out of the window & saw Celia coming home from school & a man about your size walking with her, & talking. Althea said, O Ellen! Sam is coming! I ran to the window, & sure enough, I thought it *was you*. I threw my shawl over my head & ran to meet you, & she started after me. We got to the gate & behold my *Sam*, was John Campbell![8] and you may *imagine*, my *disappointment*. I was obliged to sit down I trembled so, & did not get over it in all day. The tears I shed

8. John T. Campbell, farmer, born around 1833, lived in Coe Township according to the record of the 1860 Census. His twenty-one-year-old spouse, Sarah E. Campbell, and

were tears of bitter disappointment. I will not write more until I hear from you. This leaves us well—& I pray it may find you the same.

Ever your—Ellen.

Samuel to Ellen

Elk River. Tenn. Jan 1st 1865. [Sunday]

Ever Dear Wife—I received another of your precious letters, full of hope & love—can you ever realize how much good they do me—They cheer me on & cause me to forget my troubles, & look forward to a bright & happy future,—when I can greet one of the best women God ever gave to man. Am I worthy of her? I will try to be. O that I could be with her, & my dear children—when, O when, will that day come? God speed the time that I can return to my once happy home. This is one of the finest days that I ever saw at this time of the year—and I wish you knew how & where I am at this present hour. I feel that you are worrying, & wondering why I do not write: and perhaps will think something terrible has happened to me, & you will have to be kept in suspense till next week—but it is not my fault, as you will see. My legs are not as bad as they were one week ago—& I am feeling well—otherwise—but I expect to have to go to the Hospital—the Lieutenant says, to morrow. There is 72 dollars due me now, I dont know when I will get it—perhaps this month. I borrowed 10,00 of Caswell—for fear I might need it before I got my pay—if you can spare it, you may pay it to his girls. I hate to leave my Company—I hear we are going to our Regiment— if we do I shall get a ride on the salt water as we go by the way of New York. Sherman is at Savannah[9] & there is where we shall go—we have seen hard times for the last four weeks—but Hoods Army is whipped, & I guess will not trouble us again, very soon. I will try to keep you posted of my whereabouts.

Veppy my boy; your Papa wants to see you; but it makes my heart glad to know you are a good boy—and my little Dallie, I have not for-

---

thirty-year-old brother Thomas Campbell also resided there. *Eighth Decennial United States Census*, Coe, Isabella, Mich., 16.

9. Captured on December 21. Long, *Civil War Day by Day*, 613.

gotten you either—and you must not forget me. I hope to see you all, some day; & my prayer every day is that God will bless, & protect my dear Wife & Children.

Good bye: from your absent Husband, & Father—
Samuel Woodworth.

Samuel to Ellen

Nashville Tenn. Hospital No 15. Jan 13th 1865. [Friday]

Dear Ellen—I will send a few lines to let you know how & where I am—I am well except my leg & that is not as bad as it has been. I am in a nice, warm house, & I have a good place to sleep. I would as soon stay here the rest of the winter as any where in the Southern Confederacy. I received a letter from you last week, telling me you would not write again until you heard from me. I knew you would worry, but I was not to blame. Your anxiety was not greater than mine. I dont expect now to hear from you in a long time.

I like this place much better than I expected: I was opposed to going to a Hospital, & kept away as long as I could. We have all kinds of reading—books, papers, &c. And last night had preaching, the first white man that I have heard since I left home. I have attended a number of Negro meetings, at Stevenson. If you could see me now, just as I am—you might imagine I was some preacher, with my slippers, & morning gown on. I have seen a great deal to write about in the last two months but I will not write much this time. The war news is good; all seem to think here that the war is nearly over. God grant that it may be. The day that I left Camp, the news was that we were ordered to report to Sherman; if they go, I shall not go with them. My blood is in bad condition & it will be some time before I get entirely well. I want you should write as soon as you get this, and direct to ward 3, & Hospital, as above. Hoping this may find you all well & happy—I will close—

Faithfully yours—S. W.[10]

---

10. Samuel's service record indicates he was absent from the regiment due to being "sick in U.S. Gen Hospt Nashville Tenn. since Jan. 11 1865."

Samuel to Ellen

General Hospital No 15. Jan 22d 1865. [Sunday]

Nashville, Tenn—

Ever Dear Wife—It is with pleasure that I write a few lines to you, to say that I am well; & enjoying myself as well as I can so far away from all those that are so dear to me.

At times it seems that I must go home, & see my dear family—those little boys—I fear they will forget me—little Dallie—Vesper I am sure will not. O, how I want to see you all and I hope to in a few months. I hope you are well, but I will have to wait two long weeks to know—if you get the last letter I sent. I have a warm room, & good bed. They do not let me eat any salt meat—but I can eat all the vegetables that I want—I think my leg is improving. I have the privilege of going any where in the City that I like—I can walk around very well, now. (It is now evening): I have been to Church to day—heard three good sermons—two at the presbyterian Church & one here in the Hospital. There are about 200 sick & wounded here—some with a leg off & wounded in every possible way you can think of, but no complaining here, but they are to be pitied—brave, noble-boys—torn & mangled—giving their lives for their Country's cause. God grant that such scenes may soon come to an end and peace be restored throughout the land.

I will close trusting that our precious Saviour will guide & protect you from all harm: this is the daily prayer of your Absent Husband,

Samuel Woodworth.

To Ellen

Was home on furlough—through the Month of February.[11]

---

11. His service records include a quartermaster's document of February 9 indicating transportation was furnished from Detroit to St. Johns and return.

Samuel to Ellen

Nashville Tenn. March 18th 1865. [Saturday]

Dear Ones at Home—Here I am—back again in Old Tenn. and am feeling better than I did one week ago.—I received your letter of the 6th[12] & was glad to hear from you. You ask if I was tired when I got here? that is no name for it—I was nearly dead. I rode two nights, all night long, & the third until two o clock—but I was used well, by all.

I received $108, of pay this week Thursday—I hardly know what to do with it—but if I stay here long I will express it to you. (April 1st. 1865. In Hospital.) My Captain is here & talked with the Doctor concerning me. He told him it would not do to send me into a warmer climate. He said I was a very useful man to have about the Hospital—so I think I shall stay here some time. We are having nice warm weather & a plenty of garden sauce, such as onions, lettuce, & greens. The market is full of every thing. Eggs as low as 20 cts a dozen. It is very sickly here—the small-pox is raging fearfully—over 200 down with it: yet more deaths occur from Measles—than from *it*. (April 7th.) We have such glorious news, that I believe the end of this unjust & wicked Rebellion cannot be far off—God grant that the few remaining rebs may see the error of their ways, lay down their arms & return to the pursuits of peace, and wipe out if possible—the black stain that now rests upon them. The latest news from Sherman is that he expects to Capture Lee's whole Army.[13] I hope he may. My ankles are no worse that when I was at home. I hope you have received the money I sent you—& the box containing my winter clothes. Good bye for this time.
Love to all.
    Sam—

---

12. Missing.

13. Lee evacuated Richmond on April 2; on the April 7, Grant opened correspondence with Lee about surrendering the Army of Northern Virginia. Sherman was in North Carolina, preparing to do battle with Confederate forces under Joseph E. Johnston. Long, *Civil War Day by Day*, 668.

Samuel to Ellen

U.S. General Hospital. Nashville Tenn—

May 5th 1865. [Friday]

Ever Dear Wife—I received your kind & welcome letter[14] saying you had received the money, & box. Am glad you have got it at last, as you so much needed it. We all think the *war* is about over.[15] They are settling things up here as fast as possible & sending men home every day—and if what I hear, is true, we will all be home inside of four weeks. O can we be thankful enough? can it be that this long, & *cruel* war is over, and are we to be permitted to return once more to our dear friends & quiet homes? My heart is filled with gratitude, & joyous anticipations and words fail to give utterance to my feelings.

Praise God from whom all blessings flow:

(Later). Word has just been received that this Hospital will break up within ten day—& all that are able go to their regiments & the rest sent home. Later. *Discharged!*[16] Hoping to see you soon I remain as ever your ever faithful Husband—

Samuel Woodworth.

Co M. 1st Mich Eng. & Mech. Volunteers.

Arrived home, soon after the above letter was written.—and thus endeth *our part*, in the history of "The Great Rebellion."

E. L. W.

---

14. Missing.

15. Lee surrendered on April 9, Johnston on April 26, and for all practical purposes the Confederacy was no more. Long, *Civil War Day by Day*, 670, 682.

16. Samuel's service record states he was discharged at Nashville, Tennessee, on May 17, 1865. *Record of Service*, vol. 43, 229, "Honorably discharged 5/17/65 at hospital Nashville Tenn." *Descriptive Roll*, 170.

Acknowledgments

Founding credit for this project belongs to a first-rate gentleman and scholar, Mr. C. Wendell "Del" Dunbar of Ann Arbor, Michigan. After loaning me a typed copy of Ellen Woodworth's journal in June 2014, Del extended an invitation to visit the renowned Clarke Historical Library in Mount Pleasant for an investigation of joint possibilities. He guided our reciprocal paths of research, enlisted wife Nancy for research, and launched a creative approach that brought to life the real dimensions of the Woodworth story. His knowledge, friendship, and encouragement have been all important all along.

For gracious assistance with the manuscript, publication issues, and research, and for incisive comments and guidance all the way back to July 2014, I am indebted to now retired Clarke director Dr. Frank J. Boles, as well to the keen staff at the Clarke, most recently Bryan R. Whitledge.

To Mick Gusinde-Duffy, executive editor at the University of Georgia Press, and Dr. Judkin Browning and Dr. Susanna Lee, coeditors of this series, I am profoundly grateful for their collective support for publication. I am also grateful for their review, guidance, comments, and insights, which greatly improved this publication. I especially value Judkin's indefatigable shepherding of the manuscript through its various stages. Thank you also to Jon Davies, Matthew C. O'Neal, the series advisory board, and everyone associated with UGA Press.

I extend thanks to Fred Nachbaur, director, Fordham University Press, who pointed me toward UGA Press, and to the various anonymous readers who reviewed the proposal, validated its importance, suggested insightful improvements, and later reviewed and commented on the prepublication version.

Appreciation goes to two notable Michigan historians and authors, Mark Hoffman for loan of research materials on "Company M," and Matt VanAcker of the Michigan Capitol Tour Service for collegial support and for assistance with images.

Once more, Jackie Tinney provided unsurpassed administrative assistance for which I remain in her debt. Thank you also to Pamela R. Davis.

To selfless colleagues at the Michigan Civil War Association, thank you for inspiration and collegiality. Tuebor!

To Michael, Mom, and Dad: you are missed and ever loved.

To Dave and Tom, gratitude for brotherhood that is as enduring as the Great Lakes.

To Anna, Dan, Connor, and Emmy, thank you for your unsung sacrifices on behalf of America and its people.

To Suzzanne, whose life has enriched so many beyond measure, whose heart is always open to aiding others, and whose hands are ever engaged in beautifying this world, "my ever Dear Wife," my ardent love forever.

Last by listing, but first in priority, to, in Ellen Woodworth's words, the "Friend that sticketh closer than a brother," my humble and eternal awe, gratitude, and devotion.

Additional Writings by
Ellen Preston Woodworth

I. An Enlisted Husband

A half-century after the Civil War, Ellen Woodworth's brother-in-law
Isaac A. Fancher published a history of Isabella County. It contained
a description of the circumstances of Samuel's enlistment. Her authorship appears likely.

WAR MEETINGS

During 1863–4, after many had enlisted and the call was made
for more troops, the people became very much exercised, as it began to look as if a draft was sure to follow. The government was
sending out recruiting officers and one came to Isabella county
to see what could be done here. He was escorted through the settlements by S. Woodworth, who enlisted with others and went to
the front. They held war meetings, where the men were persuaded
to join the army of the United States. The first war meeting was
held at the house of Azariah Dunham, in the township of Lincoln,
he having the most commodious one of the settlement, and, although it had neither door or window in it, answered the purpose
and the meeting was the means of several enlisting. The meeting
had been well advertised, as they had distributed notices and had
nailed them to the trees along the trail through the timber, so that
a good crowd was secured. Chairs in those days were scarce, so
that logs were sawed off into blocks and they were placed on end
around the inside of the building, and sap troughs, with a few
loose boards placed upon them, were also in use for seats. For
lights, there were a couple of tallow dips sputtering on a rough
pine table, so that, all in all, we were all well accommodated.
Old patriotic songs were sung, speeches made and papers read
to show how things were going at the front and to what straits

the country was put to on account of the treason of the South. The songs were sung with a zest, the deep bass, the tenor and the masculine soprano, with the inspiration of Old John Brown in their hearts, made the woods ring with the old patriotic songs, and when any one stepped forward and signed the roll there came up such a shout as can only be heard connected with patriotism. These meetings were kept up at different places in the county, at Salt River and in the township of Chippewa, until nearly every able-bodied man had signed for the army.

After a few days orders came to go to the front and the sad leave-taking was had. The oxen were hitched to the old double wagon, the family placed thereon and a start was made to the Indian Mills, where the enlisted were to meet and from there were to go down the Chippewa river on a raft provided for their journey. The roads were trails through the woods across the swamps and over the corduroy, and it recalls to memory the parody on Poe's "Raven":[1]

> "Once upon a spring time dreary,
> While we plodded, weak and weary,
> Over many a bog and muddy hole,
> Of the treacherous roads of yore,
> While we bumped and splashed and floundered
> Through the swamps that we encountered,
> Oft we stopped awhile and pondered
> And sometimes I fear we swore."—E.L.W.

After an all-day's journey over these delectable roads, we arrived at our destination and put up for the night. In the morning all was made ready for the soldiers' departure. The raft that had been made to float them down the river was loaded with the luggage, blankets, rations and bedding. When at last all was ready, the bank of the river was lined with the families and friends of those departing, the last kiss was given, the last goodby was said and the raft was made loose, swung out into the current of the stream and they were afloat. Then it was that the wife and family realized what war meant and sobs could be heard, and tears were shed as they turned away from the shore of the river and once more were

---

1. The original 1845 poem is in Poe, *Raven and Other Poems*, 1.

afloat on the shore of time, little knowing what the tempest of war would bring to them. In that company were Samuel Woodworth, Daniel McLarn, Alonzo Holland, Joseph Atkins, with probably some others.

II. "A Plucky Woman"

In the chapter of Fancher's history entitled "Early Reminiscences and Incidents" appeared a story with the heading "A Plucky Woman." A short narrative provided the setting for a 26-stanza poem that was credited to Ellen Woodworth; she likely wrote the prose as well. The author looked back to the days when a couple were "then young and healthy." The date of authorship was after 1895, given a reference to a coffee substitute that first appeared on the market in that year.

A PLUCKY WOMAN.

On one occasion in the early sixties a young woman was left with two small children to do the work at home, while the husband had gone to the front to fight the battle for freedom and had left a patch of turnips and also a small field of potatoes to harvest. No help could be had, so she was compelled to go into the field and pull the turnips and dig the potatoes with the aid of the oldest boy, a lad of nine. They harvested the crop and then sold seventy-five bushels of the turnips for twenty cents a bushel.

These were used by many of the families as their staple food. The balance was fed to the stock, as there was no hay in the settlement at the time and the stock was compelled to browse upon the brush and limbs in the woods. The hard work and exposure in the field and in caring for the stock in winter caused a felon to appear on the woman's hand and, after four days and nights of intense pain and suffering, she started one starlight night for the doctor's house, some two and one-half miles away, following the trail through the woods, timid and fearful of meeting some ferocious wild animal, as the forests contained at that time many bear, some wolves, catamounts and occasionally lynx. Fortune favored the brave woman and after a long tramp she arrived at the doctor's residence about three o'clock in the morning and she rapped at his door. He soon appeared, invited her in and after examining the hand, probed it with a lance and relieved the pain and after applying some soothing applications she felt relieved and started back to her little ones at home.

At another time, not long after the above incident, a family living in the forests of Isabella, whose parents resided in western New York state, the wife learned that her parents had sold their farm and were coming to Isabella. It was in the month of March and they had made their journey by rail to the then village of St. Johns, some forty-five miles distant from the home of her daughter, and, coming into the county by wagon over the corduroy and mud roads of the country, on arriving were very much wearied and nearly exhausted so that it seemed necessary that the old lady at least should have a good strong, soothing cup of tea. She did not know that tea in the wilderness was a great luxury. The daughter knew, however, that her mother would expect it, but what could she do? There was nothing left, as it seemed to her, but procure the tea. The nearest store was at Salt River, so she donned her bonnet and shawl and started out for the beverage. It was a long journey to walk six miles and more in the month of March, but she made the trip and returned with the article, made the tea and her mother enjoyed it very much. She remarked that she thought that she must have some very good neighbors that she should stay so long and visit, or else they must be a good ways off.

> In the year '61, I remember it well,
> We came to the Michigan forests to dwell.
> No signs that the white man had yet passed that way
> Where Nature, most primitive, fully held sway.
>
> First a few trees were felled and a small space was cleared
> Where a little log-cabin was speedily reared.
> With just one small window to let in the light,
> And a wooden-hinged door that we made fast at night.
>
> We brought with us bedding, a stove and some food.
> And the axe—most important—our chief ally stood;
> We were then young and healthy, with courage quite keen,
> Though Indians and wild beasts were frequently seen.
>
> The opening around us grew broader each day,
> Letting in the blue sky and the sunlight's bright ray,

Then the birds came to greet us and sing 'mong the leaves
And build tiny nests 'neath the cabin's low eaves.

Other settlers came in and took up a claim
And the township received then its first legal name,
Which was Lincoln, and passable roads were cut through
Where each built his cabin and started anew.

Then the women found time to make calls—I should say—
Going oft in the morning and staying all day;
With knitting in hand they thought it no labor
To walk a few miles to visit a neighbor.

It may interest you to know how we made
Our pastry and puddings from things that we had;
But the maxim was just as true then as to-day
That "where there's a will, there's always a way."

We made good mince pies without apples or meat,
And the elder bush furnished us berries to eat,
Baked in pie, with a few leaves of sorrel to sour it,
You would know it was good had you seen us devour it.

Our cookies and cakes would just take the lead,
Made of nice maple sugar and caraway seed,
Cut out with a teacup or fashioned by hand,
Our pioneer cakes were the best in the land.

From barley and peas nicely roasted and ground
A fine cup of coffee could always be found;
It wasn't quite Mocha and Java, 'tis true,
But preferable far to to-day's Postum brew.

Some used the wild strawberry leaves for their tea,
And the white inner bark of the fragrant pine tree;
Its medicinal virtue no tea can excel
And the use of it daily kept each of them well.

How well I remember our first home-grown foods—
Cucumbers and turnips grown there in the woods,
And tame, juicy berries, delicious and sweet,
We now had abundance of good things to eat.

If a wood-bee was planned all the men turned out strong
And women and children of course went along;
Each carried a basket or pail full of dinner
And made no distinction between saint or sinner.

But all joined together; and while the men worked,
We women just visited—never one shirked
In doing her share of the talking and greeting
That made of that day an experience meeting.

Well, times somewhat changed as the years rolled between
When fine farms appeared, and nice homes were seen,
And fashion crept in according to station,
And visits were made only by invitation.

Some even dropped out—I am sorry to say—
And became more exclusive, like some are today,
While a spirit of rivalry if not of strife
Drove out of our midst the old simple life.

There is one more experience I will explain
Though I never should wish to explain it again.
The time for the watch-meeting service drew near
To watch out the old and to greet the New Year.

I had never attended a meeting like this.
And thought it was something I ought not to miss.
Though, to tell just the truth, I didn't feel right
In leaving my husband and children at night.

But a neighbor, his wife, and another dear friend,
Who had always accustomed themselves to attend,
Had said they would call for me if I would go,
And so I decided I would not say no.

'Twas a bitter cold night—with an old open sleigh
Drawn by oxen, and filled in with straw or with hay,
With blankets for robes to protect from the storm,
Which were quite insufficient in keeping us warm.

Then the slow pace began, for some three miles below,
To the Chippewa schoolhouse where we had to go.
It seemed we would never the meeting-place reach,
Or hear any sermon the good man might preach.

But we reached there at last, with no time to spare,
Quite chilled from the ride in the cold, frosty air,
The stove gave out warmth most grateful to all.
But no seats were provided except near the wall.

So I sat in a corner, a bench for a seat,
And the cracks in the floor gave no warmth to my feet.
'Twas a small congregation with only a few
Who had rallied to aid in the work there to do.

I patiently listened to hear what was said;
They sang a short hymn, then the minister read
A portion of Scripture, and two or three prayed,
When the minister urged them to not be afraid

But to speak a few words, some experience to give
And tell the friends present the right way to live.

Just then something ran down my shoulder and dropped
And out of my lap a poor famished mouse hopped.
　　Well, the first exclamation I made then and there,
It wasn't appropriate, was not a prayer,
And if ever I gave grateful thanks it was when
The minister said, "Happy New Year—Amen."

—Mrs. Ellen Woodworth.[2]

---

2. Fancher, *Past and Present*, 94–97 (Ellen), 312–314 (Samuel).

Bibliography

All works listed were consulted in research for this volume.

Adams, George W. *Doctors in Blue: The Medical History of the Union Army in the Civil War*. New York: Henry Schuman, 1952.

Aley, Ginette. "Inescapable Realities: Rural Midwestern Women and Families During the Civil War." In Ginette and Anderson, *Union Heartland*: 125–147.

Aley, Ginette, and J. L. Anderson, eds. *Union Heartland: The Midwestern Home Front During the Civil War*. Carbondale: Southern Illinois University Press, 2013.

Atlas to Accompany the Official Records of the Union and Confederate Armies, 1861–1865. Washington: Government Printing Office, 1891–1895.

Attie, Jeanie. *Patriotic Toil: Northern Women and the American Civil War*. Ithaca: Cornell University Press, 1998.

Attie, Jeanie. "Warwork and the Crisis of Domesticity in the North." In *Divided Houses: Gender and the Civil War*, edited by Catherine Clinton and Nina Silber, 247–259. New York: Oxford University Press, 1992.

Basler, Roy P., ed. *The Collected Works of Abraham Lincoln*. New Brunswick: Rutgers University Press, 1953.

Beazley, Samuel. *The Roue*. Vol. 2. New York: J. and J. Harper, 1828.

Benz, Charmaine M., and R. Todd Wiliamson, eds. *Diba Jimooyung, Telling Our Story: A History of the Saginaw Ojibwe Anishinabek*. Mt. Pleasant: Saginaw Chippewa Indian Tribe of Michigan, 2005.

Berkhofer, Robert F., Jr. *The White Man's Indian: Images of the American Indian from Columbus to the Present*. New York: Vintage Books, 1979.

Berry, Stephen, and Angela Esco Elder, eds. *Practical Strangers: The Courtship Correspondence of Nathaniel Dawson and Elodie Todd, Sister of Mary Todd Lincoln*. Athens: University of Georgia Press, 2017.

Billings, John D. *Hardtack and Coffee, or The Unwritten Story of Army Life*. Boston: George M. Smith & Co., 1887.

Blackbird, Andrew J. *History of the Ottawa and Chippewa Indians of Michigan*. Ypsilanti: Ypsilantian Job Printing, 1887.

Bleser, Carol K., and Lesley J. Gordon, eds. *Intimate Strategies of the Civil War: Military Commanders and Their Wives*. New York: Oxford University Press, 2001.

Boatner, Mark M., III. *The Civil War Dictionary*. New York: David Mackay Co., 1988.

Bonar, Horatious. *Hymns of Faith and Hope*. New York: Robert Carter & Bros., 1864.

Boyden, John, Jr. *The Eastern Harp: A Collection of Tunes and Hymns, Original and Selected: For the Use of Sabbath Schools*. Boston: James M. Usher, 1848.

Brockett, Linus P., and Mary C. Vaughan. *Woman's Work in the Civil War*. Philadelphia: Zeigler, McCurdy & Co., 1867.

Byrd, James P. *A Holy Baptism of Fire and Blood: The Bible and the American Civil War*. New York: Oxford University Press, 2021.

Caffrey, Margaret M. *The Register of the Kentucky Historical Society* 91, no. 1 (Winter 1993): 100–101.

Carmichael, Peter S. *The War for the Common Soldier: How Men Thought, Fought, and Survived in Civil War Armies*. Chapel Hill: University of North Carolina Press, 2018.

Cashin, Joan E., ed. *The War Was You and Me*. Princeton: Princeton University Press, 2002.

Castel, Albert. *Decision in the West: The Atlanta Campaign of 1864*. Lawrence: University of Kansas Press, 1992.

Census of the State of Michigan 1894, Soldiers, Sailors and Marines. Vol. 3. Lansing: Robert Smith & Co., 1896.

Chestnut, Mary Boykin. *Mary Chestnut's Diary*. New York: Penguin Press, 2011.

Cimbala, Paul A., and Randall M. Miller, eds. *Union Soldiers and the Northern Home Front*. New York: Fordham University Press, 2002.

Clinton, Catherine, ed. *Southern Families at War: Loyalty and Conflict in the Civil War South*. New York: Oxford University Press, 2000.

Clinton, Catherine, and Nina Silber. *Battle Scars: Gender and Sexuality in the American Civil War*. New York: Oxford University Press, 2006.

Clinton, Catherine, and Nina Silber, eds. *Divided Houses: Gender and the Civil War*. New York: Oxford University Press, 1992.

Connolly, A. P. *A Thrilling Narrative of the Minnesota Massacre and the Sioux War of 1862–63*. Chicago: A. P. Connolly, 1896.

Connelly, Thomas L. *Autumn of Glory: The Army of Tennessee, 1862–1865*. Baton Rouge: Louisiana State University Press, 1971.

Cooling, Benjamin F. *Jubal Early's Raid on Washington: 1864*. Baltimore: Nautical & Aviation Pub. Co. of America, 1989.

Cooper, Abigail. "Interactive Map of Contraband Camps." *History Digital Projects*. 2014. https://repository.upenn.edu/hist_digital/1.

Cozzens, Peter. *The Shipwreck of Their Hopes: The Battles for Chattanooga*. Urbana: University of Illinois Press, 1996.

Culpepper, Marilyn Mayer. *Trials and Triumphs: The Women of the American Civil War*. East Lansing: Michigan State University Press, 1991.

Cumming, John. *This Place Mount Pleasant*. Mt. Pleasant Centennial Commission, 1989.

Czopek, Chris. *Who Was Who in Company K: Reliable Facts about the Native American Soldiers in Company K, 1st Michigan Sharpshooters*. Lansing: Red Oak Research, 2015.

Daniel, Larry J. *Days of Glory: The Army of the Cumberland, 1861–1865*. Baton Rouge: Louisiana State University Press, 2004.

Danziger, Edmund J., Jr. *Great Lakes Indian Accommodation and Resistance During the Early Reservation Years, 1850–1900*. Ann Arbor: University of Michigan Press, 2009.

Day, J. E. *Sketch of the Settlement and Growth of Isabella County*. Lansing: Michigan Pioneer & Historical Collections, 1896.

Dean, Eric T., Jr. *Shook over Hell: Post-Traumatic Stress, Vietnam, and the Civil War*. Cambridge: Harvard University Press, 1997.

Descriptive Roll of Company M, First Michigan Engineers & Mechanics Volunteers, 1861–1866.

Devine, Shauna. *Learning from the Wounded: The Civil War and the Rise of American Medical Science*. Chapel Hill: University of North Carolina Press, 2014.

Dramatic Compositions Copyrighted in the United States, 1870 to 1916. Vol. 2. Washington: Government Printing Office, 1918.

Drinnon, Richard. *Facing West: The Metaphysics of Indian-Hating and Empire Building*. Norman: University of Oklahoma Press, 1997.

Dubin, Michael J. *United States Presidential Elections, 1788–1860: The Official Results by County and State*. Jefferson, N.C.: McFarland & Co., 2002.

Dunbar, Willis F. *Michigan: A History of the Wolverine State*. Grand Rapids: Wm. B. Eerdmans Pub. Co., 1970.

Dustin, Fred. *The Saginaw Treaty of 1819 Between General Lewis Cass and the Chippewa Indians*. Saginaw: Saginaw Pub. Co., 1919.

Dyer, Frederick H. *A Compendium of the War of the Rebellion*. Des Moines: Dyer Publishing Co., 1908.

Ellis, Franklin. *History of Shiawassee and Clinton Counties, Michigan*. Philadelphia: D. W. Ensign & Co., 1880.

Fahs, Alice, ed. "The Feminized Civil War: Gender, Northern Popular Literature, and the Memory of the War, 1861–1900." *Journal of American History* 85, no. 4 (March 1999): 1461–1494.

Fahs, Alice. *The Imagined Civil War: Popular Literature of the North and South, 1861–1865*. Chapel Hill: University of North Carolina Press, 2001.

Fahs, Alice, and Joan Waugh, eds. *The Memory of the Civil War in American Culture*. Chapel Hill: University of North Carolina Press, 2004.

Fancher, Isaac A. *Past and Present of Isabella County Michigan*. Indianapolis: B. F. Bowen & Company, 1911.

Fantina, Robert. *Desertion and the American Soldier: 1776–2006*. New York: Algora Pub., 2006.

Faust, Drew Gilpin. "'Ours as Well as that of the Men': Women and Gender in the Civil War." In *Writing the Civil War: The Quest to Understand*, edited by James M. McPherson and William J. Cooper Jr., 228–240. Columbia: University of South Carolina Press, 1998.

Faust, Drew Gilpin. *This Republic of Suffering: Death and the American Civil War*. New York: Alfred A. Knopf, 2018.

Fee, Sarah, ed. *Cloth That Changed the World: The Art and Fashion of Indian Chintz*. New Haven: Yale University Press, 2020.

Foner, Eric. *Free Soil, Free Labor, Free Men: The Ideology of the Republican Party before the Civil War*. New York: Oxford University Press, 1995.

Foote, Lorien. *The Gentleman and the Roughs: Violence, Honor, and Manhood in the Union Army*. New York: New York University Press, 2010.

Fraprie, Frank R. *American Photography*. Vol. 3. Boston: American Photographic Pub. Co., 1909.

Frederiksen, John C. *Civil War Almanac*. New York: Checkmark Books, 2008.

Freemon, Frank R. *Gangrene and Glory: Medical Care during the American Civil War.* Urbana: University of Illinois Press, 2001.

Fuchs, Richard L. *An Unerring Fire: The Massacre at Fort Pillow.* Lanham: Stackpole Books, 2017.

Gallagher, Gary W. "Blue Views: Two Northern Women Left Insightful Memoirs of Their Wartime Experiences." *Civil War Times*, 61, no. 4 (Autumn 2022). https://www.historynet.com/union-women-wartime-memoirs/.

Gallagher, Gary W. *The Union War.* Cambridge: Harvard University Press, 2011.

Gallman, J. Matthew. *Defining Duty in the Civil War: Personal Choice, Popular Culture, and the Union Home Front.* Chapel Hill: University of North Carolina Press, 2015.

Gallman, J. Matthew. *The North Fights the Civil War: The Home Front.* Chicago: Ivan R. Dee Inc., 1994.

Gardner, Sarah E. *Blood & Irony: Southern White Women's Narratives of the City War, 1861–1937.* Chapel Hill: University of North Carolina Press, 2004.

Gencarella, Stephen. *Wicked Weird & Wily Yankees: A Celebration of New England's Eccentrics and Misfits.* Lanham: Globe Pequot, 2018.

Giesberg, Judith. *Army at Home: Women and the Civil War on the Northern Home Front.* Chapel Hill: University of North Carolina Press, 2009.

Giesberg, Judith. "The Future of Civil War Era Studies: Northern Women." *Journal of the Civil War Era* 2, no. 1 (March 2012): 9.

Giesberg, Judith, and Randall M. Miller, eds. *Women and the American Civil War: North-South Counterpoints.* Kent: Kent State University Press, 2018.

Glymph, Thavolia. *The Women's Fight: The Civil War's Battles for Home, Freedom, and Nation.* Chapel Hill: University of North Carolina Press, 2019.

Grant, Ulysses S. *Personal Memoirs.* Vol. 2. New York: Charles L. Webster & Co., 1886.

Gray, Susan. *The Yankee West: Community Life on the Michigan Frontier.* Chapel Hill: University of North Carolina Press, 1996.

Greenman, Emerson F. *The Indians of Michigan.* Lansing: Michigan Historical Commission, 1961.

Hager, Christopher. *I Remain Yours: Common Lives in Civil War Letters.* Cambridge: Harvard University Press, 2018.

Hale, Sarah Josepha. *The Good Housekeeper, or The Way to Live Well and To Be Well While We Live.* Boston: Weeks, Jordan & Co., 1839.

Hauptman, Laurence M. *Between Two Fires: American Indians in the Civil War.* New York: The Free Press, 1995.

Hayes, E. L. *Atlas of Isabella County, Michigan.* Philadelphia: C. O. Titus, 1879.

Hemenway, Eric. Foreword to *Deadly Aim: The Civil War Story of Michigan's Anishinaabe Sharpshooters*, by Sally M. Walker, viii–ix. New York: Henry Holt & Co., 2019.

Hemenway, Eric, and Sammye Meadows. "Soldiers in the Shadows: Company K, 1st Michigan's Anishinaabe Sharpshooters." In Sutton and Latschar, *American Indians and the Civil War*: 48–65.

Herek, Raymond J. *These Men Have Seen Hard Service: The First Michigan Sharpshooters in the Civil War.* Detroit: Wayne State University Press, 1988.

Hershock, Martin J. *The Paradox of Progress: Economic Change, Individual Enter-*

prise, and Political Culture in Michigan, 1837–1878. Athens: Ohio University Press, 2003.

Hess, Earl J. *Braxton Bragg: The Most Hated Man of the Confederacy*. Chapel Hill: University of North Carolina Press, 2021.

Hess, Earl J. *Civil War Supply and Strategy: Feeding Men and Moving Armies*. Baton Rouge: Louisiana State University Press, 2020.

Hess, Earl J. *The Knoxville Campaign: Burnside and Longstreet in East Tennessee*. Knoxville: University of Tennessee Press, 2012.

Hewitt, Nancy A., ed. *A Companion to American Women's History*. Oxford: Blackwell Publishers, 2002.

Historical Statistics of the United States, Colonial Times to 1970. Washington: Government Printing Office, 1975.

History of the Michigan Organizations at Chickamauga, Chattanooga and Missionary Ridge, 1863. Lansing: Robert Smith Printing Co., 1899.

History of Wyoming County, N.Y. New York: F. W. Beers & Co., 1880.

Hodge, Frederick W., ed. *Handbook of American Indians North of Mexico*. Part 2. Washington: Government Printing Office, 1910.

Hoffman, Mark. *Among the Enemy: A Michigan Soldier's Civil War Journal*. Detroit: Wayne State University Press, 2013.

Hoffman, Mark. *My Brave Mechanics: The Michigan Engineers and Their Civil War*. Wayne State University Press, 2007.

Hooper, Candice Shy. *Lincoln's Generals' Wives: Four Women Who Influenced the Civil War—for Better and for Worse*. Kent: Kent State University Press, 2016.

Hooper, Robert, and Samuel Akerly. *Lexicon Medicum, or Medical Dictionary*, Vol. 2. New York: Harper & Brothers, 1860.

Hubbart, Henry C. *The Older Middle West, 1840–1880: Its Social, Economic, and Political Life and Sectional Tendencies before, during and after the Civil War*. New York: Russell & Russell, 1936.

Hurt, R. Douglas. *Food and Agriculture during the Civil War*. Santa Barbara: Praeger, 2016.

Hyman, Harold M. *American Singularity: The 1787 Northwest Ordinance, the 1862 Homestead and Morrill Acts, and the 1944 G.I. Bill*. Athens: University of Georgia Press, 1986.

Isabella County, Michigan: Families and History. Paducah: Turner Publishing Co., 2003.

Jarrow, Gail. *Blood and Germs: The Civil War Battle against Wounds and Disease*. New York: Calkins Creek, 2020.

John, Richard R. *Spreading the News: The American Postal System from Franklin to Morse*. Cambridge: Harvard University Press, 1995.

Johnson, Ludwell H. *Red River Campaign: Politics and Cotton in the Civil War*. Baltimore: Johns Hopkins University Press, 2019.

Jones, Peter. *A Collection of Chippeway and English Hymns, for the Use of the Native Indians*. New York: Carlton & Phillips, 1854.

Jordan, Brian Matthew. *Marching Home: Union Veterans and Their Unending Civil War*. New York: Liveright Pub. Corp, 2014.

Julian, John, ed. *A Dictionary of Hymnology, Setting Forth the Origin and History of Christian Hymns of All Ages and Nations*. London: John Murray, 1892.

Kappler, Charles J., ed. *Indian Affairs: Laws and Treaties*. Vol. 2: *Treaties*. Washington: Government Printing Office, 1904.

Keating, Ryan W., ed. *The Greatest Trials I Ever Had: The Civil War Letters of Margaret and Thomas Cahill*. Athens: University of Georgia Press, 2017.

Keller, Robert H. "America's Native Sweet: Chippewa Treaties and the Right to Harvest Maple Sugar." *American Indian Quarterly* 13, no. 2 (Spring 1989): 117–135.

Kennedy, Joseph C. G. *Population of the United States in 1860*. Washington: Government Printing Office, 1864.

Kertzer, David I., and Peter Laslett, eds. *Aging in the Past: Demography, Society, and Old Age*. Berkeley: University of California Press, 1995.

Klotter, James C. *The Breckinridges of Kentucky*. Lexington: University Press of Kentucky, 2006.

Lanman, Charles. *The Red Book of Michigan: A Civil, Military, and Biographical History*. Detroit: E. B. Smith & Co., 1871.

Lauck, Jon K. *The Good Country: A History of the American Midwest, 1800–1900*. Norman: University of Oklahoma Press, 2022.

Leonard, Elizabeth D. *Yankee Women: Gender Battles in the Civil War*. New York: W. W. Norton & Co., 1994.

Levin, Kevin M. *Searching for Black Confederates: The Civil War's Most Persistent Myth*. Chapel Hill: University of North Carolina Press, 2019.

Lewis, Kenneth E. *West to Far Michigan: Settling the Lower Peninsula, 1815–1860*. East Lansing: Michigan State University Press, 2002.

Linderman, Gerald F. *Embattled Courage: The Experience of Combat in the American Civil War*. New York: Free Press, 1987.

Long, E. B., and Barbara Long. *The Civil War Day by Day: An Almanac, 1861–1865*. Garden City: Doubleday, 1971.

Lonn, Ella. *Desertion during the Civil War*. New York: Century Co., 1928.

Lowenstein, Roger. *Ways and Means: Lincoln and His Cabinet and the Financing of the Civil War*. New York: Penguin Press, 2022.

Macmillan, Margaret B. *The Methodist Episcopal Church in Michigan during the Civil War*. Lansing: Michigan Civil War Centennial Observance Commission, 1965.

Mahan, Dennis H. *A Treatise on Field Fortification*. New York: John Wiley, 1861.

Manning, Chandra. *Troubled Refuge: Struggling for Freedom in the Civil War*. New York: Alfred A. Knopf, 2016.

Marks, Joseph J., ed. *Effects of the Civil War on Farming in Michigan*. Lansing: Michigan Civil War Centennial Observance Commission, 1965.

Marshall, Anne E. "A 'Sisters' War': Kentucky Women and Their Civil War Diaries." *Register of the Kentucky Historical Society* 110, nos. 3–4 (Summer/Autumn 2012): 481–502.

Marszalek, John F. *Sherman: A Soldier's Passion for Order*. Carbondale: Southern Illinois University Press, 2007.

Marten, James. *The Children's Civil War*. Chapel Hill: University of North Carolina Press, 1998.

Marten, James. *Civil War America: Voices from the Home Front*. New York: Fordham University Press, 2007.

Massey, Mary E. *Women in the Civil War*. Lincoln: University of Nebraska Press, 1994.

McConnell, Stuart. *Glorious Contentment: The Grand Army of the Republic, 1865–1900*. Chapel Hill: University of North Carolina Press, 1992.

McCune, Julia, ed. *Mary Austin Wallace: Her Diary, 1862; A Michigan Soldier's Wife Runs Their Farm*. Lansing: Michigan Civil War Centennial Observance Commission, 1963.

McCurry, Stephanie. *Women's War: Fighting and Surviving the American Civil War*. Cambridge: Belknap Press, 2019.

McDevitt, Theresa. *Women and the American Civil War: An Annotated Bibliography*. Westport: Praeger, 2003.

McDonnell, Michael A. *Masters of Empire: Great Lakes Indians and the Making of America*. New York: Hill and Wang, 2015.

McDonough, James L., and Thomas L. Connelly. *Five Tragic Hours: The Battle Of Franklin*. Knoxville: University of Tennessee Press, 1983.

McPherson, James M. *Battle Cry of Freedom: The Civil War Era*. New York: Oxford University Press, 1988.

McPherson, James M. Foreword to Clinton and Silber, *Divided Houses*: xiii-xvii.

McPherson, James M. *Tried By War: Abraham Lincoln as Commander in Chief*. New York: Penguin Press, 2008.

McPherson, James M. *What They Fought For, 1861–1865*. Baton Rouge: Louisiana University Press, 1994.

McPherson, James M., and William J. Cooper Jr. Introduction to *Writing the Civil War: The Quest to Understand*, edited by James M. McPherson and William J. Cooper Jr., 1–7. Columbia: University of South Carolina Press, 1998.

Michigan in the American Civil War. Lansing: Michigan Legislature, 2015.

Michigan Women in the Civil War. Lansing: Michigan Civil War Centennial Observance Commission, 1963.

Miles, William. *School Ma'm: The Story of Ellen L. Woodworth*. Mt. Pleasant: Tau Chapter of Delta Kappa Gamma, 1976.

Miller, Francis T., ed. *The Photographic History of the Civil War in Ten Volumes*. Vol. 2: *Two Years of Grim War*. New York: Review of Reviews Co., 1911.

Miller, R. A., and Charles J. Seely. *Faces and Places Familiar, Mt. Pleasant, Michigan*. Lynn's Printing Service, 1906.

Minot, George, and George P. Sanger, eds. *The Statutes at Large and Treaties of the United States of America*. Vol. 11. Boston: Little, Brown & Co., 1859.

Mitchell, Reid. *The Vacant Chair: The Northern Soldier Leaves Home*. New York: Oxford University Press, 1993.

Mitchell, Robert E. "Civil War Recruiting and Recruits from Ever-Changing Labor Pools: Midland County, Michigan, as a Case Study." *Michigan Historical Review* 35, no. 1 (Spring 2009): 29–60.

Mohr, James C., ed. *The Cormany Diaries: A Northern Family in the Civil War*. Pittsburgh: University of Pittsburgh Press, 1982.

Monson, Marianne. *Women of the Blue & Gray: True Civil War Stories of Mothers, Medics, Soldiers, and Spies*. Salt Lake City: Shadow Mountain, 2018.

Moore, Frank. *Women of the War: Their Heroism and Self-Sacrifice*. Hartford: S. S. Scranton & Co., 1866.

Morris, George Pope. *Poems by George P. Morris: With a Memoir of the Author*. New York: Charles Scribner, 1860.

Motz, Marilyn F. *True Sisterhood: Michigan Women and Their Kin, 1820–1920.* Albany: State University of New York Press, 1983.

Murdock, Eugene C. *Patriotism Limited, 1862–1865: The Civil War Draft and the Bounty System.* Kent: Kent State University Press, 1967.

Myers, Peter D., compiler. *The Zion Songster.* New York: Clark, Austin & Smith, 1854.

Noe, Kenneth W. *Reluctant Rebels: The Confederates Who Joined the Army after 1861.* Chapel Hill: University of North Carolina Press, 2010.

Nowlin, William. *The Bark Covered House, or, Back in the Woods Again.* Detroit: Herald Pub. House, 1876.

Oates, Stephen B. *To Purge This Land with Blood: A Biography of John Brown.* Amherst: University of Massachusetts Press, 1984.

Official Register, 1909. Vol. 2: *The Postal Service.* Washington: Government Printing Office, 1909.

Perret, Geoffrey. *Lincoln's War: The Untold Story of America's Greatest President as Commander in Chief.* New York: Random House, 2004.

Peters, Richard, ed. *The Public Statutes at Large of the United States.* Vol. 7. Boston: Charles C. Little & James Brown, 1846.

Poe, Edgar Allen. *The Raven and Other Poems by Edgar Allan Poe.* New York: Columbia University Press, 1942.

Portrait and Biographical Album, Isabella County, Mich. Chicago: Chapman Brothers, 1884.

Prokopowicz, Gerald. "The Common Soldier of the Civil War: His Rise and Fall." *Journal of the Civil War Era* 11, no. 4 (2021): 539–62.

Public Acts and Joint and Concurrent Resolutions of the Legislature of the State of Michigan, Passed at the Regular Session of 1881. Lansing: W. S. George & Co., 1881.

Quaife, Milo M., ed. *From the Cannon's Mouth: The Civil War Letters of General Alpheus S. Williams.* Detroit: Wayne State University Press, 1959; reprint, Lincoln: University of Nebraska Press, 1995.

Quist, John W., ed. *Michigan's War: The Civil War in Documents.* Athens: Ohio University Press, 2019.

Rable, George C. "Hearth, Home and Family in the Fredericksburg Campaign." In Cashin, *War Was You and Me*: 85–111.

Rafuse, Ethan S. *McClellan's War: The Failure of Moderation in the Struggle for the Union.* Bloomington: Indiana University Press, 2011.

Record of Service of Michigan Volunteers in the Civil War. Kalamazoo: Ihling Bros. & Everard [various].

Report of the Commissioner of Indian Affairs for the Year 1865. Washington: Government Printing Office, 1865.

Revised Constitution of the State of Michigan, Adopted in Convention, August 15, 1850. Lansing: R. W. Ingals, 1850.

Reynolds, David. *America, Empire of Liberty: A New History of the United States.* New York: Basic Books, 2011.

Reynolds, David S. *John Brown, Abolitionist: The Man Who Killed Slavery, Sparked the Civil War, and Seeded Civil Rights.* New York: Vintage Books, 2006.

Rhoades, Nancy L., and Lucy E. Bailey, eds. *Wanted—Correspondence: Women's Letters to a Union Soldier.* Athens: Ohio University Press, 2009.

Robbins, Sarah. *Managing Literacy, Mothering America: Women's Narratives on Reading and Writing in the Nineteenth Century*. Pittsburgh: University of Pittsburgh Press, 2006.

Robertson, John, *Michigan in the War*. Lansing: W. S. George, 1882.

Romig, Walter. *Michigan Place Names*. Detroit: Wayne State University Press, 1986.

Satz, Ronald N. "Indian Policy in the Jacksonian Era: The Old Northwest as a Test Case." In *Michigan History* 60, no. 1 (1976): 71–93.

Schwalm, Leslie A. *Emancipation's Diaspora: Race and Reconstruction in the Upper Midwest*. Chapel Hill: University of North Carolina Press, 2009.

Scott, Sean A. *A Visitation of God: Northern Civilians Interpret the Civil War*. New York: Oxford University Press, 2012.

Sears, Stephen W. *George B. McClellan: The Young Napoleon*. New York: Da Capo Press, 1999.

Shaw, Anna Howard. *The Story of a Pioneer*. New York: Harper Brothers, 1915.

Silber, Nina. *Daughters of the Union: Northern Women Fight the Civil War*. Cambridge: Harvard University Press, 2005.

Silber, Nina. *Gender and the Sectional Conflict*. Chapel Hill: University of North Carolina Press, 2008.

Sizer, Lyde Cullen. *The Political Work of Northern Women Writers and the Civil War, 1850–1872*. Chapel Hill: University of North Carolina Press, 2000.

Sligh, Charles R. *History of the Services of the First Regiment Michigan Engineers and Mechanics, during the Civil War, 1861–1865*. Grand Rapids: n.p., 1921.

Sodergren, Steven E. *The Army of the Potomac in the Overland and Petersburg Campaigns: Union Soldiers and Trench Warfare, 1864–1865*. Baton Rouge: Louisiana State University Press, 2017.

Song for the Wilderness. Kingston: James M. Creighton, 1855.

Sternhell, Yael A. *Routes of War: The World of Movement in the Confederate South*. Cambridge: Harvard University Press, 2012.

Stevenson, Louise L. "The Transatlantic Travels of James Thomson's *The Seasons* and Its Baggage of Material Culture, 1730–1870." *Proceedings of the American Antiquarian Society* (2006): 121–165.

Stout, Harry S. *Upon the Altar of the Nation: A Moral History of the Civil War*. New York: Viking Press, 2006.

Sutton, Robert K., and John A. Latschar, eds. *American Indians and the Civil War: Official National Park Service Handbook*. Fort Washington: Eastern National, 2013.

Taylor, Amy Murrell. *Embattled Freedom: Journeys Through the Civil War's Slave Refugee Camps*. Chapel Hill: University of North Carolina Press, 2018.

Thomas, Matthew M. "Historic American Indian Maple Sugar and Syrup Production: Boiling Arches in Michigan and Wisconsin." In *Midcontinental Journal of Archaeology* 30, no. 2 (Fall 2005): 299–326.

Thomson, James. *The Seasons*. Boston: Crosby & Nichols, 1862.

Trudeau, Noah A. *Bloody Roads South: The Wilderness to Cold Harbor, May–July 1864*. New York: Little, Brown & Co., 1989.

Unger, Irwin. *The Greenback Era: A Social and Political History of American Finance, 1865–1879*. Princeton: Princeton University Press, 1964.

United States General Index to Pension Files, 1861–1934.

United States Statutes at Large. Boston: Little, Brown & Co., 1859.

United States Statutes at Large. Vol. 12. Boston: Little, Brown & Co., 1863.

U.S. Census Bureau, 1910, Thirteenth United States Decennial Census.

U.S. Census Bureau, 1900, Twelfth United States Decennial Census.

U.S. Census Bureau, 1870, Ninth United States Decennial Census.

U.S. Census Bureau, 1860, Eighth United States Decennial Census.

U.S. Census Bureau, 1850, Seventh United States Decennial Census.

Wagner, Margaret E., Gary W. Gallagher, and Paul Finkelman, eds. *The Library of Congress Civil War Desk Reference.* New York: Simon & Schuster, 2002.

Walker, Sally M. *Deadly Aim: The Civil War Story of Michigan's Anishinaabe Sharpshooters.* New York: Henry Holt & Co., 2019.

The War of the Rebellion: A Compilation of the Official Records of the Union and Confederate Armies. Washington: Government Printing Office, 1880–1901.

Waugh, John C. *Reelecting Lincoln: The Battle for the 1864 Presidency.* Cambridge: Da Capo Press, 2001.

Weber, Jennifer L. *Copperheads: The Rise and Fall of Lincoln's Opponents in the North.* New York: Oxford University Press, 2006.

Weiner, Marli F. "Rural Women." In Hewitt, *Companion to American Women's History*: 150–166.

Welsh, Jack D. *Medical Histories of Union Generals.* Kent: Kent State University Press, 1996.

Wesley, Charles. *Hymns and Sacred Poems.* Vol. 1. Bristol: Felix Farley, 1749.

White, Richard. *The Middle Ground: Indians, Empires, and Republics in the Great Lakes Region, 1650–1815.* Cambridge: Cambridge University Press, 1991, 2011.

Wiley, Bell I. *The Bell Irvin Wiley Reader.* Edited by Hill Jordan and James Robertson Jr. Baton Rouge: Louisiana State University Press, 2001.

Wiley, Bell I. *The Life of Billy Yank: The Common Soldier of the Union.* Indianapolis: Bobbs-Merrill Co., 1952.

Wiley, Bell I. *The Life of Johnny Reb: The Common Soldier of the Confederacy.* Indianapolis: Bobbs-Merrill Co., 1943.

Williams, Frederick D. *Michigan Soldiers in the Civil War.* Lansing: Michigan Historical Commission, 1960.

Woods, Michael E. 2018. "Neither Snow nor Rain nor Secession? Mail Delivery and the Experience of Disunion in 1861." Muster: The Blog of the Journal of the Civil War Era. June 26. https://www.journalofthecivilwarera.org/2018/06/neither-snow-nor-rain-nor-secession-mail-delivery-and-the-experience-of-disunion-in-1861/.

Woodworth, Steven E. *Jefferson Davis and His Generals: The Failure of Confederate Command in the West.* Lawrence: University of Kansas Press, 1990.

Woodworth, Steven E. *While God Is Marching On: The Religious World of Civil War Soldiers.* Lawrence: University Press of Kansas, 2001.

Young, Elizabeth. *Disarming the Nation: Women's Writing and the American Civil War.* Chicago: University of Chicago Press, 1999.

Index

Printed in the United States
by Baker & Taylor Publisher Services